SYSTEMIC ISLAMOPHOBIA IN CANADA

A Research Agenda

Edited by Anver M. Emon

Systemic Islamophobia in Canada presents critical perspectives on systemic Islamophobia in Canadian politics, law, and society, and maps areas for future research and inquiry. The authors consist of both scholars and professionals who encounter in the ordinary course of their work the – sometimes banal, sometimes surprising – operation of systemic Islamophobia. Centring the lived realities of Muslims primarily in Canada, but internationally as well, the contributors identify the limits of democratic accountability in the operation of our shared institutions of government.

Intended as a guide, the volume identifies important points of consideration that have systemic implications for whether, how, and under what conditions Islamophobia is enabled and perpetuated, and in some cases even rendered respectable policy or bureaucratic practice in Canada. Ultimately, *Systemic Islamophobia in Canada* identifies a range of systemically Islamophobic sites in Canada to guide citizens and policymakers in fulfilling the promise of an inclusive democratic Canada.

Faculty of Law, University of Toronto

ANVER M. EMON is a professor of law and history, Canada Research Chair in Islamic Law and History, and Director of the Institute of Islamic Studies at the University of Toronto.

Dimensions: Islam, Muslims, and Critical Thought

Editors: Fahad Ahmad (Toronto Metropolitan University) and
Atiya Husain (Carleton University)

Dimensions: Islam, Muslims, and Critical Thought at University of Toronto
Press publishes empirically rich, multi-method, interdisciplinary works
that build theory and develop knowledge in the study of Islam and
Muslims. Works in this series engage urgent questions of Islamophobia
as well as the intellectual and cultural production of Muslims on their
own terms, at levels of analysis ranging from the interpersonal to the
institutional. The series promotes research on the often understudied
Canadian experience, as well as studies taking up questions of Islam
and Muslims from a comparative perspective across national sites.

Series Advisory Board

Yasmeen Abu-Laban (University of Alberta)
Cemil Aydin (University of North Carolina at Chapel Hill)
Jean Beaman (University of California Santa Barbara)
Anver M. Emon (University of Toronto)
Darryl Li (University of Chicago)
Neda Maghbouleh (University of Toronto)
Jeffrey Monaghan (Carleton University)
Nicole Nguyen (University of Illinois Chicago)
Salman Sayyid (University of Leeds)
Sunera Thobani (University of British Columbia)

Systemic Islamophobia in Canada

A Research Agenda

EDITED BY ANVER M. EMON

UNIVERSITY OF TORONTO PRESS
Toronto Buffalo London

© University of Toronto Press 2023
Toronto Buffalo London
utorontopress.com

ISBN 978-1-4875-4685-4 (cloth)   ISBN 978-1-4875-4913-8 (EPUB)
ISBN 978-1-4875-4590-1 (paper)   ISBN 978-1-4875-4773-8 (PDF)

Library and Archives Canada Cataloguing in Publication

Title: Systemic Islamophobia in Canada : a research agenda / edited by Anver
    M. Emon.
Names: Emon, Anver M., editor.
Description: Includes bibliographical references and index.
Identifiers: Canadiana (print) 20220496919 | Canadiana (ebook) 20220496927 |
    ISBN 9781487546854 (cloth) | ISBN 9781487545901 (paper) |
    ISBN 9781487549138 (EPUB) | ISBN 9781487547738 (PDF)
Subjects: LCSH: Islamophobia – Canada. | LCSH: Islamophobia – Research –
    Canada. | LCSH: Muslims – Canada. | LCSH: Canada – Ethnic relations.
Classification: LCC BP43.C3 S97 2023 | DDC 305.6/970971 – dc23

We wish to acknowledge the land on which the University of Toronto Press
operates. This land is the traditional territory of the Wendat, the Anishnaabeg,
the Haudenosaunee, the Métis, and the Mississaugas of the Credit First
Nation.

This book has been published with the help of a subvention from the Institute
of Islamic Studies at the University of Toronto.

University of Toronto Press acknowledges the financial support of the
Government of Canada, the Canada Council for the Arts, and the Ontario Arts
Council, an agency of the Government of Ontario, for its publishing activities.

 Canada Council Conseil des Arts
for the Arts du Canada

 ONTARIO ARTS COUNCIL
CONSEIL DES ARTS DE L'ONTARIO
an Ontario government agency
un organisme du gouvernement de l'Ontario

Funded by the Financé par le
Government gouvernement
of Canada du Canada

 UNIVERSITY OF
TORONTO  Institute of
Islamic Studies

Contents

Education, Memory, and Belonging

Democracy, (In)Equality, and Exclusion

Policing and the Law

Acknowledgments

This book took shape in the shadow of the Government of Canada's 2021 Summit on Islamophobia, which followed the horrific attack on a Muslim family, out for a walk in London, Ontario. That attack took the lives of the entire family, except for one, a young boy left hospitalized after the attack and now facing a future without the love, care, and protection of his family. The summit featured government leaders recognizing the government could do more to tackle Islamophobia in society, pledging among other things to launch a review of Canada Revenue Agency audits of Muslim-led charities. Looking back on the summit, it is worth remembering that it took place just weeks before a federal election was called, and during which the federal parties, asked about Quebec's Law 21 as a form of state-sponsored discrimination, hesitated to describe it as discriminatory as they vied for contested ridings in that province. Shortly after the summit, columnist Azeezah Kanji complained that the summit precluded meaningful discussion of systemic Islamophobia in the guise of law and policy across different levels of government.[1]

There is a vast literature on Islamophobia as a cultural, social, or political phenomenon, or as a subset of critical race theory or ethnic studies. That literature, often centring on the United States, the UK, or other jurisdictions, has increasingly focused on Canada as discussed in the introduction to this volume. The essays in this volume build on that scholarly corpus while directing focus on an aspect of Islamophobia that has too often gone unaddressed, namely systemic Islamophobia as enabled by government policy or action in Canada.

---

1 Kanji, Azeezah. 2021. "The 'Consultation' Racket: Report on the National Islamophobia Summit." *Centre for Free Expression Blog*. 9 August 2021. https://cfe.ryerson.ca/blog/2021/08/"consultation"-racket-report-national-islamophobia-summit.

The authors in this volume recognize that their contributions are gestures towards future research. Moreover, they are aware that future researchers bear the onus of hurdling evidentiary obstacles posed by the state's prerogative power to maintain secrets. Access to information is vital both to ensuring a transparent and accountable democracy, and to the development of robust, empirically grounded research on systemic discrimination, such as systemic Islamophobia. When the state's prerogative power creates the conditions for an absence of information, the ethical obligation to investigate is even greater, though it requires creative methodologies to ensure reliable conclusions founded on facts, data, and evidence. As the essays in this volume intimate, the challenge to any systemic study of Islamophobia will be the availability of evidence and the need for future researchers to develop creative methodologies that obviate formal, official silence.

This book was made possible by support from various units at the University of Toronto: the Faculty of Arts and Sciences, the Institute of Islamic Studies, and the Reading Muslims project at the Department of History. I'm especially grateful to Vice Dean Vince Tropepe, whose early support for the idea of this volume enabled its quick turnaround. Daniel Quinlan of University of Toronto Press quickly recognized the contribution this book could make to Canada and expertly shepherded it through the Press. Production of this volume would not have been possible without the assistance of Marya Atassi, Maaham Sachwani, and Omar Sirri, and the two anonymous reviewers for UTP who offered important advice to improve the volume. I especially want to single out Omar, who in the course of supporting this volume successfully defended his dissertation before an enthusiastic and ecstatic committee.

Introduction

ANVER M. EMON

Since the attacks in New York on 11 September 2001, Muslims have been subjected to a wide range of enhanced national security policies, which in turn have created a political narrative of "Islam" as a foreign ideology and "the Muslim" as a threat (Emon 2019; Norton 2013). Certainly, these policies pre-existed 9/11, but they took on special meaning, salience, and focus thereafter. The moral panic spurred by 9/11 informed policies, legislative agendas, and bureaucratic modes of rationality that effectively transformed Islamophobia into respectable – and institutionally sedimented – policy (Passas 2010; De Goede 2012; Bail 2014). In Canada, despite the horrific Quebec City mosque shootings in 2017, parliamentary debate on M103, a motion to study systemic discrimination, including Islamophobia, remained divided on whether the term "Islamophobia" was appropriate, as opposed to addressing the practical realities of discrimination. Avoiding the uncomfortable realities of discrimination, some members of Parliament instead complained that centring on the term "Islamophobia" would stifle freedom of speech. In other words, the value of freedom of speech gave respectable cover to what might otherwise be considered hate-promoting. For as long as the liberal constitutional legal order and its bureaucratic mechanisms can be used to give respectable cover to Islamophobia, government agencies necessarily run the risk of maintaining and enabling Islamophobia.

Bureaucratic forms of "respectable" Islamophobia are not limited to the federal branch. They cut across federal, provincial, and municipal legislative and regulatory regimes, which in the aggregate create the conditions for Islamophobia to operate bureaucratically on the bodies of Muslims and their civil society organizations. In the education sector, for instance, which operates locally but under provincial mandate, "respectable" Islamophobia infects school curricula and public debate on school board policies (Chadha, Herbert, and Richard 2020; Paradkar

2020). In the civil society sector, "respectable" Islamophobia in government policies affect the work of Muslim-led charities that support their communities in areas where the government is absent (Emon and Hasan 2021), as well as modify how they use their own properties as their communities' needs evolve (Valverde 2012). Muslim women are often considered subjects that need saving (Zero Tolerance for Barbaric Cultural Practices Act, S.C. 2015, c. 29; Razack 2008) while at the same time official provincial policies effectively exclude a segment of them from government service and employment in the name of core national values (Quebec's Law 21).

The Lexicon of "Islamophobia"

Before jumping too far afield, it is worth pausing for a moment to consider the very term that animates the studies in this volume, *Islamophobia*. As many have shown, the term found its way into public discourse when used in a 1997 Runnymede Trust report published in the UK on the topic (Green 2019). According to that report, the term is "not ideal" but nonetheless is a "useful shorthand way of referring to dread or hatred of Islam – and, therefore, to fear or dislike of all or most Muslims" (Runnymede Trust 1997, 1).

The word has generated considerable controversy in some circles and has led many to question whether it is the right term, or if it is overinclusive, ambiguous, or simply inapt for a study centring on systemic considerations. The lexically inclined might break down the term into its etymological parts, noting that the suffix *phobia* denotes a type of irrational fear. Critics argue that on this lexical approach, the term reduces the phenomena to clinical and therapeutic terms. This does not adequately capture how the phenomena characterized as "Islamophobic" is more than about feelings or emotion, but instead is deeply political and institutional (Green 2019, 14). For instance, as witnessed in Canada's 2015 federal election, where fears of "barbaric cultural practices" were instrumentalized by political elites, Islamophobia can have important electoral implications, especially if an electoral base is swayed by such rhetoric (Bronskill 2021). In such cases, the Islamophobia at issue is hardly irrational or fearful, but rather is instrumentally weaponized for political gain. In other words, Islamophobia is strategically deployed to achieve certain political outcomes or government policies.

Others argue that the term is overinclusive of what might otherwise be valid criticism of a religious tradition and its modern manifestations. This particular view was dominant among Conservative MPs in Canada's Parliament as they debated M103, in particular the inclusion of Islamophobia in the motion. In its minority report appended to the final report of the Standing Committee on Canadian Heritage, the Conservative Party of Canada (CPC) stated that the term is not well defined, can be weaponized against those merely issuing dissenting views, and ultimately infringes core values such as the freedom of expression (CPC 2018; Green 2019, 14). Alternative terms of art that have been proffered centre on the identity of the believer, not the religion itself. Rather than Islamophobia, the preference is for anti-Muslim hate, for instance.

Yet others still contend that the term improperly draws upon the theoretical architecture of racism. It is improper since "Muslimness" is not reducible to the biological, phenotypical focal points of racializing logics. On this point, Ghassan Hage offers a rather straightforward rebuke that questions such reifying analyses of racism by reference to the politics of anti-racism:

> [S]uch approaches have all the hallmarks of what Pierre Bourdieu critically identifies as a form of scholastic thought [reference omitted]. "Scholastic" here refers to a mode of thinking that detaches racism from its practical/usage context and conceives it as an academic exercise aimed at some kind of pure knowledge, a desire to classify for classification's sake. (Hage 2017, 6)

While academics and theorists may debate the term and its implications, the tenor of debate in Canada on its usage seems to have changed as events have transpired, new elections have taken place, and government has changed parties. After a horrific attack against a Muslim family in London, Ontario in 2021, the federal government announced a summit on Islamophobia, without any need to explain the term or justify its use. Erin O'Toole, then-leader of the CPC, labelled the attack in London, Ontario a terror attack and said that "police services have warned of a dramatic increase in hate crime, violate extremism, Islamophobia and other signs of intolerance from one part of our country to another" (*House of Commons Debates* 2021). The seemingly unproblematic usage of "Islamophobia" now as a term of reprobation in Canada, in contrast to the earlier seemingly acceptable use of Islamophobic rhetoric in Canadian public discourse, plays out Hage's concept of "generalized domestication" (2017). The "domesticated" use of *Islamophobia* as an official term of art allows us to move beyond terminological debates and train our scrutinizing gaze on how the structures of power across Canadian governmental institutions pursue the ambiguous task of threat assessment and neutralization in which the "Muslim" remains a (if not "the") figure of suspicion.

The Limited Literature on Government-Enabled Systemic Islamophobia in Canada

A number of scholars have addressed the phenomenon of state-sponsored Islamophobia in Europe and North America generally, and Canada specifically. In Europe, many have written about states that ban burkas and now sponsor "moderate" Islam projects (Al-Azmeh and Fokas 2007; Amiraux 2012a, 2012b; Barras 2013, 2014; Cesari 2006, 2014). In the United States, a growing archive documents formal state endeavours to legislate "Sharia bans," and to ban travel from Muslim-majority states (Marzouki 2017; Corbett 2016; *Trump v. Hawaii*, 138 S. Ct. 2392 (2018)). Canada is no stranger to these debates – Ontario's Sharia arbitration debate of 2004–5, Quebec's Charter of Values and Law 21, the federal government's 2015 proposed "barbaric cultural practices hotline," and the debates on M103 regarding Islamophobia are just a few examples (Bakali 2015; Bouchard and Taylor 2008; Brodeur 2008; Bunting and Mokhtari 2007; Korteweg and Selby 2012; Amiraux 2012c; Amiraux and Araya-Moreno 2014; Eid 2012a, 2012b; Emon 2009; Chaudhry 2018; Barras 2016; Zine 2007, 2012). In the literature on these formal state acts, the theoretical/analytic emphasis is on core questions of belonging, citizenship, security, and policing (e.g., Bakht 2020). These are theoretically framed arguments that locate formal government acts and pronouncements within the broad themes of Orientalism, Islamophobia, and the culture of "othering" (Emon 2019).

The discourse on Islamophobia and/or anti-Muslim hate recognizes it as a social construct. In that sense, the theoretical and methodological literature draws on the scholarship that feminist, critical race, and critical Indigenous theorists have already done to map gender, race, and Indigeneity as topographical features of an encultured world. In addition, as Rabiat Akande in this volume suggests, "Islamophobia" offers an opportunity to develop best practices in intersectional analysis given the internal diversity within the category "Muslim." The added term "systemic" – as in systemic Islamophobia – works to embed these topographical features in the formal institutions that make up and regulate the same world. This move from culture to institution is meant to take the experience of Islamophobia from the street corner where Joe Ahmed and Joe Schmo might meet, and instead locate it as an instantiation of a different reality – a reality that governs the corner as a site upon which sovereign authority is effected, even if only through the unseen abstractions of law and administrative regulations. This turn to the systemic reflects new lines of scholarship in which the lived experiences of communities with government bureaucrats inform innovations in research design into the bureaucratic rationality that often makes coercive government action possible and legitimate, despite being tainted by apparent Islamophobic bias (Emon and Hasan 2021). Indeed, the essays in this volume are entirely committed to exploring this turn to the systemic, which integrates lived experiences and government/institutional bureaucracy. The thematic unity across the volume is meant to recast the state and its institutions from being viewed as neutral umpire and/or peacekeeper on the streets where everyday Islamophobia may occur, to an instrument that makes cultural articulations and expressions of Islamophobia possible and respectable – and often even heightens them.

The essays in this volume are short interventions that introduce readers to particular sites of systemic Islamophobia. As introductions, they are explicitly designed as gestures to future researchers on Islam and Muslims in Canada who may take these introductions as inspiration for their own research. Together, then, these essays outline a future research agenda that fills a two-fold gap in the broader, global literature on Islamophobia, state practice, and bureaucratic rationalities. First, while humanities and social sciences scholarship examines state-based bureaucratic processes (e.g., Latour 2009; Mitchell 2002; Scott 1999; Evans, Rueschemeyer, and Skocpol 2010), the literature on Islamophobia often takes formal state endeavours as empirical givens rather than as markers of a deliberative, bureaucratic process. The studies do not gauge the bureaucratic epistemologies that give formal decisions the character of respectability even as they enable and perpetuate Islamophobic biases to structure the discretionary authority of civil servants (Passas 2010). Literature on how bureaucratic epistemologies effect systemic racism is a growing field with respect to anti-Black and anti-Asian racism (Crenshaw 1991; Williams 1991; Backhouse 1999). Moreover, in Canada, with the Truth and Reconciliation Commission and the subsequent National Centre for Truth and Reconciliation's archival mandate, research is now growing on the violence of law and policy on the history and well-being of Canada's Indigenous Peoples. This particular development in Canada's recent institutional and political history ultimately makes Canada an important case study that can be used to interrogate systemic paradigms in Europe and the US.

Despite Canada's unique positionality on the world stage, the academic literature on systemic Islamophobia across Canadian levels of government is not robust. This absence is hardly surprising given that the relevant evidence required for such study is hidden behind the prerogative power of the state to insist on secrecy. Moreover, in the case of policy-based literature, Canada is somewhat unique: foundations and policy think tanks in the UK, Europe, and the US that combat all forms of racism issue self-published reports that address this gap in the academic literature, and they remain touchpoints in the study of state-sponsored Islamophobia. The Runnymede Trust in the UK coined the term Islamophobia in its 1997 report on the phenomenon in Britain (Runnymede Trust 1997). The Institute for Social Policy and Understanding has developed in collaboration with Georgetown University various surveys and measures of Islamophobia in the US (Institute for Social Policy and Understanding, n.d.). In Europe, the European Network against Racism integrates academics and civil society organizations to identify sites of systemic Islamophobia and the democratic mechanisms that enable it as formal policy, as evinced in its 2018 recommendations from civil society organizations in Europe (European Network against Racism 2018). But in Canada, there is little coordination between academics and the non-profit sector, thereby maintaining a disconnect between academic research and civil society groups advocating for communities on the margins. For instance, the leading not-for-profit advocate Imagine Canada and the not-for-profit sector's leading journal, *The Philanthropist*, did not robustly address systemic Islamophobia and the charitable sector until academe and civil society partnered to produce the study *Under Layered Suspicion* (Shaheen 2021; Nakua 2021).

Second, the academic study of Islam and Muslims in North America is itself situated within a disciplinary contest that maintains a distance from the lived realities of communities marginalized by state activity. The field remains structured around an area studies model informed by Cold War politics; a German philological model that centres textuality in the study of Islam; and an ethnographic approach that locates the study of Muslims and Islam through field work that decentres formal government policies to centre the lived experiences of Muslims (Emon 2019; Selby, Barras, and Beaman 2019). But the dominant approaches in the field do not regularly integrate state bureaucratic practices *and* lived realities in the construction of Islam and Muslim life (*contra*, Salomon 2016).

The essays in this volume recognize that sustained interrogation of government-enabled systemic Islamophobia must examine the epistemologies and bureaucratic modes of enquiry that make state policies and decisions *both* institutionally possible *and* embodied in the lived realities of Muslim communities. This research agenda focuses attention on the state as a disaggregated, complex entity operating across an increasingly diverse set of sectors, embracing and/or contending with rapidly changing technologies, and assuming the monopoly of coercive authority and violence at a time when its settler colonial origins call into question its very legitimacy. The research agenda requires interrogating the artefacts and remnants of bureaucratic decision-making as it relates to the study of Islam, or affects the lives of Muslims, whether openly stated as such or not (e.g., Emon and Mahmood 2021). However, the possibility of fulfilling this agenda is contingent on the transparency and accountability we can expect of representative democratic government in Canada. Put differently, the study of government-enabled systemic Islamophobia is also a litmus test on the scope to which Canada's representative democratic institutions are also accountable to the public. As such, this research agenda is not simply about documenting the lived experience of a community on the margins. It shifts the gaze of Canadian national security from the construct of "Islam" and "the Muslim" to the state itself. The proposed research agenda, captured in each essay in this volume, reverses the gaze by centring the vantage point of a historical Islam and an embodied Muslim in Canada to render powerful institutions across Canada's governmental landscape as objects of enquiry and critique. The capacity of this agenda to yield important insights will depend on acknowledging the *instability* and *inconstancy* in both the gazing subject and the gazed object.

This volume takes a specific interest in how institutions in the public and private sectors enable and perpetuate Islamophobia. At the same time, the essays do not pretend to go into the level of research detail needed to prove one thesis or another. Rather, they uncover a series of themes, topics, and arguments with the express aim of outlining the beginnings of a research agenda for future researchers to carry to completion. Some authors draw upon their time and experience in professions where they encounter Islamophobia in the ordinary course of business. For others, their essays reflect the kind of instinctive vision that comes from years of research in areas that touch upon, but don't necessarily centre in, the study of systemic Islamophobia. And, for others, their essays reflect a zooming out from prior research undertaken on narrower topics that hinted at something broader and more systemic that has yet to be fully understood and appreciated.

Organized under four themes (outlined further below), these essays were purposely written to be short, direct, and methodologically inquisitive. They identify an issue or problem area, explain the nexus of the topic to the broader concern about systemic Islamophobia, and address the research challenges that will necessarily attend to anyone who might pursue the directions outlined herein. As map or guide, the essays identify important points of consideration that have systemic implications for whether, how, and under what conditions Islamophobia in Canada is enabled and perpetuated, and in some cases even rendered respectable policy or bureaucratic practice. The contributions were drafted with the express interest of inspiring younger researchers to assume the mantle of interrogating the dynamics of government-enabled systemic Islamophobia in Canada.

Theme 1: Islamophobia in Canada: Representation and Perspective

The first theme centres the importance of thinking intersectionally and transnationally about Islamophobia. Not all who experience Islamophobia are positioned the same or subject to similar modalities of Islamophobic rationality. Rabiat Akande takes an approach on the experience of Islamophobia by addressing Islamophobia as experienced by Black Muslim women, while Sarah Shah and Maryam Khan focus on Muslims who are sexually and gender diverse. Akande's contribution is especially timely given the too-regular news of Black Muslim women in Alberta facing threats to their safety (Mosleh 2021). In both essays, the authors adopt an intersectional analysis to differentiate the experiences of Islamophobia in a Muslim Canadian community beset by differences, with some deemed more socially and religiously acceptable than others. Recognizing the ways in which these subsets of Muslim are neither in-group nor out-group but somewhere in-between creates the need for more calibrated research to examine the systemic impact of Islamophobia on their lives in Canada. As Akande remarks in this volume, "the pervasive understanding of Islamophobia as a singular and undifferentiated form of oppression – and suffering – obscures the uniqueness of the suffering of different positioned Muslim subjects."

Whereas in Canada national security services increasingly turn their attention to White Extremism, John Smith, Wafaa Hasan, and Zarah Khan remind us that Islamophobia is constructed without limits to national borders. Indeed, one cannot appreciate the operation of Islamophobia without reflecting on transnational dimensions. Smith recognizes and appreciates the tendency of North American and European discourse on Islamophobia to centre a critical race lens, which in turn is often structured by a majoritarian whiteness. As John Smith reminds us though, Islamophobia is not merely an artefact of a majoritarian whiteness in the so-called West. Rather, examining the exportation of Hindutva ideology from official Indian state agencies into Canada through diasporic links, Smith identifies the ways in which Hindutva-promoting organizations are enabled by a Canadian regulatory environment that fails to see such organizations contributing to the landscape of Islamophobia. Hasan and Khan focus on the attacks in London, Ontario, in 2021 and the transnational dimensions linking violence in the streets of Canada to violence in the streets in Gaza. Their analysis illustrates the way in which Canadian efforts, such as the 2021 Summit on Islamophobia, so centred domestic Canada that it severed "the Muslim body from its transnational connections even while imposing the transnational on it."

These intersectional and transnational prompts contribute to a more robust demand on Canada's media sector to consider its editorial policies and how it represents the "Muslim" to a broader Canadian public. Faisal Bhabha's contribution looks at the case of Toronto-based imam Ayman Elkasrawy, who was accused of anti-Semitism by a media industry that, Bhabha argues, did its homework too late. Tracing the travails of Elkasrawy, Bhabha illustrates the politics of (mis)translation, a legal system with limited capacity to provide effective redress, and the failures of critical journalistic methodologies. On this last point, Zeinab Farokhi and Yasmin Jiwani remind us how Western media portrayals have long cast Muslims in unflattering if not outright prejudicial terms. Of the various representations, they focus on the Muslim – and in particular the Muslim refugee – as terrorist, and the Muslim woman as helpless and needing protection. These media templates, they argue, require both examination and proactive standards of representation by media professionals and their institutions.

Theme 2: Education, Memory, and Belonging

Syed Adnan Hussain opens the section on education, memory, and belonging with his essay on imperial amnesia, setting up the story of Muslims in Canada in part by remembering their constitutive role in the very formation of the Commonwealth in which Canada takes shape. Reflecting on contemporary Canadian debates about so-called *sharia creep*, Hussein recalls the irony of how imperial British common law, which informs the public law of Canada, has a long history of thinking with both Muslims and Sharia as mutually constitutive. The juxtaposition of contemporary Canadian angst about sharia and imperial common law highlights the need to remain vigilant against multiple strands of settler imperial practices of statecraft.

Hussain's article sets the stage for the following essays that address the institutions of learning and memory in Canada that often enable various forms of Islamophobia, whether in terms of how stories are told or what stories are erased. These essays examine the systemic operationalization of Islamophobia closer to home, specifically local schools, libraries, and archives. These institutions take shape differently across each province and of course draw on national and international standards of professionalization. At the same time, their localized operation offers one path of enquiry into the systemic design of Islamophobia.

This reminder leads to two essays that address the local context of education as a site of memory and meaning-making. Melanie Adrian focuses on the more local context of primary public schools and Islamophobia, while Sheliza Ibrahim reflects on Islamophobia and pedagogic design at post-secondary educational institutions. Recognizing an increased enrolment in private Islamic schools, Adrian recognizes the need to examine the ways in which Islamophobia is embedded in the public school system and motivates Muslim students and their families to find alternatives. At the same time, she enquires of Islamic private schools about their capacity to foster a sense of inclusion in Canada among their students in a context of rising Islamophobia. Her essay sets out a series of questions that call for greater research at the intersection of education policy, youth, and Islamophobia. Ibrahim starts where Adrian leaves off and examines post-secondary pedagogies and curriculum to address whether and to what extent post-secondary institutions both address Islamophobia and prepare the Muslim student on campus for a complex and sometime antagonistic world. Read alongside Akande's contribution to this volume, Ibrahim's essay centres on the Muslim university student as a conceptual device to reflect on the pedagogic possibilities of integrating an intersectional teaching lens to help students grapple with their futures, an approach that consists of more than metrics of job placement. By conceptually centring the Muslim student though, she also illustrates gaps in the way policies on equity and inclusion take shape within higher education.

Moska Rokay, archivist for the Muslims in Canada Archives, examines the history of archives and archival practices in Europe and North America and outlines how the scale and scope of their mandate makes a social justice orientation difficult to institutionalize. Addressing the relative absence of Muslims in Canada's archival landscape, she lays out a mode of systemic redress that centres on the integration of marginalized communities and focuses on community-engaged archives that make the unseen and unheard stories of Muslims legible as part of Canada's democratic fabric.

Theme 3: Democracy, (In)Equality, and Exclusion

The third theme involves the cultural promises of equality and freedom embedded in the Charter of Rights and Freedoms (sections 2 and

15) as well as in the national commitment to multiculturalism. The two essays in this section identify these promises as peculiarly broken in the case of the Muslim subject. Natasha Bakht's essay interrogates the constitutional foundation for Law 21 in Quebec, namely section 33 of the Charter of Rights and Freedoms, the so-called "notwithstanding clause." As she convincingly argues, the notwithstanding clause, if read without limitation and constraint, provides governments with the legal trump card to trample rights that we otherwise consider fundamental. Reading section 33 in light of the unwritten constitutional principles enunciated by the Supreme Court of Canada in *Reference re Secession of Quebec*, Bakht illuminates how the notwithstanding clause of Law 21 systemically infringes on the fundamental rights of some of the most visible targets of Islamophobia in Canada, namely Muslim women.

Shifting registers from the federal and the constitutional to the private and financial, Anver M. Emon's essay outlines how Canada's financial investigation regime renders suspect the very movement of Muslim money. Expanding on his prior work concerning tax audits of Muslim-led charities, Emon illustrates how the Canadian government has effectively conscripted Canada's financial sector in the War on Terror, in particular the war on terrorism financing. Juxtaposing Canada's policies on both terrorism financing and financial intelligence, Emon identifies Islamophobic policies that have the potential to inform biases in how the private sector assesses risk and fulfils its regulatory requirements, with the risk of fiscal penalties for failure to do so. These risk-assessment models are implemented against daily transactions using computer software with algorithms that are vulnerable to certain biases in their design. But because these computerized risk-assessment mechanisms are the stuff of intellectual property, they are also insulated from scrutiny. Citizens and civil society organizations are now subject to private sector risk-assessment metrics that can potentially exclude them from the ordinary financial services sector that Canadians across the country otherwise take for granted (e.g., Interac, PayPal, and others), with limited public accountability metrics.

Theme 4: Policing and Law

The final section concerns issues of national security. This area of systemic enquiry is not necessarily a new area of concern; it remains a significant site through which Muslims in Canada continue to feel the sting of systemic, government-enabled Islamophobia. But it appears last in the volume if only to showcase by reference to the above thematic sections the various scales at which systemic Islamophobia operates across Canada.

Kent Roach draws on the experience of Canada's Indigenous communities to hypothesize that Canada's Muslims are both over-policed, resulting in the abuse of their human rights, and under-protected from hate crimes and White extremism. This hypothesis rests on publicly available information that echoes the documented experiences of racialized and Indigenous groups in Canada. Roach suggests that this disparity calls for greater research to identify the forces within security institutions that create the conditions for over-policing Muslims, as well as work to examine the internal dynamics and capacities of Muslim communities themselves as they contend with increasing incidents of hateful speech, conduct, and violence directed at them. Studies of social capital might interrogate the absence of trust between Muslim communities and the state, which may perpetuate both the state's paradigms of suspicion, while also precluding Muslim communities from seeking assistance from the state.

Fahad Ahmad's essay complements Roach's hypothesis by examining the impact of national security and radicalization policies from the ground up, with specific reference to Muslim civil society organizations. As he shows, national security agencies wield the power of legitimacy over and against segments of civil society. Counter-radicalization policies offer a sharp tool that has the capacity, based on potentially biased evidence and prejudices, to preclude Muslims from leveraging the potential of effective civil society in contributing to Canada's democratic landscape.

Naseem Mithoowani develops the national security theme by showing how immigration and refugee policy are its tools. She brings the laser focus of an immigration lawyer to the task of identifying the ordinary sites of systemic Islamophobia at Immigration, Refugees, and Citizenship Canada (IRCC). Her analysis of how bureaucrats within the IRCC review case files, enable implicit bias, and adopt machine learning tools to make such implicit bias more hidden presents a revealing account of systemic Islamophobia in action on the front lines of client representation.

Michael Nesbitt takes aim at the terrorism offence provisions in the Criminal Code, in particular the special motive requirement that defines a terrorist act as one motivated by religion, politics, or ideology. As he ably demonstrates, this special motive requirement remains ambiguous and unclarified by Parliament or the courts. In terrorism cases, this has been operationalized by using certain movements or groups as a proxy for motive. When read alongside Canada's terrorist entity list, which overwhelmingly lists Muslim-identified organizations, there is unsurprisingly a disproportionate focus in terrorism prosecutions against Muslim defendants. Simply increasing the number of groups on the terrorist entity list will only allow law enforcement and the courts to continue to use "outgroups" as proxies for a motive requirement that remains unclear, unambiguous, and vulnerable to a range of systemic biases.

In his essay for this volume, Youcef Soufi examines the US-Canada border as a site at which Islamophobia structures the experience of Muslim Canadians. Soufi examines three cases of Muslim Canadians hampered from traversing that border due to practices of information sharing between the Government of Canada and the United States' Department of Homeland Security. Throwing light on the metrics of suspicion, he questions the prevailing "guilt by association" model employed by CSIS, the RCMP, and the US Department of Homeland Security in determining how, when, and why a Muslim is precluded from crossing. Examining this particular practice of data sharing and border management, Soufi critiques the epistemic presumptions that make systemic Islamophobia at the border possible.

Conclusion

Setting out a research agenda, this volume offers critical examinations of Canada's institutions of governance as sites of embedded, systemic, institutionalized Islamophobia. The authors were tasked with writing short essays that identify sites of systemic Islamophobia and how it operates. There are, of course, other sites that could have been written about, and we hope that they will be someday. As a collection of essays, the volume is tied together by a central focal point, namely the operation of Islamophobic logics as respectable policy within formal institutions across all levels of government. For some, that has meant examining local public schools, while for others, the focus is on bureaucratic decision-making in a federal ministry such as Immigration, Refugees, and Citizenship Canada. The scales of governance may vary, but the focus on Islamophobia as respectable policy remains consistent.

Four themes structure this volume. The first theme on representation and perspective is a reminder that Islamophobia is an embodied experience that cannot help but vary across intersectional lines of difference. Moreover, it is does not operate in a domestic vacuum; transnational communities and networks as well as global information sharing inform both the construction of Islam and Muslims and the ways in which Islamophobic practices take shape. The second theme on education, memory, and belonging begins with a story of imperial forgetting that enables a contemporary national – if not nationalist – hostility and fear to rise to the surface. Critical care in developing classroom pedagogy and memory making institutions is required to reverse the accretion of Islamophobia that has gradually become institutionally sedimented.

The third theme examines Islamophobia in light of Canadian commitments to democracy, equality, and inclusion. For those committed to an image of Canada as multicultural, welcoming, and accepting of others, this may not be a particularly comfortable starting point. Of course, Canada is no stranger to exclusionary, discriminatory policies given the histories of residential schools and the Chinese head tax, to give but two examples. In this volume, the authors appreciate that Canada's promise is most meaningful and most plausible when these uncomfortable realities are faced head on, without apology. To identify and expose systemic Islamophobia in Canada, in other words, does not benefit one interest group over another, one identity group over another. Rather, pinpointing ways in which the state systemically enables Islamophobia is a project in and for the benefit of Canada's democratic commitments. In other words, this research agenda is built on the hope that all Canadians can reap the benefits of an inclusive, democratic Canada. And where they cannot, we have a collective obligation to diagnose the problem and propose modes of redress.

Perhaps the most notorious diagnoses of exclusionary and discriminatory policies lie in the realm of safety and policing, the fourth theme of the book. There, authors identify how Islamophobia informs, if not captures, whole aspects of the state's national security apparatus: police, immigration, counter-radicalization, and intelligence sharing with foreign states.

Across these four themes, each essay presents a different systemic site in which Islamophobia structures and informs what passes as respectable bureaucratic policy, much of which is backed by the coercive monopoly the state exercises in the name of all Canadians. While not exhaustive, this volume offers an enterprising research agenda designed to bring forth a Canada within which all can flourish and thrive. It is commonplace that living collectively as we do entails an implicit social contract, where we give up some freedoms to enjoy so many others. The ironic virtue of the social contract is that it maximizes freedom and human flourishing by requiring that we all make sacrifices. But as we all too readily know from history, the benefits of freedom and the costs of sacrifice are not always borne equally. A research agenda on systemic Islamophobia tests Canada's social contract for whether the costs for security are equally shared, and whether the imperatives of security do not override the equally important imperatives of transparent and accountable government.

WORKS CITED

Al-Azmeh, Aziz, and Effie Fokas, eds. 2007. *Islam in Europe: Diversity, Identity and Influence*. Cambridge: Cambridge University Press.

Amiraux, Valerie, and Javierra Araya-Moreno. 2014. "Pluralism and Radicalization: Mind the Gap!" In *Religious Radicalization and Securitization in Canada and Beyond*, edited by Paul Bramadat and Lorne Dawson, 92–120. Toronto: University of Toronto Press.

Amiraux, Valérie. 2012a. "État de la littérature. l'Islam et les musulmans en Europe: un objet périphérique converti en incontournable des sciences sociales." *Critique Internationale* 56, no. 3: 141–57. https://doi.org/10.3917/crii.056.0141.

–. 2012b. "Radicalization and the Challenge of Muslim Integration in the European Union." In *Handbook of Political Islam*, edited by Shahram Akbarzadeh, 205–24. London: Routledge.

–. 2012c. "Visibility, Transparency and Gossip: How Did the Religion of Some (Muslims) Become the Public Concern of Others?" *Critical Research on Religion* 4, no. 1: 37–56. https://doi.org/10.1177/2050303216640399.

Backhouse, Constance. 1999. *Colour-Coded: A Legal History of Racism in Canada, 1900–1950*. Toronto: University of Toronto Press.

Bail, Chris. 2014. *Terrified: How Anti-Muslim Fringe Organizations Became Mainstream*. Princeton, NJ: Princeton University Press.

Bakali, Naved. 2015. "Contextualising the Quebec Charter of Values: How the Muslim 'Other' Is Conceptualized in Quebec." *Culture and Religion* 16, no. 4: 412–29. https://doi.org/10.1080/14755610.2015.1090468.

Bakht, Natasha. 2020. *In Your Face: Law, Justice, and Niqab-Wearing Women in Canada*. Toronto: Irwin Law.

Barras, Amélie. 2013. "Sacred Laïcité and the Politics of Religious Resurgence in France: Wither Religious Freedom?" *Mediterranean Politics* 18, no. 2: 276–93. https://doi.org/10.1080/13629395.2013.799345.

–. 2014. *Refashioning Secularisms in France and Turkey: The Case of the Headscarf Ban*. London: Routledge.

–. 2016. "Exploring the Intricacies and Dissonances of Religious Governance: The Case of Quebec and the Discourse of Request." *Critical Research on Religion* 4, no. 1: 57–71. https://doi.org/10.1177/2050303216630066.

Bouchard, Gérard, and Charles Taylor. 2008. *Building the Future: A Time for Reconciliation*. Québec commission de consultation sur les pratiques

d'accommodement reliées aux differences culturelles. http://collections
.banq.qc.ca/ark:/52327/bs1565996.

Brodeur, Patrice. 2008. "La commission Bouchard-Taylor et la perception des
rapports entre 'Québécois' et 'musulmans' au Québec." *Cahiers de recherche
sociologique* 46: 95–107. https://doi.org/10.7202/1002510ar.

Bronskill, Jim. 2021. "Conservative MP Tim Uppal Sorry for Role in
'Divisiveness' of Harper-Era Politics." CBC News. 14 June 2021. https://
www.cbc.ca/news/politics/uppal-harper-conservative-muslim
-niqab-1.6065058.

Bunting, Annie, and Shado Mokhtari. 2007. "Migrant Muslim Women's
Interests and the Case of 'Sharia Tribunals' in Ontario." *Racialized Migrant
Women in Canada: Essays on Health, Violence, and Equity*, edited by Vigay
Agnew, 233–64. Toronto: Toronto University Press.

Cesari, Jocelyne. 2006. *When Islam and Democracy Meet: Muslims in Europe and
the United States*. London: Palgrave MacMillan.

–, ed. 2014. *The Oxford Handbook of European Islam*. Oxford: Oxford University
Press.

Chadha, Ena, Suzanne Herbert, and Shawn Richard. 2020. *Review of the Peel
District School Board*. Toronto: Ontario Ministry of Education.

Chaudhry, Ayesha S. 2018. "Islamic Legal Studies: A Critical Historiography."
Oxford Handbook of Islamic Law, edited by Anver M. Emon and Rumee
Ahmed, 1–40. Oxford: Oxford University Press.

Conservative Party of Canada (CPC). 2018. "Minority Report of the Standing
Committee on Canadian Heritage on Systemic Racism and Religious
Discrimination." In *Taking Action against Systemic Racism and Religious
Discrimination Including Islamophobia: Report of the Standing Committee on
Canadian Heritage*. 42nd Parliament, 1st Session, February 2018.

Corbett, Rosemary R. 2016. *Making Moderate Islam: Sufism, Service and the
"Ground Zero Mosque" Controversy*. Redwood City, CA: Stanford University
Press.

Crenshaw, Kimberlé. 1991. "Mapping the Margins: Intersectionality, Identity
Politics, and Violence against Women of Color. *Stanford Law Review* 43, no. 6:
1241–99. https://doi.org/10.2307/1229039.

De Goede, Marieke. 2012. *Speculative Security: The Politics of Pursuing Terrorist
Monies*. Minneapolis: University of Minnesota Press.

Eid, Paul. 2012a. "Les inégalités 'ethnoraciales' dans l'accès à l'emploi à
Montréal: le poids de la discrimination." *Recherches sociographiques* 53, no. 2
(May–August): 415–50. https://doi.org/10.7202/1012407ar.

–. 2012b. "Mesurer la discrimination à l'embauche subie par les minorités
racisées: résultats d'un "testing" mené dans le grand Montréal." Commission
des droits de la personne et des droits de la jeunesse. 13 June 2012.

Emon, Anver M. 2009. "Islamic Law and the Canadian Mosaic: Politics, Jurisprudence, and Multicultural Accommodation." *Canadian Bar Review* 87, no. 2: 391–425. https://cbr.cba.org/index.php/cbr/issue/view/528.

–. 2019. "The 'Islamic' Deployed. The Study of Islam in Four Registers." *Middle East Law and Governance* 11, no 3: 347–403. https://doi.org/10.1163/18763375-01103001.

Emon, Anver M., and Nadia Z. Hasan. 2021. *Under Layered Suspicion: A Review of CRA Audits of Muslim-Led Charities.* Toronto: Institute of Islamic Studies. www.layeredsuspicion.ca.

Emon, Anver, and Aaqib Mahmood. 2021. "*Canada v. Asad Ansari*: Avatars, Inexpertise and Racial Bias in Canadian Anti-Terrorism Litigation." *Manitoba Law Journal* 44, no. 1: 255–94. https://ssrn.com/abstract=3614107.

European Network against Racism. 2018. "Key Recommendations to Tackle Islamophobia from a Coalition of Civil Society Organisations." 3 December 2018. https://www.enar-eu.org/Key-recommendations-to-tackle-Islamophobia-from-a-coalition-of-civil-society.

Green, Todd. 2019. *The Fear of Islam: An Introduction to Islamophobia in the West.* 2nd ed. Minneapolis, MN: Fortress Press.

Hage, Ghassan. 2017. *Is Racism an Environmental Threat?* Cambridge: Polity Press.

House of Commons Debates. 2021. 43rd Parliament, 2nd Session, Vol. 150, No. 113 (8 June 2021).

Institute for Social Policy and Understanding. n.d. "Islamophobia: A Threat to Us All." Accessed 26 March 2022. https://www.ispu.org/public-policy/islamophobia/.

Korteweg, Anna C., and Jennifer A. Selby, eds. 2012. *Debating Sharia: Islam, Gender, Politics, and Family Law Arbitration.* Toronto: University of Toronto Press.

Latour, Bruno. 2009. *The Making of Law: An Ethnography of the Conseil d'Etat.* Hoboken, NJ: Wiley.

Marzouki, Nadia. 2017. *Islam: An American Religion? (Religion, Culture, and Public Life)*, translated by C. Jon Deglou. New York: Columbia University Press.

Mitchell, Timothy. 2002. *Rule of Experts: Egypt, Techno-Politics, Modernity.* Oakland, CA: University of California Press.

Mosleh, Omar. 2021. "As Muslim Women Are Attacked in Alberta, a Community Asks: Can Canada Face Its Islamophobia Problem?" *Toronto Star*, 4 July 2021. https://www.thestar.com/news/canada/2021/07/04/they-only-call-it-a-hate-crime-after-you-get-killed-as-muslim-women-are-attacked-in-alberta-a-community-asks-can-canada-face-its-islamophobia-problem.html.

Nakua, Abdussalam. 2021. "An Agenda for Equitable Recovery: Balancing Economic Outputs with Social Wellbeing Outcomes." Imagine Canada (blog). 8 April 2021. https://imaginecanada.ca/en/360/agenda-equitable-recovery-balancing-economic-outputs-social-wellbeing-outcomes.

Norton, Anne. 2013. *On the Muslim Question*. Princeton, NJ: Princeton University Press.

Paradkar, Shree. 2020. "Students, Teachers, Parents Feel the Sting of Islamophobia in Peel Schools. They Share Their Stories." *Toronto Star*, 16 June 2020. https://www.thestar.com/opinion/star-columnists/2020/06/16/students-teachers-parents-feel-the-sting-of-islamophobia-in-peel-schools-they-share-their-stories.html.

Passas, Nikos. 2010. "Understanding Terrorism Financing." *Commission of Inquiry into the Investigation of the Bombing of Air India Flight 182*. Terrorism Financing, Charities, and Aviation Security. Commission of Inquiry into the Investigation of the Bombing of Air India Flight 182 Research Studies, vol. 2. 15–118. Ottawa: Minister of Public Works and Government Services.

Razack, Sherene. 2008. *Casting Out: The Eviction of Muslims From Western Law and Politics*. Toronto: University of Toronto Press.

Runnymede Trust. 1997. *Islamophobia: A Challenge for Us All*. London: Runnymede Trust.

Salomon, Noah. 2016. *For Love of the Prophet: An Ethnography of Sudan's Islamic State*. Princeton, NJ: Princeton University Press.

Scott, James C. 1999. *Seeing Like a State*. New Haven, CT: Yale University Press.

Selby, Jennifer A., Amélie Barras, and Lori G. Beaman. 2019. *Beyond Accommodation: Everyday Narratives of Muslim Canadians*. Vancouver: UBC Press.

Shaheen, Kareem. 2021. "Does CRA's Charities Directorate Have an Islamophobia Problem?" Philanthropist Journal. 21 September 2021. https://thephilanthropist.ca/2021/09/does-cras-charities-directorate-have-an-islamophobia-problem.

Evans, Peter B., Dietrich Rueschemeyer, and Theda Skocpol. 2010. *Bringing the State Back In*. Cambridge: Cambridge University Press.

Valverde, Mariana. 2012. *Everyday Law in the Street: City Governance in an Age of Diversity*. Chicago Series in Law and Society. Chicago: University of Chicago Press.

Williams, Patricia. 1991. *The Alchemy of Race and Rights: Diary of a Law Professor*. Cambridge, MA: Harvard University Press.

Zine, Jasmin. 2007. "Safe Havens or Religious 'Ghettos'? Narratives of Islamic Schooling in Canada." *Race, Ethnicity and Education* 10, no. 1: 71–92. https://doi.org/10.1080/13613320601100385.

–. 2012. "Introduction: Muslim Cultural Politics in the Canadian Hinterlands. *Islam in the Hinterlands: Muslim Cultural Politics in Canada*, edited by Jasmin Zine, 1–38. Vancouver: UBC Press.

Islamophobia in Canada: Representation and Perspective

1 Centring the Black Muslimah: Interrogating Gendered, Anti-Black Islamophobia

RABIAT AKANDE

Islamophobia is an everyday reality for Muslims. It takes spectacular acts of violence, such as the brutal 2021 slaying of a London, Ontario, family, to bring this common Muslim experience to public consciousness (Zardosky and Thompson 2021). Yet, extensive studies show that Islamophobia has a firm foothold in Canada as it does in much of the contemporary world (Allen 2016; Bouchard and Taylor 2008; Wilkins-Laflamme 2018). For all the generality of the Muslim experience of discrimination, however, Islamophobia is, like all forms of systemic oppression, more acutely experienced at particular intersections. Perhaps the most palpable of these intersections is the meeting of the Muslim identity not only with gender but also specifically with race. If the body of the Muslim woman is constantly marked and othered, that of the Black Muslim woman inhabits an even more precarious intersection. Studies of Islamophobia and the state's complicity in its systemic and structural forms, including those that pay attention to gender and those that interrogate Islamophobia as anti-Muslim racism, have, however, been inattentive to the precarity of the Black Muslim woman. This essay tentatively interrogates how Islamophobia in its systemic forms encounters the Black Muslim woman, mapping out what the interrogation of this encounter might entail, the voices it will foreground, the forms of questions it might enable scholars and activists to ask, and its possible contributions to scholarly and policy debates.

I proceed in two parts. Part 1 considers what is elided by the pervasive tendency to homogenize the forms of oppression that Islamophobia engenders. Arising from the flawed understanding of Muslims as a monolith, the pervasive understanding of Islamophobia as a singular and undifferentiated form of oppression – and suffering – obscures the uniqueness of the suffering of differently positioned Muslim subjects. Moreover, it elides intra-Muslim forms of domination that foster the heightened vulnerability of discretely situated Muslims. I further argue that this inattention to unique realities, and specifically, intersectional ones, partly arises from the term *Islamophobia*'s ostensible focus on "Islam," the religion. By understanding Islamophobia as a form of oppression directed at Islam, the term risks homogenizing the target of the hostility, privileging the experience of dominant groups among them. Departing from this tendency, theorizing Islamophobia through the lens of intersectionality pays attention to the systemic and structural oppression that Muslims face while also paying attention to the particularities of Muslim experiences. Doing so helps to foreground both the intergroup differentiation and ultimately the discrimination that instantiates and sustains Islamophobia, as well as the intragroup positioning that makes certain Muslims more vulnerable than others. Building on this foregrounding of the "particular," part 2 then proceeds to map a specific intersection – the Black Muslim woman. Black Muslimahs are intersectionals who easily fall through the cracks in the current discourse, which focuses on hegemonic Muslim representations – typically male, Middle Eastern or South Asian. In contrast to this approach, I attempt to centre the figure of the Black Muslimah, a marginalized experience, in interrogating Islamophobia. I conclude by arguing that intersectionalizing the study of Islamophobia illuminates the distributive effects of Islamophobia on differently situated Muslims while also nuancing our understanding of the shared Muslim experience of oppression.

1. Intersectionalizing Islamophobia

Muslims, and in particular Arabo-Muslims are, with Blacks, the group hardest hit by various forms of discrimination. (Bouchard and Taylor 2008)

Islamophobia, as defined by the often-cited UK Runnymede Trust report, is "unfounded hostility towards Islam" having "practical consequences" in "unfair discrimination," including the "exclusion of Muslims from mainstream political and social affairs" (Runnymede Trust 1997, 4; Elahi and Khan 2017, 7). If pervasive anti-Muslim discrimination informed the 1997 Runnymede enquiry, global Islamophobia has only proliferated exponentially since its publication, particularly in the aftermath of the 11 September 2001 attacks and the Euro-America-championed global War on Terror that followed. Even as scholars and activists have grappled with the distant roots and recent iterations of anti-Muslim hate – a drive continuously renewed by frequent bursts of spectacular acts of Islamophobic violence – much continues to be elusive including the lived experiences of Muslims encountering Islamophobia. The term "Islamo-phobia" centres Islam as the subject of anti-Muslim vitriol, portraying anti-Muslim bias as arising from hostility towards the religion of Islam itself. This foregrounding of Islam has paradoxically served to arm pur-veyors of anti-Muslim rhetoric who cite transnational liberal commit-ments to free speech and debate to defend anti-Muslim vitriol masked as a critique of Islam as an ideology (Islam 2018a). Anti-Muslim rhetoric is hardly an engagement with Islam as an ideology; yet, presenting anti-Muslim hate as a critique of Islam is possible precisely because of the essentialization of the Muslim at the centre of Islamophobic discourse. That discourse produces Muslims as a homogenous racial category, of-ten relying on stereotypical tropes of the brown Arab or South Asian, typically male or male-dependent (Hill 2015). By racializing Muslims as a homogenous category with essentialized cultural or social markers while attributing those differences to the natural difference of Muslims, Islamophobic discourse creates an essentialized and differentiated cate-gory while insisting that the hostility is directed at the ideology rather than the people.

This essentialization, paradoxically, finds a place in the discourse seeking to dismantle Islamophobia (Islam 2018a). Often, well-meaning advocates adopt the experience of the dominant Muslim prototype to understand the Muslim experience of oppression, with the conse-quence that advocates respond to a relentless and homogenizing Islam-ophobic discourse with an equally homogenizing and essentializing representation. Such a response eclipses the stories of Muslims whose experiences of oppression are conditioned by the unique interplay of various identities that heighten their vulnerability. The outcome is the displacement of these experiences to the periphery, intensifying the vulnerability of these intersectionals, and ultimately undermining the project of dismantling anti-Muslim discrimination that these advo-cates pursue. Furthermore, by siloing anti-Muslim discrimination from other forms of oppression, the homogenization that continues to be pop-ular in advocacy and policy reform discourse obscures the entrenched systemic and structural violence that sustains and perpetuates anti-Muslim oppression. Integral to that violence is the homogenization of ways of being Muslim and of the Muslim experience. De-marginaliz-ing those experiences calls for theorizing the relations of power that produces, others, and renders Muslims vulnerable in divergent ways (Abdul Khabeer, n.d.; Alexander 2017).

The marginalization of the experiences of non-dominant members of minority groups is hardly unique to the context of anti-Muslim dis-crimination. Critical race theorists have long interrogated this issue in the context of racialized minorities, attempting to map the experience at the "margins" by deploying the theory of intersectionality. The theory of intersectionality suggests that a focus on a single axis in interrogating the experience of discrimination and formulating legal and policy responses tends to privilege the experience of dominant members of minority groups, eliding the experience of persons at the margins. Far from arising from a single identity, this experience of marginalization is the culmination of the simultaneity of multiple minority identities. Consequently, no single-axis analysis can apprehend the experience of persons at the intersection of multiple minority identities. By viewing marginalized persons merely through the lens of a single identity, both laws that seek to address discrimination and discourses of emancipation fail to account for the heightened vulnerability of intersectionals. This failure to engage with intersectional realities dooms the quest to remedy discrimination or achieve substantive equality (Crenshaw 1989, 139; 1991, 1242). If the experience of working-class Black women first inspired intersectional analysis, the theory has productively theorized the power relations and marginalization that speaks to a range of experiences, including Indigeneity, disability, and religion, among others (Crenshaw 1989, 139; 1991, 1242; Clutterbuck 2015, 51; Hammer 2013). Interrogating the experience of Muslims at the margins calls for intersectionalizing the Muslim experience of discrimination.

In recognition of this insight that "intergroup discrimination" can be "based on intragroup difference" (Aziz 2015, 391), studies of anti-Muslim discrimination are increasingly illuminating the ways particularly situated Muslims more keenly experience Islamophobic oppression (Aziz 2014, 2015; Islam 2018a; Runnymede Trust 1997). This shift has led to calls to foreground the experience of Muslim women, racialized groups, and those with non-dominant ethnic-national origins. Nevertheless, this emerging attention to intersectionality in understanding Islamophobia continues to ignore certain intersections. Perhaps no elided intersection carries a more heightened precarity than that of the Black Muslim woman.

2. Centring the Black Muslimah

Solidarity is centring the most affected. (Islam 2018b)

The figure of the Muslim woman is an object of intense scrutiny. Long an object of occidental fascination and exoticization, Muslim women are "caught in the crosshairs of bias at the intersection of religion, gender, and race or ethnicity" (Aziz 2015, 342; Aziz, 2012, 262). Popular discourse, therefore, continues to foreground the ostensible need to emancipate Muslim women, invoking age-long tropes of the Muslim woman's subordination by her male counterparts and calling for liberation through the state's regulation of the Muslim woman's body. Indeed, what Muslim women wear or uncover continues to be hotly contested and the subject of a social, political, and legal discourse that often elides the agency of Muslim women, foreclosing their participation in the ostensibly democratic liberal discourse that is supposed to emancipate them. As Faiza Hijri states, "the obsession with Muslim women's bodies – whether they are covered, how they are covered, what those bodies are capable of – never seems to go out of style, as it were, and the obsession is held by many different groups that feel they should control these bodies in some way" (Hirji 2021, 80). At the same time, however, the vision of the meek, docile, and repressed female on which this first representation of the Muslim woman relies has long collided with the post-9/11 view of the Muslim woman as a vector of dangerous ideologies, a disloyal terrorist, or, at least, an enabler of her terrorist male counterpart. As a result, Muslim women are simultaneously stereotyped as meek, passive, and docile while also portrayed as aggressive and violent. This representation of Muslim women, itself based on the stereotypes of Muslim men in a post-9/11 global War on Terror context, genders Islamophobia (Zine 2004). Gendered Islamophobia culminates in Muslim women's heightened vulnerability in employment, education, law enforcement, and political participation – especially when the Muslim woman wears a visible religious marker such as the hijab (Aziz 2014; 2015; Zine 2006, 239; Zempi and Chakraborti 2014).

The vulnerability is heightened in the case of the Black Muslim woman. The added axis of blackness compounds the Black Muslim woman's experience of anti-Muslim oppression and marginalization. Anti-Black racism conditions the Black Muslimah to an entrenched system of racial oppression that has treated Black persons as second-class humans and, in not a few jurisdictions, as chattel to be transported abroad or brutally colonized at home. This long history of colonization, slavery, and socio-economic and cultural exploitation does not only survive through Black memories haunted by intergenerational trauma. It also lives on in stark socio-economic disparities, in the continuing brutalization of Black bodies by forms of state-sponsored and state-enabled violence. Everyday violence, sometimes life-ending, remains the global experience of Black people. Despite claims to multiculturalism, Canada is far from an exception (Maynard 2017; Backhouse 1999).

For the Black Muslim woman, the simultaneity of bias along the multiple axes of race, gender, and religion arises from a complex relation of power between these uniquely situated Muslim intersectionals and non-Muslims, and between these intersectionals and differently situated Muslims. That intergroup relation of power is instantiated by the casting of Muslims as an "other" to world civilization and global progress. While Islamophobia invents a homogenized notion of a Muslim and sustains its othering through that homogenization, Islamophobia is perpetuated and thrives through its interconnection with other forms of oppression. Those forms of oppression are not absent from Muslim intragroup relations. The outcome is the uneven distribution of Islamophobia among differently positioned Muslims. It is by mapping that distribution that scholarship can unveil Muslim women's heightened burden of Islamophobic oppression.

Grasping the Black Muslim woman's encounter with Islamophobia calls for interrogating both intergroup and intragroup relations of power. Examining the stereotypes attached to the Black, female, Muslim intersection is one productive way to apprehend the marginalization of the Black Muslim woman. Stereotyping is itself an act of power. When the Black Muslimah's blackness meets her gender, she is subject to the age-long stereotype of the angry Black woman. Economic assumptions also travel with this stereotypical portrayal of a Black woman; the Black woman is imagined to be poor and dependent on social welfare. On the one hand, the conditions that overdetermine the Black woman's subjugation are also implicated in the economic conditions that make her economic advancement impossible without radical reform. At the same time, any denunciations of the system that conditions her oppression and advocacy for reform only reinstate the a priori conclusion that rage defines the Black woman. These self-perpetuating and therefore irrefutable presumptions about the Black woman's rage are only intensified when the Black woman is Muslim. The post-9/11 understanding of the Muslim woman as aggressive, disloyal, and violent only heightens when it encounters a Black and stereotypically portrayed angry woman. At the same time, however, agency-eliding occidental presumptions of the meek, docile, and submissive Muslim woman persist with these stereotypes and serve not to neutralize the stereotypes of aggression but instead, peculiarly coexist with it. The simultaneity of these identities and the experiences that follow them intensify the psychological burden for Black Muslim women.

An agenda to centre the Black Muslim woman requires interrogating the experience at that unique intersection. That storytelling, to be deployed in projects to reform state institutions, foregrounded in possible societal reconciliation and remediation projects, and conceivably in corrective litigations, cannot merely rely on archives of formal encounters with legal and bureaucratic institutions. Those archives, including of the police where Black bodies have always been a target of violence, in national security where Muslims continue to be scapegoated, of the workplace where the labour of Black women continues to be exploited, and of the family where both Black and Muslim women continue to be governed by the overreaching hands of the state while also battling entrenched patriarchy, will be useful for what they reveal of the precarity of the Black Muslim woman. However, apprehending this experience will call for far more than a voyage into state and institutional archives. Scrutinizing this elided intersection will call for live histories and forms of storytelling that keep mediation of these accounts at a minimum. If this essay's attempt to account for the experiences of Black Muslim women spotlights the vulnerability of these intersectionals, the storytelling it calls for resists domination by centring the self-told narrative of the Black Muslimah experience.

Conclusion

Anti-Muslim hate and discrimination is unevenly distributed among Muslims. The continued legacy of Western colonialism, slavery, anti-blackness, patriarchy, the War on Terror, and several other global events have culminated in relations of power that heighten the Black Muslim woman's vulnerability to Islamophobia. This essay has, therefore, made a case for demarginalizing the intersection of race, gender, and religion that accounts for the Black Muslim woman's experience. To intersectionalize the study of Islamophobia is to pay attention to the unique vulnerabilities that arise from multiple and interconnected systems of oppression. Such a study will not only map the intra-Muslim and external relations of power that heighten the vulnerability of the Black Muslim woman. Mapping the margin inhabited by the Black Muslim woman will also illuminate, not occlude, the general Muslim experience of oppression. For one, the intersection of race, gender, and religion that culminates in the Black Muslim woman's experience may implicate other identities, including class, immigration, and the intergenerational inheritance of Western colonization. Interrogating the vulnerability of the Black Muslimah will mean paying closer attention to these other identities with the consequence that centring the story of the Black Muslimah will foreground the experience of differently positioned Muslims. For all its attention to particularity, however, this focus on the unique realities of differently positioned Muslims does not discount the structural context within which Islamophobia emerges and in which it thrives. Because that context is one that has always insisted on homogenizing Muslims even while its consequences lead to uneven distributive effects among adherents of the Islamic faith, a critical intersectional analysis of Islamophobia necessitates awareness of that structural context linking the experience of differently situated Muslims. In sum, mapping the margin inhabited by the Black Muslimah coheres with spotlighting the shared Muslim experience of oppression.

WORKS CITED

Abdul Khabeer, Su'ad. n.d. "Islamophobia Is Racism: Resource for Teaching & Learning about Anti-Muslim Racism in the United States." Islamophobia Is Racism. Accessed 29 March 2022. https://islamophobiaisracism.wordpress.com.

Alexander, Claire. 2017. "Raceing Islamophobia." In *Islamophobia: Still a Challenge for Us All*, edited by Farah Elahi and Omar Khan, 13–17. London: Runnymede Trust.

Allen, Chris. 2016. *Islamophobia*. New York: Routledge.

Aziz, Sahar. 2012. "From the Oppressed to the Terrorist: Muslim American Women Caught in the Crosshairs of Intersectionality." *Hastings Race & Poverty Law Journal* 9, no. 1: 191– 264. https://ssrn.com/abstract=1981777.

–. 2014. "Coercive Assimilationism: The Perils of Muslim Women's Identity Performance in the Workplace." *Michigan Journal of Race and Law* 20, no. 1: 1–64. https://dx.doi.org/10.2139/ssrn.2404074.

–. 2015. "Coercing Assimilationism: The Case of Muslim Women of Color." *Journal of Race, Gender and Justice* 18, no. 1: 389–99. https://ssrn.com/abstract=2719651.

Backhouse, Constance. 1999. *Colour-Coded: A Legal History of Racism in Canada, 1900–1950*. Toronto: University of Toronto Press.

Bouchard, Gérard, and Charles Taylor. 2008. *Building the Future: A Time for Reconciliation*. Commission de consultation sur les pratiques d'accommodement reliées aux differences culturelles. http://collections.banq.qc.ca/ark:/52327/bs1565996.

Clutterbuck, Alyssa. 2015. "Rethinking Baker: A Critical Race Feminist Theory of Disability." *Appeal: Review of Current Law & Legal Reform* 20: 51–70. https://journals.uvic.ca/index.php/appeal/article/view/13594.

Crenshaw, Kimberlé. 1989. "Demarginalizing the Intersection of Race and Sex: A Black Feminist Critique of Antidiscrimination Doctrine, Feminist Theory and Antiracist Politics." *University of Chicago Legal Forum*, no. 1: 139–67. http://chicagounbound.uchicago.edu/uclf/vol1989/iss1/8.

–. 1991. "Mapping the Margins: Intersectionality, Identity Politics, and Violence against Women of Color." *Stanford Law Review* 43, no. 6: 1241–99. https://doi.org/10.2307/1229039.

Elahi, Farah, and Omar Khan. 2017. "Introduction: What Is Islamophobia?" In *Islamophobia: Still A Challenge for Us All*, edited by Farah Elahi and Omar Khan, 5–12. London: Runnymede Trust.

Hammer, J. 2013. "Center Stage: Gendered Islamophobia and Muslim Women." In *Islamophobia in America: The Anatomy of Intolerance*, edited by C.W. Ernst, 107–44. London: Palgrave Macmillan.

Hill, Margari. 2015. "What's in a Name? Using Muslim as a Cultural Category Erases and Stereotypes." Margariaziza (blog). 23 March 2015. https:// margariaziza.com/2015/03/23/whats-in-a-name-using-muslim-as -a-cultural-category-erases-and-stereotypes/.

Hirji, Faiza. 2021. "Claiming our Space: Muslim Women, Activism, and Social Media." *Islamophobia Studies Journal* 6, no. 1: 78–92. https://doi.org /10.13169/islastudj.6.1.0078.

Islam, Namira. 2018a. "Soft Islamophobia." *Religions* 9, no. 9: 280–96. https:// doi.org/10.3390/rel9090280.

–. 2018b. "Modifying Silk Ring Theory for Allyship." *Medium* (blog). 16 April 2018. https://medium.com/@namira.islam/modifying-silk-ring-theory -for-allyship-c7ae4963912d

Maynard, Robyn. 2017. *Policing Black Lives: State Violence in Canada from Slavery to the Present*. Halifax: Fernwood.

Runnymede Trust. 1997. *Islamophobia: A Challenge for Us All*. London: Runnymede Trust.

Wilkins-Laflamme, Sarah. 2018. "Islamophobia in Canada: Measuring the Realities of Negative Attitudes towards Muslims and Religious Discrimination." *Canadian Review of Sociology* 55, no. 1: 86–110. https://doi .org/10.1111/cars.12180.

Zardosky, Justin, and Matt Thompson. 2021. "Police Say Driver 'Intentionally' Crashed into Muslim Family in London, Ont., Killing 4." CTV News. 6 June 2021. https://london.ctvnews.ca/police-say-driver-intentionally-crashed -into-muslim-family-in-london-ont-killing-4-1.5458887.

Zempi, I., and N. Chakraborti. 2014. *Islamophobia, Victimisation and the Veil*. Palgrave Macmillan.

Zine, Jasmin. 2004. "Anti-Islamophobia Education as Transformative Pedagogy: Reflections from the Educational Front Lines." *American Journal of Islamic Social Sciences* 21, no. 3: 110–19. https://doi.org/10.35632/ajiss .v21i3.510.

–. 2006. "Unveiled Sentiments: Gendered Islamophobia and Experiences of Veiling among Muslim Girls in a Canadian Islamic School." *Equity & Excellence in Education* 39, no. 3 (2006): 239–52. https://doi.org/10.1080 /10665680600788503.

2 The Impact of Systemic Islamophobia on Sexually Diverse and Gender Diverse Muslims in Canada

SARAH SHAH AND MARYAM KHAN

Introduction

Sexually and gender diverse (SGD) Muslims living in Canada face intersectional discrimination in mainstream LGBTQ+, ethno-racial, and Muslim communities of belonging and origin (Alvi and Zaidi 2021; Golriz 2021; Khan and Mulé 2021; Javaid 2020; Maulod 2021; Minwalla, Rosser, Feldman, and Varga 2005). This multifaceted, intersectional discrimination is based on social and cultural identities straddling spirituality, race, religiosity, sexuality, ability, ethnicity, and gender identity and expression. This in turn contributes to poor socio-economic and health outcomes, including poor mental health and social isolation, and it may lead to substance abuse and suicide (Siraj 2009, 2012; Mulé and Gamble 2018). There is a dire need to better understand and address the structural and institutional (e.g., systemic) experiences and impacts of Islamophobia among SGD Muslims.

We assess *Islamophobia* as insidious ideological, cultural, political, historical, and social forces that systemically operate through various mechanisms and mediums of social organization such as laws, practices, policies, attitudes, discourse, and structures to promote fear and violence through making *other* the bodies, regions and geographies, identities, and ultimately anything to do with *Muslimness* and Islam. This also includes omissions and prejudices grounded in internalized oppressions, Orientalism, and civilizational discourses (Mullaly and West 2018; Puar 2017; Said 1978). While there has been a significant increase in the study of Islamophobia since 9/11, there remains a gap in research on SGD Muslims' experiences of Islamophobia.

Research on SGD Muslims has been limited due to multiple methodological challenges. Quantitative analyses with SGD samples have been limited due to the lack of representation within survey samples

(Shah 2019). Qualitative analyses tend to focus on case studies, which allow us a better understanding of the processes and problems SGD Muslims experience; however, in the absence of quantitative data, the prevalence and relevance of such findings are difficult to extrapolate beyond the limited and often selective qualitative study samples. Additionally, research on SGD Muslims is often conducted by researchers who themselves do not believe in Islam's validity (e.g., by non-Muslims or former Muslims); thus, this body of research tends to reflect researcher bias and emerge from Orientalist assumptions, fixating on how SGD Muslims negotiate their identities. As devout Muslim queers, we call on researchers to go beyond tired tropes and strawmen arguments about the incompatibility of SGD Muslims' identities in order to better understand their experiences and needs. We call on researchers to centre the voices of SGD Muslims and involve them in the research process to ensure ethical reciprocation (Shah and Khan 2023).

Despite these methodological challenges, a limited body of scholarship on SGD Muslims exists. This body of scholarship demonstrates the value of exploring the experiences of SGD Muslims through an intersectional lens. There is much theoretical richness in exploring the experiences of social actors who live at the margins of multiple intersections like SGD Muslims. Intersectional approaches value lived experiences as knowledge and support the individual and communal strengths that can fuel resistance and agency. An intersectional research approach considers how SGD Muslims navigate and live the multiple and compounding oppressions in identity facets of race, ethnicity, sexuality, gender identity and expression, and religion and spirituality without problematizing identities as "competing" as would an Orientalist approach (Collins 2009; Rahman 2010; Said 1978; Shah, Khan, and Abdel-Latif 2021; Sterzing, Gartner, Woodford, and Fisher 2017). Further, lived experiences of identity facets, which can take the form of resistance, oppression, agency, and so on, are sources of knowledge which can inform service provision (Meyer 2015; Rahman 2010, 2014, 2018). Intersectional research, moreover, moves from theory to action to advocate on behalf of disadvantaged groups with a focus on social justice (Rahman 2010). This theoretical approach is ideally suited for partnered research that aims to challenge stigma at the nexus of SGD identities, ethnicities, and religion.

We provide two examples of potential research projects that explore and address the ways systemic Islamophobia impacts SGD Muslims. Both studies are qualitative, take intersectional approaches, and provide ethical considerations in reciprocity – e.g., the studies incorporate the communities from which the samples are drawn in knowledge mobilization processes.

Avenues for Research

As in other homonationalist states (Puar 2017), Canadian national identity is defined by acceptance of sexual and gender diversity. However, Canadian national identity is also defined by multiculturalism and inclusion of diverse populations (Alba and Foner 2015). To honestly hail itself a mosaic, Canada needs a population motivated to support *all* its members, not just the mainstream. The LGBTQ+ communities are not homogenous, and creating awareness, services, programming, practices, and policies inclusive of SGD Muslims will enhance equity. An important step in that process is to identify how systemic Islamophobia in policies and practices impact SGD Muslims.

To better understand the experiences of systemic Islamophobia among and unique to SGD Muslims in Canada, we offer two directions for research. The first study proposes a robust policy analysis on how federal, provincial, and local health and mental health care policies create unsafe situations and deny access to care for SGD domestic Muslims (i.e., Muslims already in Canada). The second proposes an analysis of Canadian immigration and refugee policies that are not sensitive to the circumstances and lived realities of SGD Muslims. Each study integrates direct benefits to the communities from which the samples are drawn, through such means as knowledge mobilization, resource development, and community forums.

Study 1: Health Care Policies

The first avenue for research is a robust policy analysis on how federal, provincial, and local health and mental health care policies create unsafe situations and deny access to care for SGD Muslims. Such research could yield several benefits for SGD Muslims as well as other equity seeking groups in Canada. This project would identify specific mental, spiritual, emotional, and health needs of SGD Muslims, which would facilitate identifying and addressing service gaps related to psychological distress and isolation, leading to culturally relevant services, programs, and policies. In 2019, a policy brief submitted to the House of Commons Standing Committee on Health argued that "in addition to using a population health approach to address the social determinants of health, a comprehensive Federal LGBTQ2 Health Equity Strategy must also ensure that we improve our understanding of SOGIESC [sexual orientation, gender identity, gender expression, and sex characteristics] within a health equity and intersectional lens" (Mulé, Khan, and McKenzie 2020, 2). The imperative of adopting this strategy has become even more prominent given the existing inequities experienced by LGBTQ+ Muslim communities are further exacerbated by the COVID-19 pandemic.

Many Canadian LGBTQ+ organizations do not have policies and practices appropriate for diverse and intersectional subgroups such as SGD Muslims. For example, there are major programming and service gaps in Canadian LGBTQ+ organizations which tend to focus on "coming out," promoting identity and rights-based perspectives while ignoring communities where being public about sexuality is not safe (Khan and Mulé 2021). For SGD Muslims, who like other Canadian Muslims may rely on immigrant networks for social and economic resources (Moghissi, Rahnema, and Goodman 2009), "coming out" could mean losing access to valuable support in their most vulnerable time. Research documents that Muslim newcomers, both refugees and immigrants, draw on religion as a tool of social support during settlement in their new host countries (McMichael 2002; Shoeb, Weinstein, and Halpern 2007).

Another example of gaps in programming and practices impacting SGD Muslims includes the secular approach many LGBTQ+ organizations take, divorcing sexuality from spirituality. This is notably not a feature of queer Indigenous spaces – which is why, in this chapter, we retain use of LGBTQ+ and omit "2S," given the colonial approach to sexuality we critique is absent in many two-spirited spaces. While the significance of the interconnectedness of sexuality, spirituality, culture, and identity are recognized in two-spirited spaces (Alaers 2010), such spaces are created because of the colonial, categorical, and secular approaches of mainstream LGBTQ+ organizations. This secular approach is alienating for some SGD Muslims, for whom religiosity and spirituality are part and parcel of their identity. Especially in a post-9/11 social world, where ascribed Muslim-identity is difficult to escape (Peucker 2021), the value of religion-based mental health resources, especially for religious minorities, cannot be ignored (Shah 2018).

These issues remain unaddressed as there is a gap in Canadian research, and thus there remain very limited and culturally relevant social service provisions for nonbinary, queer, and trans Muslims in both mainstream Canadian LGBTQ+ and Muslim organizations. The proposed study will address these gaps to better support this "minority within a minority" in therapeutic milieus including counselling, health care, and social work service provision. Researchers may conduct community-based explorations to better understand the social service and programming needs of SGD Muslims in Canada.

Such a project would have three main tasks: identifying and assessing SGD Muslims' heterogeneous psychosocial and intersectional needs for social service and programming; documenting and analysing barriers and facilitators to SGD Muslims' psychosocial well-being in mainstream social service agencies; and determining how mainstream agencies can more meaningfully respond to and engage in culturally relevant ways to the service and programming needs of SGD Muslims in Canada.

Study 2: Immigration and Refugee Asylum Policies

The second proposed avenue for research is a robust policy analysis on how Canadian immigration and refugee policies create barriers for SGD Muslims coming to Canada, as these policies are not sensitive to the circumstances, identities, and lived experiences of SGD Muslims. The Immigration and Refugee Board (IRB) is self-described as the largest "independent administrative tribunal. It is responsible for making well-reasoned decisions on immigration and refugee matters, efficiently, fairly and in accordance with the law" (IRB 2021). This arm of the government evaluates the large numbers of refugee claimants, and works alongside Immigration, Refugees, and Citizenship Canada on refugee and immigration particulars (IRB 2021). Research has documented that white refugee claimants are at the top of the hierarchy, as state actors and institutions render African, Middle Eastern, and Asian claimants at the bottom (Iacovetta 2006; Lee and Brotman 2013; Mulé and Gamble 2018). Many scholars are critical of IRB's inner workings as it relates to claimant application evaluation and how decisions about who is accepted and who is denied are made.

For example, efforts are needed to address the impacts of race, gender identity and expression, ethnicity, religion, and ability as they intersect with geographies and legacies of colonialism and imperialism. Notably, there are historical accounts of same-sex themes, references, acts, and characters featured in poetry, fiction, and non-fiction found in historic Muslim societies, alongside practices of "homosexuality," which were made illegal by former colonial states (Gopinath 2005; Ibrahim 2016; Massad 2007; Najmabadi 2008, 2013; see also Shah, Khan, and Abdel-Latif 2021). Thus, research documents the current biphobic, homophobic, and transphobic legislation, policies, and attitudes found in Muslim regions and societies, which lead to persecution, torture, and death of many SGD Muslims (Kahn 2015a, 2015b; Lennox and

Waites 2013). Kinsman (2018, 99) argues that the IRB assesses claimant applications based on Western understandings of sexuality and gender that are mainly grounded in "essentialist theories of differences in SOGI [sexual orientation and gender identity]. This perspective views LGBT characteristics as innate, essential and often as physiologically based." The proposed project would identify assumptions made about LGBTQ+ applicants, how such assumptions fail to capture the realities of SGD Muslims, and how the policies in turn prevent SGD Muslims from gaining entry or legal status in Canada. Such an analysis would yield better insight for policy and practice recommendations.

Current immigration and refugee policies are not sensitive to the social realities and the threats of violence experienced by SGD Muslims in Muslim-majority contexts. For example, in November 2015, Prime Minister Justin Trudeau announced that Canada would accept children, single women, and families fleeing Syria, but not single men. The justification for this decision was to help those "most vulnerable." This exclusion of single men in turn excludes sexually diverse men, who may in fact be partnered, but present as single due to the homophobic context they are fleeing (Yurdakul and Korteweg 2021).

Likewise, there exists discrimination against bisexual sexual orientations, and this is also present in refugee status hearings as claimants identifying as bisexual are more likely to have their cases rejected (Rehaag 2008). Thus, even applicants who are homosexual but have had heterosexual relations are suspect. This can raise barriers for SGD Muslims, whose families may have pressured or even forced them to get married in apparently heterosexual unions to save face in their social networks and/or as a form of conversion therapy. Furthermore, refugee application processes require claimants to provide proof of one's same-sex relationship when most SGD Muslims go to painstaking lengths to hide and erase any evidence of such relations for the sake of safety given the homophobic social environments they occupy. This is also a barrier for immigrants seeking family reunification through family-class immigration: without proof of one's same-sex relationship, applicants cannot reunite with loved ones.

Research on SGD immigrants and refugees to the US and Canada tends to focus on the challenges experienced in countries of origin with a mixed sample of participants from Muslim and non-Muslim majority nation-states (Alessi, 2016; Alessi, Kahn, and Van Der Horn 2017; Munro et al. 2013). Research also documents that SGD refugees and immigrants encounter *othering* via racist and discriminatory practices upon arrival and throughout the settlement process in Canada and the US (Alessi 2016; Fournier, Hamelin Brabant, Dupéré, and Chamberland

2018; Kahn 2015a, 2015b). While there is research on how Canadian immigration and refugee policies impact LGBTQ+ applicants, there is a gap in how these policies impact SGD Muslims specifically. The proposed study would assess the policies as they impact SGD Muslims to provide better access for this vulnerable population. In addition to policy reviews, researchers may conduct community-based explorations to better understand the lived experiences and consequences among SGD Muslim immigrant and refugee applicants already in Canada, or with service agencies that are facilitating applicants' cases.

Thus, the main goals of this research avenue would include assessing immigration and refugee policies and practices in the ways they may create barriers for SGD Muslim applicants; better understanding the lived experiences, social realities, and consequences of such policies on SGD Muslims; and creating recommendations for policies and practices that would reflect the needs of and be inclusive towards SGD Muslims.

Conclusion

Dominant discourses present Islam as antithetical to sexual and gender diversity. This results from Islamophobia and normative assumptions about Muslim homophobia, gender-conservative interpretations of Islam that support heteronormativity, and internationalization of LGBTQ+ identity-rights politics that are not indigenous to Muslim-majority contexts (Shah, Khan, and Abdel-Latif 2021). The proposed research avenues would challenge these normative discourses. Additionally, the proposed inclusion of target populations in the knowledge mobilization process would provide researchers opportunities to reciprocate and co-create resources, programs, and policies in meaningful ways.

Knowledge derived from the studies can be disseminated in research and practice communities through presentations at scholarly conferences and workshops, written reports in publication outlets, and student training within classrooms. These are the more typical routes of knowledge mobilization that also advance the researchers' careers. Beyond these more typical forms of knowledge mobilization, and to decolonize the production and extraction of knowledge from marginalized communities, we urge researchers to consider ethical concerns around reciprocity (Shah and Khan 2023). Knowledge should be mobilized among researchers' networks, but it should also be mobilized in the communities from which it is drawn.

There are also benefits in community consultation processes. Consultation gives an opportunity to further revise and refine resources, policies, or other products emerging from research findings so that they can be implemented on service-receiving populations in more culturally sensitive and relevant ways. Consultation also creates opportunities to bridge gaps and build relationships between academic communities and marginalized communities. Individuals living at the intersections of multiple identities may find it difficult to build trust with those in positions of authority including researchers or health care providers, and an established relationship between communities and researchers can help to overcome this rift. Additionally, given the suggestion to mobilize the knowledge produced from the research within communities from which samples are drawn, the research would allow for SGD Muslims to better understand their experiences through the sociological imagination, reframing apparently personal issues as actual social problems created through dysfunctional social institutions. Such awareness, or consciousness in Foucauldian terms, would better situate SGD Muslims to advocate for themselves and challenge instances of systemic Islamophobia.

WORKS CITED

Alaers, J. 2010. "Two-Spirited People and Social Work Practice." *Critical Social Work* 11, no. 1: 63–79. https://doi.org/10.22329/csw.v11i1.5817.

Alba, R.D., and N. Foner. 2015. *Strangers No More: Immigration and the Challenges of Integration in North America and Western Europe*. Princeton, NJ: Princeton University Press.

Alessi, E.J. 2016. "Resilience in Sexual and Gender Minority Forced Migrants: A Qualitative Exploration." *Traumatology* 22, no. 3: 203–13. https://doi.org /10.1037/trm0000077.

Alessi, E.J., S. Kahn, and R. Van Der Horn. 2017. "A Qualitative Exploration of the Premigration Victimization Experiences of Sexual and Gender Minority Refugees and Asylees in the United States and Canada." *The Journal of Sex Research* 54, no. 7: 936–48. https://doi.org/10.1080/00224499.2016.1229738.

Alvi, S., and A. Zaidi. 2021. "My Existence Is Not Haram": Intersectional Lives in LGBTQ Muslims Living in Canada. *Journal of Homosexuality* 68 no. 6: 993–1014. https://doi.org/10.1080/00918369.2019.1695422.

Collins, P.H. 2009. *Black Feminist Thought*. New York: Routledge Classics.

Fournier, C., L. Hamelin Brabant, S. Dupéré, and L. Chamberland. 2018. "Lesbian and Gay Immigrants' Post-migration Experiences: An Integrative Literature Review." *Journal of Immigrant & Refugee Studies* 16, no. 3: 331–50. https://doi.org/10.1080/15562948.2017.1299269.

Golriz, G. 2021. "'I Am Enough': Why LGBTQ Muslim Groups Resist Mainstreaming." *Sexuality & Culture* 25, no. 2: 355–76. https://doi.org /10.1007/s12119-020-09773-x.

Gopinath, G. 2005. *Impossible Desires: Queer Diasporas and South Asian Public Cultures.* Durham, NC: Duke University Press.

Ibrahim, N.A. 2016. "Homophobic Muslims: Emerging Trends in Multireligious Singapore." *Comparative Studies in Society and History* 58, no. 4: 955–81. https://doi.org/10.1017/S0010417516000499.

IRB. 2021. "Mandate." About the Board. Last modified 10 October 2021. https://irb.gc.ca/en/board/Pages/index.aspx.

Javaid, A. 2020. "The Haunting of Shame: Autoethnography and the Multivalent Stigma of Being Queer, Muslim, and Single." *Symbolic Interaction* 43, no. 1 (February): 72–101. https://doi.org/10.1002/symb.441.

Kahn, S. 2015a. "Experiences of Faith for Gender Role Non-conforming Muslims in Resettlement: Preliminary Considerations for Social Work Practitioners." *British Journal of Social Work* 45, no. 7: 2038–55. https://doi.org/10.1093/bjsw/bcu060.

Kahn, S. 2015b. "Cast Out: 'Gender Role Outlaws' Seeking Asylum in the West and the Quest for Social Connections." *Journal of Immigrant & Refugee Studies* 13, no. 1: 58–79. https://doi.org/10.1080/15562948.2014.894169.

Khan, M. and N.J. Mulé. 2021. "Voices of Resistance and Agency: LBTQ Muslim Women Living Out Intersectional Lives in North America." *Journal of Homosexuality: Special Issue on the LGBTQ Muslim Experience* 68, no. 7: 1144–68. https://doi.org/10.1080/00918369.2021.1888583.

Kinsman, G. 2018. "Policing Borders and Sexual/Gender Identities: Queer Refugees in the Years of Canadian Neoliberalism and Homonationalism." In *Envisioning Global LGBT Human Rights: (Neo)colonialism, Neoliberalism, Resistance and Hope,* edited by N. Nicol, A. Jjuuko, R. Lusimbo, N.J. Mulé, S. Ursell, A. Wahab, and P. Waugh, 97–130. London: Human Rights Consortium, Institute of Commonwealth Studies, University of London.

Lee, E.O.J., and S. Brotman. 2013. "SPEAK OUT! Structural intersectionality and anti-oppressive practice with LGBTQ refugees in Canada." *Canadian Social Work Review/Revue Canadienne de Service Social* 30, no. 2: 157–83. https://www.jstor.org/stable/43486768.

Lennox, C., and M. Waites, eds. 2013. *Human Rights, Sexual Orientation and Gender Identity in the Commonwealth: Struggles for Decriminalisation and Change.* London: Human Rights Consortium, Institute of Commonwealth Studies.

Massad, J.A. 2007. *Desiring Arabs.* Chicago: The University of Chicago Press.

Maulod, A. 2021. "Coming Home to One's Self: Butch Muslim Masculinities and Negotiations of Piety, Sex, and Parenthood in Singapore." *Journal of Homosexuality* 68, no. 7: 1106–43. https://doi.org/10.1080/00918369.2021.1888584.

McMichael, C. 2002. "'Everywhere Is Allah's Place': Islam and the Everyday Life of Somali Women in Melbourne, Australia." *Journal of Refugee Studies* 15, no. 2: 171–88. https://doi.org/10.1093/jrs/15.2.171.

Meyer, I.H. 2015. "Resilience in the Study of Minority Stress and Health of Sexual and Gender Minorities." *Psychology of Sexual Orientation and Gender Diversity* 2, no. 3: 209–13. https://doi.org/10.1037/sgd0000132.

Minwalla, O., B.R.S. Rosser, J. Feldman, and C. Varga. 2005. "Identity Experience among Progressive Gay Muslims in North America: A Qualitative Study within Al-Fatiha." *Culture, Health & Sexuality* 7, no. 2: 113–28. https://doi.org/10.1080/13691050412331321294.

Moghissi, H., S. Rahnema, and M.J. Goodman. 2009. *Diaspora by Design: Muslims in Canada and Beyond.* Toronto: University of Toronto Press.

Mulé, N.J., and K. Gamble. 2018. "Haven or Precarity: The Mental Health of LGBT Asylum Seekers and Refugees." In *Envisioning Global LGBT Human Rights: (Neo)colonialism, Neoliberalism, Resistance and Hope*, edited by N. Nicol, A. Jjuuko, R. Lusimbo, N.J. Mulé, S. Ursell, A. Wahab, and P. Waugh, 205–20. London: Human Rights Consortium, Institute of Commonwealth Studies, University of London.

Mulé, N.J., M. Khan, and C. McKenzie. 2020. "Queering Canadian Social Work Accreditation Standards and Procedures: A Content Analysis." *Social Work Education* 39, no. 3: 1–14. https://doi.org/10.1080/02615479.2019.1648408.

Mullaly, B., and J. West. 2018. *Challenging Oppression and Confronting Privilege: A Critical Approach to Anti-oppressive and Anti-privilege Theory and Practice.* 3rd ed. Don Mills, ON: Oxford University Press.

Munro, L., R. Travers, A. St. John, K. Klein, H. Hunter, D. Brennan, and C. Brett. 2013. "A Bed of Roses? Exploring the Experiences of LGBT Newcomer Youth Who Migrate to Toronto." *Ethnicity and Inequalities in Health and Social Care* 6, no. 4: 137–50. https://doi.org/10.1108/EIHSC-09-2013-0018.

Najmabadi, A. 2008. "Types, Acts, or What? Regulation of Sexuality in Nineteenth-Century Iran." In *Islamicate Sexualities: Translations across Temporal Geographies of Desire*, edited by K. Babayan and A. Najmabadi, 275–96. Cambridge, MA: Harvard University Press.

–. 2013. *Professing Selves: Transsexuality and Same-Sex Desire in Contemporary Iran.* Durham, NC: Duke University Press.

Peucker, M. 2021. "'You Are Essentially Forced into Being an Activist': The Interplay between Islamophobia and Muslims' Civic Engagement in Australia." *Religion, State and Society* 49, no. 1: 23–40. https://doi.org/10.1080/09637494.2021.1900766.

Puar, J.K. 2017. *Terrorist Assemblages: Homonationalism in Queer Times.* 10th ed. Durham, NC: Duke University Press. https://www.jstor.org/stable/j.ctv1131fg5..

Rahman, M. 2010. "Queer as Intersectionality: Theorizing Gay Muslim Identities." *Sociology* 44, no. 5: 944–61. https://doi.org/10.1177/0038038510375733.

–. 2014. *Homosexualities, Muslim Cultures and Modernity.* Basingstoke: Palgrave Macmillan.

–. 2018. "Postcolonialism and International Relations: Intersections of Sexuality, Religion and Race." In *Race, Gender and Culture in International Relations*, edited by R. Persaud and S.A. Sajed, 99–115. New York: Routledge.

Rehaag, S. 2008. "Patrolling the Borders of Sexual Orientation: Bisexual Refugee Claims in Canada." *McGill Law Journal* 53, no. 1: 59–102. https://lawjournal.mcgill.ca/article/patrolling-the-borders-of-sexual-orientation-bisexual-refugee-claims-in-canada/.

Said, E. 1978. *Orientalism*. New York: Pantheon Books.

Shah, S. 2018. "Does Religion Buffer the Effects of Discrimination on Distress for Religious Minorities? The Case of Arab Americans." *Society and Mental Health* 9, no. 2: 171–91. https://doi.org/10.1177/2156869318799145.

–. 2019. *Canadian Muslims: Demographics, Discrimination, Religiosity, and Voting*. Toronto: Institute of Islamic Studies Occasional Paper Series, The University of Toronto.

Shah, S., and M. Khan. 2023. "The Search for Ethics in Research: Learning from Non-binary, Queer, and Trans Muslims." In *Reading Sociology: Decolonizing Canada*, edited by Johanne Jean-Pierre et al. Oxford: Oxford University Press.

Shah, S., M. Khan, and S. Abdel-Latif. 2021. "Decolonizing Muslim Same-Sex Relations: Reframing Queerness as Gender Flexibility to Build Positive Relationships in Muslim Communities." In *Toward a Positive Psychology of Islam and Muslims*, edited by N. Pasha-Zaidi, 261–83. Vol. 15, *Cross-Cultural Advancements in Positive Psychology*. Cham, Switzerland: Springer. https://doi.org/10.1007/978-3-030-72606-5_12.

Shoeb, M., H. Weinstein, and J. Halpern. 2007. "Living in Religious Time and Space: Iraqi Refugees in Dearborn, Michigan." *Journal of Refugee Studies* 20, no. 3: 441–60. https://doi.org/10.1093/jrs/fem003.

Siraj, A. 2009. "The Construction of the Homosexual 'Other' by British Muslim Heterosexuals." *Contemporary Islam* 3: 41–57. https://doi.org/10.1007/s11562-008-0076-5.

–. 2012. "'I Don't Want to Taint the Name of Islam': The Influence of Religion on the Lives of Muslim Lesbians." *Journal of Lesbian Studies* 16, no. 4: 449–67. https://doi.org/10.1080/10894160.2012.681268.

Sterzing, P.R., R.E. Gartner, M.R. Woodford, and C.M. Fisher. 2017. "Sexual Orientation, Gender, and Gender Identity Microaggressions: Toward an Intersectional Framework for Social Work Research." *Journal of Ethnic & Cultural Diversity in Social Work: Innovation in Theory, Research & Practice* 26, no. 1–2: 81–94. https://doi.org/10.1080/15313204.2016.1263819.

Yurdakul, Gökçe, and Anna C. Korteweg. 2021. "Boundary Regimes and the Gendered Racialized Production of Muslim Masculinities: Cases from Canada and Germany." *Journal of Immigrant & Refugee Studies* 19, no. 1: 39–54. https://doi.org/10.1080/15562948.2020.1833271.

3 Transnational Disinformation Networks and Islamophobic International Charities in Canada

JOHN SMITH

Following the horrific attacks in London, Ontario in 2021, some outlets reported that a "Hindutva" organization called "Canadian Hindu Advocacy" tried to organize a rally to support Nathaniel Veltman – the man who ruthlessly murdered four of five family members for simply looking and being Muslim (News Desk 2021). Why would a group purportedly representing Hindu interests, as its name suggests, rally to absolve a white supremacist for the brutal murder of a Muslim family? To understand this seemingly perplexing phenomenon where some Brown bodies are pitting themselves against other Brown (and Black) bodies in "multicultural Canada," it is necessary to understand the international politics of Hindu Nationalism, also known as Hindutva, and its distinction from Hinduism.

Hinduism is a religion that has traditionally featured myriad forms of regional, cultural, and linguistic forms of religious expression and devotion stratified by notions of purity and pollution in its caste system. Hindutva, however, is an ideology that seeks to convert India's culturally and religiously diverse polity into an exclusively Hindu *rashtra* (nation-state), thereby challenging the country's secular and egalitarian constitution, which was pioneered by its Dalit (so-called "untouchable") visionary, Bhim Rao Ambedkar. Notably, India is home to the world's second largest population of Muslims, who have experienced violence and discrimination as religious minorities in the country. This includes recent legislation like the Citizenship Amendment Act of 2019, which stands to render millions of Muslims in the country stateless. Kashmir also continues to face a severe lockdown since 2019 with human rights violations taking place, aided by restrictions placed on international media from covering these issues (UN News 2016; News HRW 2020). In over a century of its existence, Hindutva has explicitly upheld an Islamophobic agenda (through centralizing state mechanisms) as a key ingredient of its ideology and, since the 1940s, has sought to spread its influence in the diverse and geographically dispersed Hindu diaspora. The rise of Hindu Nationalism in India with the election and re-election of Narendra Modi in 2014 and 2019 came in no small part due to the support and funding from many diasporic quarters outside India's borders, in a phenomenon dubbed by Christopher Jaffrelot and Ingrid Therwath (2007) as "long distance Hindu Nationalism."

Diaspora Hindutva Organizations and Charities

The Hindutva movement and political organizing can be traced to 1921 with the establishment of the Hindu Mahasabha, followed by the still dominant neo-Nazi paramilitary organization Rashtra Swayam Sevak (RSS). Founding members of Hindu Nationalism dubiously claimed that upper caste Hindus were the "original Aryans," and India was the cradle of Aryan civilization – a concept that has made inroads globally among several white supremacist idealogues including in the manifesto of the Norwegian mass killer Anders Breivik (Nanda 2011). The anti-Black connotations of such ideologies are self-evident. However, in recent times scholars and activists have noted that diaspora Hindutva actors have diversified their strategies and seemingly even support progressive causes in Canada and America while also supporting anti-minority and exclusionary perspectives and policies in India (Umar 2017; Upadhyay 2020; Rajagopal 2020). The founder of the RSS, Veer Damodar Savarkar, infamously idolized Nazi Germany's treatment of Jewish people and called for a similar treatment of Muslims in India (Bridge Initiative Team 2021). Narendra Modi was a member of the RSS before joining its political wing, the Bharatiya Janata Party (BJP) (Jaffrelot and Schoch 2021). While Modi was the chief minister of the province of Gujarat in 2002, by the BJP's own estimates more than a thousand Muslims, including children, were killed by Hindu extremists in the region (Ghassem-Fachand 2012). Many activists viewed this as a failure of Modi's leadership, but his popularity in the Canadian diaspora has soared as indicated by the huge turnout to celebrate his visit to Toronto in 2015 (Mangione 2015).

The first diasporic Hindu Nationalist organization established outside India was the Hindu Swayam Sevak (HSS) in Kenya in 1940. Since then, it has spread to various parts of the world, including Canada. In 2018, the then-Indian Consular General, Dinesh Bhatia, spoke at an HSS event in Brampton, triggering fear and concern among Indian-origin minorities in Canada that the Indian consulate in Canada was under the influence of the RSS (NH Web Desk 2018). Meanwhile, HSS seems to operate in Canada as both a charity and an NGO, and it seems to be thriving in the Peel Region of the Greater Toronto Area – forging favourable ties with the local police and holding festive functions of brotherhood or *Rakshabandhan* with them (Peel Regional Police News 2018). For those familiar with the landscape of Islamophobia in Canada, the Peel School District has come under scrutiny over Islamophobic prayer room controversies. As documented by several media reports, Ron Banerjee has also been at the forefront of Islamophobic protests in the Peel School District in Mississauga, campaigning not just against Muslim prayer spaces in schools, but also spurring the destruction of the Qur'an in the name of "free speech" (Khandaker 2017). Mainstream media outlets in Canada also widely covered the story of Ravi Hooda, a real estate agent who was fired from his job and as an executive member of the Peel School District Council in 2020 after he tweeted that permitting evening *azaans* or calls to prayer during Ramadan in Brampton was catering to "camel and goat riders," along with other Islamophobic tropes (Nasser 2020). It is incumbent upon the Canadian government to not underestimate the role of such home-grown and diaspora Hindutva ideologues and organizations within and outside Canada in spreading Islamophobic sentiments.

Since the 1980s, well before the sixteenth century mosque known as Babri Masjid was notoriously demolished by Hindu militants in 1992, organizations such as the Vishwa Hindu Parishad (VHP) in Canada had actively sent funds to India to build the Ram Mandir (a temple honouring the alleged birthplace of the mythical god Rama) on the land where the historic mosque stood (India Today Web Desk 2018). The American CIA listed the VHP as a "militant religious organization" in North America in its 2018 World Factbook (Bal 2019). The organization continues to operate in Canada as a registered charity. Other registered charities such as SEWA Canada (under the ambit of SEWA International) operate here, with the latter openly affiliated with and promoted by the RSS. UK human rights activists have decried how SEWA organizations across the world have sent significant donations to fund Hindu Nationalist schools and other projects in India (Awaaz – South Asia Watch 2004). It is vital to note here that SEWA International has allegedly sponsored controversial projects with RSS offshoots such as the Vanvasi Kalyan Ashram (Awaaz – South Asia Watch 2004). This organization has been accused of committing violence against Christian missionaries who proselytize in tribal and remote areas in India, as well as spreading propaganda against Muslims, including instigating mass violence against them (Chattopadhyay 2020).

It is imperative to understand that Islamophobia is not unique to white and/or Western quarters exclusively, and several transnational actors in Canada use multiple strategies to further this agenda for their own political and social interests (Chattopadhyay 2020). Undeniably, more efforts need to be made by the Canadian government to prevent Islamophobia both institutionally and normatively in Canada. In a recent independent report published by the International Civil Liberties Monitoring Group, it was discovered that the Canadian Revenue Agency had specifically targeted Muslim charities for audits in the name of "counter-terrorism" (McSorley 2021). These charities were subject to intense scrutiny for giving donations to humanitarian projects, including aiding persecuted Muslims in Kashmir. Yet Islamophobic foreign charities and diasporic NGOs including Hindutva organizations such as VHP, SEWA Canada, and HSS have not received similar regulation and scrutiny as Muslim charities by the Canada Revenue Agency. Meanwhile, India has prevented local and transnational NGOs such as Greenpeace and Amnesty International from operating in the country (Hukil 2019), including those seeking justice for Muslim victims of the Gujarat massacre of 2002 – despite the UN Special Rapporteur on human rights defenders noting that India was placing unreasonable restrictions on transnational advocacy networks (OHCHR 2016).

Disinformation

In addition to controversial diasporic charities and organizations that fund questionable politics and projects in India, an important strategy for Hindu Nationalists has been to spread Islamophobic content via disinformation networks in Canada. While this has consequences for the ethnically diverse Muslim community beyond India, online hate speech and content against Muslims on platforms such as Facebook and WhatsApp have led to offline killings of several innocent Muslims in India and wider calls for genocide (Leideg 2020; Amarasingam and Desai 2020). In 2019, the EU Disinformation Lab reported that over 265 misinformation networks emerged from India or Indian diaspora communities and sought to "influence international institutions and elected representatives with coverage of specific events and demonstrations" and "provide NGOs with useful press material to reinforce their credibility and thus be impactful" (Alaphilippe et al. 2019). The report noted that "most of [the websites] are named after an extinct local newspaper or spoof real media outlets," in a bid to manipulate the audience; over a dozen of these outlets were reported by CBC as existing in Canada (Yates and Bellemare 2019).

This phenomenon of organized disinformation in the North American diaspora has been termed as "Cyber Hindutva," and often IT professionals from India have played a critical role in spreading Islamophobic content online while also "discretely" developing strategies that evade the gaze of authorities in their countries of residence (Therwath 2012). Canadian media outlets such as Global News have highlighted how disinformation networks are being used by foreign intelligence agencies to lobby diasporic members of Indian descent and influence Canadian politicians to view Muslims as funders of terrorism – particularly those of Pakistani origin (Bell 2020). Although many of these websites have been taken down as result of work done by the EU Disinformation Lab, they were all reportedly tied to one Srivastava Group, an Indian corporation run by Ankit Srivastava based in New Delhi. Srivastava also claims to be "friends" with Tarek Fatah, a Canadian columnist writing for the *Toronto Sun* (Yates and Bellemare 2019). Ankit Srivastava, through his websites, regularly republishes Fatah's articles. Fatah has been accused (with evidence) of tweeting Islamophobic fake news and not removing the content once errors have been pointed out (Chaudhari and AltNews.in 2020).

Given the deeply Islamophobic ideology of Hindutva politics in India and abroad, Middle Eastern Muslims have not been spared by some individuals such as Ron Banerjee, who had to publicly apologize for defaming the Lebanese owner of Paramount Restaurant as a "jihadist" and rapist (Yang 2018, para. 1). Furthermore, amid growing concerns of genocide against Muslims in India, Bollywood propaganda films such as "Kashmir Files" (endorsed by Modi himself) have been released in Canadian film theatres. This has led some human rights organizations and activists to raise alarm about the Islamophobic violence such movies seek to normalize through historically distorted narratives and questionable portrayals of Muslims, while strengthening outlooks that favour India's military occupation of Kashmir despite widespread human rights violations by the Indian army in the region (Justice for All 2022).

Other than targeting Muslims in India and spreading fake news including Islamophobic content in Canada, Hindutva actors have also targeted Dalit scholars and other progressive academics online in Canada who are critical of the BJP and/or public lynching of minorities carried out by emboldened Hindu nationalists in India (Ahmed, Chopra, and Truschke 2021; Zhou 2021b). While the Canadian media obsessed over Prime Minister Justin Trudeau's choice of attire during his visit to India in 2018, hardly any reporting considered how Hindu nationalists have targeted minorities in India, including Indian Christians (NBC

News 2015). Importantly, the complicity of "big tech" in targeting and surveilling environmental activists in India, leading to their imprisonment on dubious grounds, has been condemned by prominent Canadian activists such as Naomi Klein (Klein 2021). Some Hindutva actors have even disrupted events featuring Sikh journalists in Canadian universities for speaking out against Hindutva, including reinvigorating tropes of the Sikh community as "Khalistani terrorists," or "anti-India" for decrying the BJP government and its polemical policies (Gangdev 2017, paras. 3–11).

Unironically downplaying its own exclusionary and often deeply violent nationalist politics, diaspora Hindutva and its spread have implications for how Sikhs and Muslims are represented in converging tropes of religious racialization as threats and as terrorists. As has been well documented by several activists and academics, the Sikh community already bears the brunt of Islamophobic attacks for being perceived as Muslims in turbans (Sian 2017). Such stereotypes and ignorance have ramifications for the lives of innocent people, particularly for those who do not have representation on mainstream platforms that consistently portray them in a bad light (WSO 2019).[1] It is critical to challenge Hindutva actors who seek to further marginalize Sikhs, Muslims, Dalits, and other secular Hindu Indians for questioning the current government's exclusionary and discriminatory ideology against minorities and farmers in India, yet we must not reinforce stigmatizing tropes against other South Asians. This entails in part being empathic and supportive for Hindus in Canada who also face racism as visible minorities, as well as challenging the casteist and anti-minority politics of Hindutva ideology that cleverly seeks to conflate Hinduism with Hindutva. Fighting against Islamophobia and other racialized, religious, and gendered persecuted minorities anywhere requires solidarity and empathy with groups similarly and differently oppressed than ourselves.

There are several limitations and obstacles in mapping the far reach of the Hindutva diaspora and its implications for Canadians and Muslims in Canada specifically. Tracing the funding trail of several other home-grown "screen" Hindutva organizations that claim to represent "India" is even harder to determine for ordinary researchers in Canada. An upcoming and important study has observed how

---

1   Furthermore, the World Sikh Organization of Canada (2019) has also raised concerns that "many Sikhs, including current and former elected officials, have been denied visas to visit India due to their having spoken out about human rights abuses in India."

Hindutva ideology is gradually spreading its ethnonationalist and Islamophobic content through media channels of the Hindu Canadian diaspora (Datta and Chakroborty 2021). However, more awareness about these issues in the country including among progressive members of the Hindu diaspora needs to be built (Chiu 2020). In addition, disinformation networks using the names of defunct Canadian websites or even "official-sounding" names to influence the perceptions of ordinary Canadians and Canadian politicians must be regulated with responsibility instead of being left unchecked to circulate hate content and false narratives against Muslims. Worryingly, the Canadian Anti-Hate Network has reported that the current Indian High Commissioner to Canada allegedly cited an Islamophobic and anti-Sikh conspiracy site in the consulate's official memo bearing its seal and ignored the Network's attempts to confirm the authenticity of said memo (Zhou 2021a).

Conclusion

Indians with permanent residency, as well as Indian immigrant students, have become one of Canada's largest immigrant populations (Anderson 2020). And yet the immense power and reach of Hindutva in the diaspora remains woefully understudied in Canada compared to other Western countries such as the US and UK. Reports have recently been released that consider how some Indian-origin students and Hindutva groups protested against the academic freedom of scholars in Canadian universities who are interrogating Hindutva, claiming their work is "Hinduphobic" or "anti-Hindu"; several academics in North America who have spoken out about these actions have faced rape and death threats, leading them to withdraw from academic conferences (Ellis-Petersen 2021). In some cases, university staff members of Indian origin have demonstrated disturbing behaviour and attitudes towards Muslims, providing a list on "how to boycott Muslims" and how non-Muslims should "educate their children to avoid Muslims," in addition to labelling Muslims who stand in solidarity with Palestine as "jehadi's [sic]" (CBC News 2021).

Such instances of Islamophobia should not be seen in isolation but rather as the product of ideologies that seek to propagate and normalize Islamophobia to legitimize ethnonationalist projects that discriminate against Muslims as undesirable people globally (Chopra 2019, 36). It is important to pay heed to the warnings of human rights activists and progressive Hindus. The hate speeches, questionable "charities and NGOs," surveillance, circulation of disinformation through social media platforms, and intimidation methods including attempts by some members of the Indian diaspora to silence critics of Hindutva and its deeply Islamophobic worldview must not be viewed as a peripheral matter in Canada.

Histories and politics of Islamophobia beyond the West matter transnationally, including in Canada. Carrying anti-Muslim prejudices from India to Canada, Hindutva networks in the country should warrant urgent attention to combat Islamophobia across different spaces and geographies. This includes the sphere of overt and subtle foreign interference precisely because of its impacts on the lives of ordinary Muslims in Canada and beyond.

WORKS CITED

Ahmed, Manan, Rohit Chopra, and Audrey Truschke. 2021. "North America Has a Hindu Nationalist Problem, and Scholars Are on the Frontlines of These Right-Wing Attacks." Religion Dispatches. 19 October 2021. https://religiondispatches.org/north-america-has-a-hindu-nationalist-problem-and-scholars-are-on-the-frontlines-of-these-right-wing-attacks/.

Alaphilippe, Alexandre, Gary Machado, Roman Adamczyk, and Antoine Grégoire. 2019. "Uncovered: 265 Fake Local Media Outlets Serving Indian Interests." EU Disinfo Lab. 26 November 2019. https://www.disinfo.eu/publications/uncovered-265-coordinated-fake-local-media-outlets-serving-indian-interests/.

Amarasingam, Amarnath, and Shweta Desai. 2020. "#CoronaJihad: COVID-19, Misinformation, and Anti-Muslim Violence in India." Strong Cities. 26 May 2020. https://strongcitiesnetwork.org/en/coronajihad-covid-19-misinformation-and-anti-muslim-violence-in-india/.

Anderson, Stuart. 2020. "Indians Immigrating to Canada at an Astonishing Rate." *Forbes*. 3 February 2020. https://www.forbes.com/sites/stuartanderson/2020/02/03/indians-immigrating-to-canada-at-an-astonishing-rate/?sh=36fc54cb2b5f.

Awaaz – South Asia Watch. 2004. "In Bad Faith? British Charity & Hindu Extremism: Report Summary." South Asia Citizens Web. http://www.sacw.net/DC/CommunalismCollection/ArticlesArchive/British_charity_and_Hindu_extremism_a_report_summary.pdf.

Bal, Hartosh Singh. 2019. "The Transformation of India Is Nearly Complete." *New York Times*, 11 November 2019. https://www.nytimes.com/2019/11/11/opinion/india-ayodhya-temple-ruling.html.

Bell, Stewart. 2020. "Canadian Politicians Were Targets of Indian Intelligence Covert Influence Operation: Document." Global News. 17 April 2020.

https://globalnews.ca/news/6823170/canadian-politicians-targeted
-indian-intelligence/.

Bridge Initiative Team. 2021. "Factsheet: Rashtriya Swayamsevak Sangh
(RSS)." The Bridge Initiative. 18 May 2021. https://bridge.georgetown.edu
/research/factsheet-rashtriya-swayamsevak-sangh-rss/.

CBC News. 2021. "Wilfrid Laurier Employee Put on Leave after Alleged
Islamophobic Posts." 28 May 2021. https://www.cbc.ca/news/canada
/kitchener-waterloo/
waterloo-region-wilfrid-laurier-islamophobic-posts-1.6044847.

Chattopadhyay, Sohini. 2020. "EXCLUSIVE: Inside a Hindutva Hostel: How
RSS Is Rewiring the Tribal Mind." CatchNews. 4 May 2020. https://www
.catchnews.com/india-news/exclusive-inside-a-hindutva-hostel-how
-rss-is-rewiring-the-tribal-mind-1450354461.html.

Chaudhari, Pooja, and AltNews.in. 2020. "20 Times Pakistani-Canadian Writer
Tarek Fatah Has Tweeted Fake News – Often with a Communal Bite."
Scroll.in. 27 January 2020. https://scroll.in/article/951291/20-times
-pakistani-canadian-writer-tarek-fatah-has-tweeted-fake-news-often-with
-a-communal-bite.

Chiu, Joanna. 2020. "Should Canada Try to Forge Closer Ties with India?
Experts Are Raising Red Flags. Here's Why." Toronto Star, 4 December 2020.
https://www.thestar.com/news/canada/2020/12/04/should-canada
-try-to-forge-closer-ties-with-india-experts-are-raising-red-flags-heres
-why.html.

Chopra, Rohit. 2019. Virtual Hindu Rashtra: Saffron Nationalism and New Media.
Gurugram, India: HarperCollins India.

Datta, Anisha, and Indranil Chakraborty. 2021. "The Ideology of Hindutva
in the Canadian Hindu Diaspora's Media: A Critical Examination of the
Integrative and Non-Integrative Discourses." Revisiting Ethnic Media in
Canada: Policies, Practises and Integration (Accepted for Editorial Review).

Ellis-Petersen, Hannah. 2021. "Death Threats Sent to Participants of US
Conference on Hindu Nationalism." Guardian, 9 September 2021. https://
www.theguardian.com/world/2021/sep/09/death-threats-sent-to
-participants-of-us-conference-on-hindu-nationalism.

Gangdev, Srushti. 2017. "Vancouver Journalist Says He Was Threatened by
Hindu Nationalists at UBC Event." Global News. 20 February 2017. https://
globalnews.ca/news/6602149/vancouver-ubc-india-protest-threats/.

Ghassem-Fachandi, Parvis. 2012. Pogrom in Gujarat: Hindu Nationalism and
Anti-Muslim Violence in India. Princeton, NJ: Princeton University Press.

Hukil, Roomana. 2019. "NGOs Need Protection from Hindu Nationalism in
India." The Conversation. 30 May 2019. https://theconversation.com
/ngos-need-international-protection-from-hindu-nationalism-in
-india-117238.

India Today Web Desk. 2018. "VHP Warns CIA: Global Movement against You If Militant Tag Not Changed." *India Today*, 15 June 2018. https://www .indiatoday.in/india/story/vishwa-hindu-parishad-statement-cia-world -factbook-1260955-2018-06-15.

Jaffrelot, Christopher, and Cynthia Schoch. 2021. *Modi's India: Hindu Nationalism and the Rise of Ethnic Democracy.* Princeton, NJ: Princeton University Press.

Jaffrelot, Christopher, and Ingrid Therwath. 2007. "The Sangh Parivar and the Hindu Diaspora in the West: What Kind of 'Long-Distance Nationalism'?" *International Political Sociology* 1, no. 3 (2007): 278–95. https://doi.org /10.1111/j.1749-5687.2007.00018.x.

Justice for All. 2022. "Cineplex and Canadian Theatres Enable Genocide by Featuring Propaganda Film, 'The Kashmiri Files.'" 31 March 2022. https:// www.justiceforallcanada.org/kashmir_files_cineplex_canada_propaganda _film_2022_03_31.html.

Khandaker, Tamara. 2017. "The Quran Was Torn to Shreds in a Raucous School Board Meeting in Peel Region." VICE. 23 March 2017. https://www .vice.com/en/article/j5d37y/the-quran-was-torn-to-shreds-at-a-raucous -school-board-meeting-in-peel-region.

Klein, Naomi. 2021. "How Big Tech Helps India Target Climate Activists." *Guardian*, 4 March 2021. https://www.theguardian.com/news/2021 /mar/04/how-big-tech-helps-india-target-climate-activists-naomi-klein.

Leideg, Eviane. 2020. "The Far-Right Is Going Global." *Foreign Policy.* 21 January 2020. https://foreignpolicy.com/2020/01/21/india-kashmir -modi-eu-hindu-nationalists-rss-the-far-right-is-going-global/.

Mangione, Kendra. 2015. "'Modi-Mania' Hits Toronto During Indian PM's Visit." CTV News. 15 April 2015. https://www.ctvnews.ca/canada /modi-mania-hits-toronto-during-indian-pm-s-visit-1.2328282.

McSorley, Tim. 2021. "The CRA's Prejudiced Audits: Counter-Terrorism and the Targeting of Muslim Charities in Canada." International Civil Liberties Monitoring Group. May 2021. https://iclmg.ca/prejudiced-audits/.

Nanda, Meera. 2011. "Ideological Convergences: Hindutva and the Norway Massacre." *Economic and Political Weekly* 46, no. 53: 61–8. https://www.jstor .org/stable/23065638.

Nasser, Shanifa. 2020. "'Disturbing, Islamophobic' Tweet about Call to Prayers Prompts Firing of Peel Council Chair." CBC News. 5 May 2020. https:// www.cbc.ca/news/canada/toronto/brampton-call-to-prayer -peel-1.5556043.

NBC News. 2015. "Indian Christians Protest against PM Narendra Modi after Nun's Rape, Attacks." 16 March 2015. https://www.nbcnews.com/news /world/indian-christians-protest-against-pm-narendra-modi-after-nuns -rape-n324266.

News Desk. 2021. "Hindutva Group in Canada Shows Support to the London Attack Culprit." *Global Village Space*, 17 June 2021. www.globalvillagespace. com/hindutva-group-in-canada-shows-support-to-the-london-attack -culprit/.

News HRW. 2020. "India: Abuses Persist in Jammu and Kashmir – Internet Restrictions amid Pandemic Exacerbate Year Long Crackdowns." Human Rights Watch. 4 August 2020. https://www.hrw.org/news/2020/08/04 /india-abuses-persist-jammu-and-kashmir.

NH Web Desk. 2018. "Indian Ambassadors around the World Appear for RSS's 'Hindu Nationalism' events." *National Herald*, 15 November 2018. https://www.nationalheraldindia.com/international/indian-consulates -around-the-world-fraternise-with-rsss-international-wing.

Peel Regional Police News. 2018. "Peel Regional Police Celebrates the Festival of Raksha Bandhan." 5 September 2018. https://www.peelpolice.ca/Modules /News/index.aspx?newsId=1b2e16da-64ae-4fdf-a30b-0faa3dd36f3f#.

Rajagopal, Raju. 2020. "Hindutva Groups in the US Are Calling Out Anti-Black Racism, but Support Bigotry in India." Scroll.in. 21 July 2020. https:// scroll.in/article/967964/hindutva-groups-in-the-us-are-calling-out -anti-black-racism-but-their-support-rings-hollow.

Sian, Katy P. 2017. "Surveillance, Islamophobia, and Sikh Bodies in the War on Terror." *Islamophobia Studies Journal* 4, no. 1 (October): 37–52. https://doi .org/10.13169/islastudj.4.1.0037.

Therwath, Ingrid. 2012. "Cyber-*Hindutva*: Hindu Nationalism, the Diaspora and the Web." *Journal of Social Science Information* 51, no. 4 (December): 551–77. https://doi.org/10.1177/0539018412456782.

Umar, Sanober. 2017. "Beyond Whiteness: Rethinking Aryan Nationalisms in Multicultural Canada." Active History. 14 December 2017. http:// activehistory.ca/2017/12/beyond-whiteness-rethinking-aryan-nationalisms -in-multicultural-canada/.

UN News. 2019. "New Citizenship Law in India 'Fundamentally Discriminatory': UN Human Rights Office." United Nations. 13 December 2019. https://news.un.org/en/story/2019/12/1053511.

United Nations Human Rights Office of the High Commissioner (OHCHR). 2016. "UN Rights Experts Urge India to Repeal Law Restricting NGO's Access to Crucial Foreign Funding." United Nations. 16 June 2016. https://www.ohchr.org/EN/NewsEvents/Pages/DisplayNews. aspx?NewsID=20112&LangID=E.

Upadhyay, Nishant. 2020. "Hindu Nation and Its Queers: Caste, Islamophobia, and De/coloniality in India." *Interventions* 22, no. 4: 464–80. https://doi.org/10.1080/1369801X.2020.1749709.

World Sikh Organization of Canada (WSO). 2019. "WSO Expresses Concern over Indian Interference in Canada." World Sikh Organization. 17 April

2019. https://www.worldsikh.org/wso_expresses_concern_over_indian
_interference_in_canada.

Yang, Jennifer. 2018. "Anti-Muslim Agitator Gives Video Apology to Owner
of Paramount Fine Foods over 'Jihadist' Comments." *Toronto Star*, 17
December 2018. https://www.thestar.com/news/gta/2018/12/17
/anti-muslim-agitator-gives-video-apology-to-owner-of-paramount
-fine-foods-over-jihadist-comments.html.

Yates, Jeff, and Andrea Bellemare. 2019. "Huge Pro-India Fake News
Networks Include Canadian Sites, Links to Canadian Think-Tanks."
CBC News. 21 November 2019. https://www.cbc.ca/news/politics
/india-fake-news-sites-canada-1.5366591.

Zhou, Steven. 2021a. "Indian High Commissioner to Canada Cites Anti-Sikh,
Islamophobic Canadian Publication in Alleged Official Memo." Canadian
Anti-Hate Network. 15 April 2021. https://www.antihate.ca/indian
_ambassador_cites_anti_sikh_islamophobic_canadian_publication_official
_memo.

–. 2021b. "Indian Scholars in Canada Face Hate and Intimidation Online
for Speaking Out against Modi Government's Discriminatory Policies."
Canadian Anti-Hate Network. 29 April 2021. https://www.antihate.ca
/indian_scholars_canada_face_hate_intimidation_online_speaking_out
_against_modi_government_discriminatory_policies.

4 Fragmented Bodies "Dancing on the Spot": The Transnational Lives of Canadian Muslims and the Limits of Contemporary Anti-Islamophobia Advocacy

WAFAA HASAN AND ZARAH KHAN

A framework that emphasizes transnationalism rejects traditional notions of assimilation that conceive of acculturation as a linear process of shedding one's association with native countries and developing ties and associations with new countries ... According to ... xenophobic discourse, immigrants' transnational connections and attachments are threatening to the national community. (Jaffe-Walter and Lee 2018, 259)

Nationality, background, real origins, and past actions all seemed to be the sources of my problem ... so beginning in America I resolved to live as if I were a simple, transparent soul and not to speak about my family or origins except as required, and then very sparingly. To become in other words, like the others, as anonymous as possible. (Said 2000, 137)

We cannot isolate ourselves from a global phenomenon which is manifesting itself now very clearly ... [Without] a change in foreign policy ... we will be basically dancing on the spot and not moving anywhere. (Dr. Munir El-Kassem, imam in London, Ontario; speaker at the "Our London Family"[1] vigil)

This chapter illustrates the ways in which the recent National Summit on Islamophobia in Canada (spring 2021)[2] as well as other state

---

1 The family in London who was victimized by Islamophobic violence in the spring of 2021 wishes for their name not to be used. Instead, we will be referring to them as "Our London Family."

2 The National Summit on Islamophobia was hosted virtually on 22 July 2022, organized by the Federal Anti-Racism Secretariat, and convened by Bardish Chagger, Minister of Diversity and Inclusion and Youth. In attendance were Prime Minister Justin Trudeau, federal ministers, members of Parliament, and officials from provincial and municipal governments.

initiatives such as the implementation of Islamic Heritage Month continue to operate with limitations, severing the Muslim body from its transnational connections even while imposing the transnational onto it. Participants and organizers necessarily continue to censor against and divorce critiques of Canadian foreign policies and their complicities with transnationalized systems of Islamophobic violence from mainstream anti-Islamophobia advocacy work. However, we argue that these critiques are required to trouble the "sedative politics" (Kamboureli 2009, 82) of multiculturalist and assimilationist models of anti-Islamophobia advocacy, currently prevalent in Canada. Sedative politics that operate in ways to acknowledge ethnic difference while "containing" and "managing" it maintains the political articulations of dominant Canadian society, and they have not proven to alleviate the frightening growth of Islamophobic violence within our borders. This chapter highlights the transnational lives of Canadian Muslims as they experienced their identity formations through social/institutional relations while also highlighting the simultaneous transnationalization of Canada's *outward* Islamophobic military and cultural projects through the interrogation and surveillance of the Muslim Canadian body, at home. We argue that while the Muslim Canadian body is a constitutive target of transnationalized Islamophobic violence, it cannot articulate its liberation in transnational terms without public and political reprisal.

The Transnational Lives of Canadian Muslims

The transnational lives of Canadian Muslims are a key consideration for effective anti-Islamophobia advocacy in Canada. For the purposes of this chapter, we focus on the concept of "transnational life" as embodied in "identities and social structures that help form the life world of immigrants and their children and [that] is constructed in relations among people, institutions and places" (Smith 2006, 7). We live in a world that is not simply bounded by the borders of a nation. We are part of a complex and connected world that is undoubtedly transnational (Grewal and Kaplan 2006, xxvi), and which some scholars have called a globalized "new world order marked by one superpower, the United States" (xxii) with support from their military and economic allies. We take this notion of the "transnational life" – the identities and social structures that help form many Canadian Muslims' relationships with people, institutions, and places which are elsewhere or in many places at once – as our starting point for studying anti-Islamophobia advocacy in Canada.

Canadian Muslims' lives are transnationalized through familial, social, and economic networks. Various generations of Canadian Muslims envision their work as contributing economically, politically, or culturally to families "back home," like many other immigrant communities in North America (Jaffe-Walter and Lee 2018). Moreover, spaces and places worldwide constitute the psychic geographies of the *ummah*, a transnational concept of the Muslim community. An Nu'man ibn Bashir reported that Prophet Muhammad said: "The believers, in their mutual love, compassion, and sympathy are like a single body; if one of its organs suffers, the whole body will respond to it with sleeplessness and fever" (Sahih Muslim 45:84). Such Islamic theological paradigms inform diaspora politics among many Muslim Canadian communities. Moreover, many of these communities express postcolonial critiques of Euro-American imperial hegemony in the political happenings of many Muslim-majority countries. Canadian Muslims contend with imperial and colonial histories as well as economic globalization in relation to contemporary experiences of impoverishment, displacement, familial fragmentations, and loss of cultural connections. These imperial and colonial histories have been historically rationalized and propagated through centuries of Orientalist and Islamophobic colonial and neo-colonial discursive cultures (Said 2003).

Even if Canadian Muslims were to acquiesce to the Canadian nation-state's fantasy of immigrant assimilation – that is, as Said notes, if Canadian Muslims were to become "anonymous," speaking very little of their families or origins (137) – the transnational would continue to impact their bodies, locally and violently. The Canadian state is deeply implicated in the elsewhere violence against Muslims through transnational military, economic, and cultural allyships with American imperial projects (Shipley 2021). Further, the Canadian state has historically interrogated and surveilled its Muslim Canadian populations in direct parallel to the particularized coordinates of foreign wars and invasions. There are many examples, but for the sake of brevity, we will offer a couple: during the Gulf War, Canadian Security Intelligence Services targeted and interrogated Iraqi Canadian citizens, pulling them out of workplaces and calling them at home, asking threatening questions on their position on the Gulf War and whether they supported Canadian allies in the war (Kashmeri 1991). In June 2006, while the Canadian government was seeking to send more troops to Afghanistan, seventeen young Muslim men, five of whom were teenagers, were arrested with various terrorism charges in Toronto. The coverage of these young men relied on the "spectacle of the 'dangerous' Muslim" using language such as "brown skinned," and the attendant heavy presence of police snipers and leg cuffs (Razack 2008, 5). Afghan Canadians and other Muslims in Canada were even spied on and interrogated by the Canadian carceral system (Baksh and Heroux 2017; Nasser 2018). Canada has historically brought so-called "foreign" wars home, discursively and materially. This phenomenon has direly impacted local Muslim communities' freedoms and rights. In both ways outlined above (organic familial/ cultural connections and through imposed political accusations from the state) Muslim Canadian bodies are transnationalized.

Muslims' historical memories of this type of here and there violence are embroiled in the Gulf War, the invasion of Afghanistan, the ethnic cleansing of Palestine (Pappé 2006; Khalidi 2020; Masalha 1997), and other imperial/settler colonial projects in Muslim-majority countries. The paradox is that while the Canadian state brings wars home by intimidating, imprisoning, and discriminating against Canadian Muslims, Canadian Muslims cannot meaningfully engage with this violent homecoming.[3] Moreover, if Muslims travel to those elsewhere spaces, they themselves become targets of Islamophobic political and military campaigns. The double paradox of being targets of transnational violence and muzzled from articulating their/our relationships to the transnational manifests in most contemporary models of anti-Islamophobia advocacy in Canada.

State Institutions and the Limits of Anti-Islamophobia Advocacy

On 6 June 2021, five members of the same Muslim family were out for a walk in London, Ontario, when a truck jumped the curb and ran them over in a deadly attack that devastated the entire Muslim community. The youngest family member and lone survivor was hospitalized (Hasham 2021a). In the same week, three white people showed up at a mosque in Toronto, threatening to detonate a bomb (Hasham 2021b), and a Black Muslim woman was attacked in Edmonton (Mosleh 2021). The Muslim community was barely recovering from the grief of the Quebec shootings (during which six Muslims were killed and eight injured in prayer in 2017) when mosque caretaker Mohamed-Aslim Zafis was brutally slain by a white supremacist in Toronto on 13 September 2020 (Elpa 2020). On 25 June 2021, the Canadian government finally officially named the Three Percenters (a US right-wing

---

3   Further, Canadian Muslims endure the traumatic experience of being complicit in violence against one's "own." Canadian Muslims must contend with the fact that their tax dollars fund the very same violence that might be harming their own family (Hasan 2013, 207) or their own bodies when they travel to these spaces.

militia group) a terrorist entity (Reynolds 2021). However, on the same day, a Muslim man in Saskatoon was stabbed in the back multiple times while his attackers yelled, "we hate Muslims" (Piller 2021). All these events were happening around the same time that bombs were raining down on Gaza; Israeli troops attacked Al-Aqsa Mosque; Palestinians were subject to increased and brutal settler-colonial violence; and evictions of Palestinians in Jerusalem went viral on social media (Al Jazeera 2021). Canadian Muslims who see Al-Aqsa Mosque as a sacred space for Muslims and identify with the Palestinian plight (as a manifestation of Islamophobic and Orientalist cultures) were dizzied with grief; grief for here and there. Many Muslim communities were concerned with Islamophobic violence in their backyards and with Canadian complicities in violence (against Muslims and those perceived to be Muslims) elsewhere (Nasser 2018; Engler 2010).

The public school system, despite adopting Islamic Heritage Month and anti-Islamophobia resources in Ontario, as well as their public claims of commitment to "culturally responsive" classrooms (TDSB, n.d.), failed to address any of this violence in announcements, check-ins with Muslim students, or in curriculum applications. The Toronto District School Board (TDSB), in particular, failed to address this here-and-there violence, despite the fact that the student population of the TDSB is 19 per cent Muslim (TDSB 2018). When Muslim students brought up the ongoing event in Jerusalem and Gaza in class, they were quickly hushed (Ayyash 2021) by educators and senior executives.[4] Such events illustrate the limits of anti-Islamophobia advocacy through Islamic Heritage Month in schools, e.g., the repulsions of the transnational.

Islamic Heritage Month (IHM) was first proclaimed in 2016 and is often celebrated in public school boards by noting cultural festivities, foods, and learning about the ways in which Muslims have contributed to Canadian society (Saleh and Aoudeh 2021). In October 2016, the TDSB announced its own initiatives related to implementing IHM.[5] The TDSB's website cites the Islamic Heritage Month Act, stating that IHM

---

4 Information which emerged in personal conversations and Muslim community groups in the Greater Toronto and Hamilton area in Ontario.

5 This was a hard-won victory by TDSB parents who had been systematically harassed through the years – and who had to defend every resource selection against accusations of promoting terrorism, anti-Semitism, or referring to elsewhere conflicts related to Islamophobia.

will provide all Ontarians, both today and in future generations, with an opportunity to reflect, celebrate, and learn about the rich and longstanding Islamic history in the Province and the diverse roles and contributions of Muslim people in communities across Ontario. This new understanding will in turn help combat anti-Islamic sentiment." (Islamic Heritage Month Act, 2016, S.O. 2016, c. 20 – Bill 38)

This statement is distinctly local in its focus on Islamic history within the province, contemporary or otherwise. Educators attempting to implement IHM curricula became painfully aware that any resources reflecting Canada's political policies in Muslim-majority countries are censored and often rejected by school board administrators.[6] This muzzling within public school boards reflects a larger political culture that seeks to fragment the Muslim body from other parts of itself (its relationships to the extra-national and/or transnational) and violently punish that body for even its symbolic resemblance to elsewhere Muslims.

The Transnational Threat: Reconstituting the Muslim Body

On 8 June, two days after the attack on the London family, ten thousand people gathered in support of the family, and politicians from all levels of government spoke outside the London Muslim Mosque at a special

---

6 Wafaa Hasan, co-author of this chapter, was asked to speak at various events on Islamophobia in 2021. The first was for a Toronto private school, alongside famous Olympian Ibtihaj Mohamad. At the time of the talk, bombs were raining down on Gaza and the eviction campaigns were ongoing in Jerusalem. The student organizers called her a few minutes before her talk and told her that the educators were requesting that she does not mention Palestine in her talk. It was clear that there was a kind of widely understood limitation to what could be said in a talk on Islamophobia. Later that month, the Muslim Educators Network of Durham (in Ontario) asked Hasan to join a presentation on Islamophobia and the Muslim educators (who are supporters of Palestinian human rights) noted that there would be senior staff there, and it was important not to mention Palestine for fear of reprisals to them and their livelihoods. This fear was a result of widespread intimidation of educators in the Ontario public school system for doing things as innocuous as responding to student questions about Palestine in classrooms and/or liking a tweet or Facebook post related to Palestinian human rights. Interestingly, during these events, young students insisted on bringing up their relationships and identifications with Muslim majority countries of origin when asked about their experiences of Islamophobia during the question-and-answer periods. Some referenced the temporal relationship between the harassment of their bodies and the invasion of Afghanistan, for example. This illustrates the relevance of the transnational for racialized and Muslim youth.

vigil. Ontario Premier Doug Ford stated, "We need to work every day to ensure Ontario is a safe and inclusive home for everyone who lives here," and "I want every single Muslim family to know that we're with them, we'll always have your backs" (CBC News 2021, para. 4). Prime Minister Justin Trudeau said, "Together we will take action. Together we will find our way forward" (CBC News 2021, para. 5). Erin O'Toole said, "We have to work across party lines … to end the kind of violence and hatred that took these lives … The [London] family was entitled to the same freedom from fear and freedom to worship as every Canadian family. And we have to commit ourselves that it is a reality for all Canadians" (Jackson 2021, para. 25).

When it came time for the Muslim community to speak, Dr. Munir El-Kassem, a public figure in the London Muslim community, took the podium. His speech went viral among some Muslim communities and caused an uproar in other communities. It became the definitive case study of Canada's bounds of multicultural political expression. Speaking at the vigil, Dr. El-Kassem said, "There's a reason why they say the world is a small village. Every country has a foreign policy. I just want to say, whatever is happening in Jerusalem and Gaza is related to whatever happened in London, Ontario – period." His statements were featured in the Canadian Jewish News, Centre for Israel and Jewish affairs, and on the social media accounts of B'nai Brith, a self-ascribed Jewish Human Rights Organization, where they were named "inflammatory," "incendiary" (Bessner 2021), and "deeply disturbing" (B'nai Brith Canada 2021). Dr. El-Kassem faced defamatory comments.[7] El-Kassem explained that

> I was threatened by Bnai Brith with legal action and one rabbi even went as far as leaving me a voice message saying that if any Jewish person would be killed as a result of the violence which I am calling for in my speech, then I will be responsible and I will not be able to live comfortably for the rest of my life.

El-Kassem's speech connecting the violence against Muslims in London with the violence against Muslims and those perceived to be Muslim in Jerusalem and Gaza was read by these prominent Canadian

---

7 Responding to the uproar the day after the vigil, the public figure Munir El-Kassem posted on Facebook saying that "it has been painful to see my words twisted in a moment of incredible grief … The deaths of families here in London has happened too in Palestine. Our love and pain is universal. Any other interpretation is nonsensical and potentially defamatory. I will not be responding further."

organizations to be a call for violence instead of a reflection of the globalization of Islamophobic discourse, which makes the Muslim body (and those misread as or perceived to be Muslim) disposable. El-Kassem's signalling of the violence against the Muslim body is narrated as inciting violence – a discursive scheme of Orientalist and Islamophobic semiology itself. Indeed, the transnationalism of immigrants in North America has historically been perceived to be a threat to the national project (Jaffe-Walter and Lee 2018, 259) of assimilationist multicultural politics.

In a personal interview, El-Kassem shared that "close to 300 people … sent [him] hate messages and threatening messages on [his] Facebook page."[8] He was called a "terrorist leader" and was accused of "advocating violence." He continued: "The main critique was that the 'connection between Gaza and al Quds and London ON is … dumb' … Some asked me how I could reach this conclusion."[9] According to El-Kassem, it took "close to 2 months before things started to die down."[10] Opinion pieces were published in the *Toronto Star*, calling his words "disgraceful" (Cabessa 2021). B'nai Brith Canada called his comments "disturbing" because "the London suspect is not Jewish" (2021). Dr. El-Kassem was not reductively accusing the killer of being Jewish or Israeli but was pointing to a globalized discourse of Islamophobia and Orientalism that is killing Muslims and those perceived to be Muslim in geographical spaces entangled in Canada's imperial-ally matrix. This kind of reprisal – related to both "the Palestine exception"[11] and the anchoring of the ideal Muslim Canadian citizen – is not uncommon in the Canadian landscape (Wills et al. 2022).

Notably, politicians speaking about Islamophobia continued their work of supporting ethnic cleansing in Palestine. Just two months after the London Muslim family tragedy, Erin O'Toole, who had previously

---

8   Personal Interview, 9 January 2022.
9   Personal Interview, 9 January 2022.
10 Personal Interview, 9 January 2022.
11 This is explicated in Marc Lamont Hill and Mitchell Plitnick's 2021 book *Except for Palestine*. They write: "The United States repeatedly isolates itself on the world stage in order to shield Israel as much as possible from any consequences that it might face as a result of its policies and actions. Questioning this lockstep support in any but the mildest terms has long been seen as a political third rail and is often greeted by charges of bias against the world's only Jewish state, or even allegations of outright anti-Semitism. Against the backdrop of these realities, the American political left has normalized a world in which it is acceptable, through words and policies, to embrace the ethical and political contradiction of being 'progressive except for Palestine'" (10).

stated that we must "end the kind of violence and hatred that took these lives" (Jackson 2021, para. 24), announced that he would move the Canadian embassy in Israel to Jerusalem (a controversial move as Jerusalem is considered a sacred site in Islamic historical tradition and the Palestinian struggle) (Kahana 2021; O'Toole 2021), which parallels the "slow violence" (Nixon 2011) of Orientalist and Islamophobic ethnic cleansing in Jerusalem (Kingsley 2021). This announcement was on the heels of devastating and violent "evictions" of Palestinians in Jerusalem, justified predominantly according to their racialization as Arab/ Muslim others. For Muslims in Canada, this move by O'Toole is rooted in an Islamophobic and Orientalist conception of the Arabs in Palestine as non-existent and with non-rightful objections to this decision. Endemic to the erasure of Palestinians in Jerusalem and their objections to claiming Jerusalem as the capital of Israel[12] is the sense that Palestinians, by their proximity to Islam (even though many Palestinians are not Muslim), are disposable and expendable outsiders to the project of Western civility-making and its attendant imperial project (Berenstain 2020; Bell and Schreiner 2018). Therefore, under current models of anti-Islamophobia advocacy, politicians like O'Toole can simultaneously express their disdain for Islamophobia at the vigil and support the ethnic cleansing of Palestinians. For him, Canadian Muslims are amputated from their transnational relationships and the project of protecting them is separate from internationalized Islamophobic discourses that rationalize the erasure of their bodies elsewhere.[13]

The Transnational Life of Islamophobia

Important to note in this analysis are the ways that those enacting Islamophobic violence carry the discursive world of Islamophobic transnational Canadian military campaigns with them when they come home. Even the sight of their local Muslim neighbours (and those perceived to be Muslim) in Canada can trigger this discursive schematic. Indeed, many white supremacists and neo-Nazi terrorist groups look to the Canadian military to channel their racism and advance their combat skills (Lamoureux and Makuch 2018; Shephard, Mak, and Kaschor 2021). This persistent pattern has led to formal investigations and more

---

12 This is despite United Nations regulations maintaining that Israel's claim on Jerusalem is null and void. See United Nations Security Council Resolution 478, adopted on 20 August 1980.
13 For Canadian Muslim Palestinians, evictions of Palestinians from Jerusalem harm their access to their ancestral lands and affect their families directly and violently.

stringent screening processes by the Canadian Armed Forces to "weed out" white supremacists (Mukbil 2020). This demonstrates that the war is not only brought home for those who are victims of Islamophobic violence and harassment, but also for those who are expected to serve in the name of Canada and are asked to live harmoniously with Muslims upon their return. What we saw in London is that even the visual reminder of the Muslim body walking down the street is enough to activate Islamophobic hatred. This is consistent with how a politics of diversity understands difference "as something that exists 'in' the bodies or culture of others … difference is something 'they are'" (Ahmed 2007, 234). This is paired with civilizational discourse that binarizes that difference with "Canadian values" and freedom.

These dichotomous beliefs and their cultural effect became particularly clear in 2008 when the Israeli Ambassador to Canada, Alan Baker, admitted to fearing that the growing population of Canadian Muslims might impact Canada's foreign policy. "Do you expect from these greater numbers that they will absorb themselves into Canadian society as Canadians or that they'll try to push Canadians to adopt their own values and principles?" According to Baker, these values and principles "wouldn't gel with Canadian values of mutual respect" (CTV News 2008). We argue the phraseology of "immigrant/Muslim values" and the fear it stokes functions predominantly to silence rich Muslim knowledges and embodied experiences – the epistemological products of their transnational lives.

Canadian Multiculturalism

Current models of Islamophobia advocacy by Canadian Liberal and Conservative Parties and state institutions like the public education system continue to regulate the bounds of Canadian multiculturalism as well as the failures of the "sedative politics" (Kamboureli 2009, 82) of terms like inclusion and diversity. These boundaries were demonstrated in the carefully sieved agenda for the Summit, noticeably excluding discussions on foreign policy – staple points of conversation about Islamophobia within Muslim communities in Canada. The National Summit on Islamophobia (in spring 2021) in Canada failed to address the relevance of the transnational lives of Canadian Muslims by avoiding conversations about foreign policy and, as such, ignored the ways that Canadian foreign policy (re)produces systems and discourses of Islamophobia.

Sedative politics, Kamboureli argues, is "a politics that attempts to recognize ethnic differences, but only in a contained fashion, in order to manage them" (82). She elaborates that this form of Canadian multi-culturalism responds to the call of ethnic communities for recognition but does so "without disturbing the conventional articulation of the Canadian dominant society" (82). The language of Canada's "diver-sity" and politics of inclusion can be understood to "conceal the opera-tion of systematic inequalities under the banner of difference" (Ahmed 2007, 236).

During the summit, the government of Canada agreed to engage more actively with Muslim communities on anti-racism initiatives, tackle misinformation, and address the tax concerns of Muslim-led charities (Canadian Heritage 2021). However, Muslim academics and community members shared their scepticism even before the sum-mit took place, considering the history of inaction on Islamophobia (Bowden 2021) and the perfunctory rehearsal of hope and sorrow (Patel 2021). In the summit, the logics of diversity and multiculturalism were instrumentalized to contain dissent. In this way, it "secures rather than threatens" (Ahmed 2007, 238) the form of governmentality that is invested in transnational Islamophobia, and through the summit, the rhetoric of diversity was utilized "in ways that reproduce rather than challenge social privilege" (2007, 240).

However, as Ahmed writes, "the whiteness of organizations might be reproduced at the very moment they 'embrace diversity,' as if di-versity is what adds spice and colour to 'mainstream white culture'" (2007, 246). Islamic Heritage Month is one example of offering Mus-lims a form of inclusion into Canadian nationhood at "the cost of their increased subservience, across generations, to the grand narrative of national supremacy" (Thobani 2007, 150). Tactics like Islamic Heritage Month not only work as a perfunctory tool to absolve the Canadian state of its crisis of whiteness by being inclusive to outsiders, but also works as a disciplinary tool towards Muslims by laying out the strin-gent conditions upon which their inclusion is dependent. Through fo-cusing on multiculturalism as opposed to anti-racism, Canada masks the ways in which difference is constituted through Muslim bodies while also offering a distraction from its violence and complicity in violence towards Muslims in other parts of the world. What remains missing in multiculturalism is a politics of plurality that understands difference as a quality within a nation and not a difference from. The commitment to political pluralism enables the religious belonging to Islam as something that does not compete with Canadian nationhood but meaningfully constitutes it.

In fact, the depoliticized model of anti-Islamophobia advocacy en-acted at the summit further damages the anti-racist movement against

Muslims by providing a performative evidence-making of anti-racist practice. This practice relies on liberal models of diversity and cultural pluralism that invoke notions of inclusion and reproduce the referent point of Canadian whiteness as the includers and the Muslims as "fetishized as the origin of the difference" (145). In the logic of diversity and multiculturalism, "difference has become an essence to be recognized rather than a process, a social and historical construction, to be deconstructed" (Razack 1998, 164). Rhetoric of multiculturalism and the attendant language of "mosaic" in Canada vs. the "melting pot" in the United States dominated governmental and academic discussions, making clear that "either one identifies with a group that is defined by its difference from other Canadians or one identifies with what we all have in common" (Angus 2008, 86). This idea of multiculturalism sets up national identity and ethnic identity as mutually exclusive because the foundational assumption of multicultural inclusivity maintains that racialized communities are the origin of difference in a national space that is necessarily white. While being seen as Islamophobic can be understood as an "injury" to the reputation of the Canadian government, narratives of diversity and multiculturalism are offered as solutions that assuage those injuries by concealing the racism (Ahmed 2012, 28).

This practice further runs the risk of reinforcing forms of Islamophobia by gatekeeping Muslims' ability to speak about Canadian foreign policy or Canada's role and complicity in the vilification of Muslims elsewhere. Through the rhetoric of multiculturalism, Canada presents itself as benevolent, liberal, and tolerant, and it falsely reinforces its transition from a white settler-colony to a multi-ethnic and diverse nation, which also works to conceal Canada's genocidal origin. As Thobani's work highlights, Canada only eliminated the overt racial categorization in state policy "after the whiteness of the 'nation' and its 'citizens' had been consolidated by the policies" (2007, 147). Indeed, the rhetoric of multiculturalism works to rearticulate whiteness as culturally tolerant and immigrant friendly, traits that hold more traction in the current neoliberal global order. In this way, the language of diversity and multiculturalism earns its currency precisely through transforming difference into pleasure. While dominant political institutions and public school boards in Ontario have recently been more enthusiastically addressing Islamophobic violence through the Summit and in adopting programs like Islamic Heritage Month, we are continuing to see an uptick in violence against Muslims and those associated with or perceived to be Muslim, nationally.

Conclusion

Until Canada's foreign policy and Canada's transnational relations are critiqued openly for producing Islamophobic cultures, it will be a long and ineffective fight against Islamophobia. Until Muslims can critique the Islamophobia that allows the Canadian public to consent to the pillaging of Muslim-majority nations and to justify the interrogations, harassments, entrapments, and surveillance of Canadian Muslims for "deviant" political thoughts that challenge and seek to transform the settler colonial and imperial projects of the Canadian state, Muslims and their allies will only scratch the surface of fixing Canada's Islamophobia problem. It will continue to grow despite a performative theatre of anti-Islamophobia initiatives. To combat Islamophobia meaningfully, Muslims must be able to articulate transnational connections and educate against them without reprisal and without accusations of inciting violence.

WORKS CITED

Al Jazeera. 2021. "Palestinians Condemn 'Raiding' of Al-Aqsa by Israeli Forces." 18 July 2021. https://www.aljazeera.com/news/2021/7/18/israeli-forces-storm-al-aqsa-compound-on-eve-of-hajj-pilgrimage.
Ahmed, Sara. 2007. "The Language of Diversity." *Ethnic and Racial Studies* 30, no. 2: 235–56. https://doi.org/10.1080/01419870601143927.
–. 2012. *On Being Included: Racism and Diversity in Institutional Life*. Durham, NC: Duke University Press.
Angus, Ian H. 2008. *Identity and Justice*. Toronto: University of Toronto Press.
Ayyash, Mark Muhannad. 2021. "The Toronto District School Board's Real Scandal Is Anti-Palestinian Racism." The Breach. 6 October 2021. https://breachmedia.ca/the-toronto-district-school-boards-real-scandal-is-anti-palestinian-racism/.
B'nai Brith Canada [@bnaibrithcanada]. 2021. "Deeply disturbing to hear a speaker at tonight's vigil for the London hate attack victims claim that the tragedy Is linked to 'whatever Is happening in Jerusalem and Gaza.' The London suspect is not Jewish." Twitter, 8 June 2021, 7:39 p.m. https://twitter.com/bnaibrithcanada/status/1402455214133764096.
Baksh, Nazim, and Devin Heroux. 2017. "'My Life Was Ripped Apart': Two Calgary Muslim Men Say CSIS Wrongfully Targeted Them." CBC. 22 November 2017. https://www.cbc.ca/news/canada/calgary/yacine-meziane-and-abderrahmane-ghanem-want-their-names-cleared-1.4407331.

Bell, Colleen, and Kendra Schreiner. 2018. "The International Relations of Police Power in Settler Colonialism: The 'Civilizing' Mission of Canada's Mounties." *International Journal* 73, no. 1 (March): 111–28. https://doi .org/10.1177/0020702018768480.

Berenstain, Nora. 2020. "'Civility' and the Civilizing Project." *Philosophical Papers* 49, no. 2: 305–37. https://doi.org/10.1080/05568641.2020.1780148.

Bessner, Ellin. 2021. "London Imam's 'Inflammatory' Remarks at Vigil Link Israel to Local Killings." Canadian Jewish News. 9 June 2021. https://thecjn.ca/news/london-imams-inflammatory-remarks-at-vigil -link-israel-to-local-murders/.

Bowden, Olivia. 2021. "'Another Political Extravaganza?' Muslim Academics, Community Members Skeptical about What Might Be Achieved." *Toronto Star*, 2 July 2021. https://www.thestar.com/news/gta/2021/07/02 /another-political-extravaganza-muslim-academics-community-members -skeptical-about-what-might-be-achieved-at-islamophobia-summit.html.

Cabessa, Liad. 2021. "Disgraceful Words at a Vigil for Members of Muslim Family Killed." *Toronto Star*, 12 June 2021. https://www.thestar.com /opinion/letters_to_the_editors/2021/06/12/disgraceful-words-at-a-vigil -for-members-of-muslim-family-killed.html.

Canadian Heritage. 2021. "The Government of Canada Concludes National Summit on Islamophobia." Government of Canada. 23 July 2021. https:// www.canada.ca/en/canadian-heritage/news/2021/07/the-government -of-canada-concludes-national-summit-on-islamophobia.html.

CBC News. 2021. "It's Been 6 Months Since Members of the Afzaal Family in London, Ont., Were Killed. What's Changed?" 6 December 2021. https:// www.cbc.ca/news/canada/london/it-s-been-6-months-since-members -of-the-afzaal-family-in-london-ont-were-killed-what-s-changed-1.6274751.

CTV News. 2008. "Israel Ambassador's Comments 'Unjustified': Critics." 8 May 2008. https://www.ctvnews.ca/israel-ambassador-s-comments -unjustified-critics-1.294539.

Elpa, Ann Marie. 2020. "Toronto Police Urged to Investigate Fatal Stabbing outside Rexdale Mosque as Potential Hate Crime." *Toronto Star*, 19 September 2020. https://www.thestar.com/news/gta/2020/09/19 /toronto-police-urged-to-investigate-fatal-stabbing-outside-rexdale -mosque-as-potential-hate-crime.html.

Engler, Yves. 2010. *Canada and Israel: Building Apartheid*. Winnipeg: Fernwood.

Grewal, Inderpal, and Caren Kaplan. 2006. *An Introduction to Women's Studies: Gender in a Transnational World*. 2nd ed. Boston. McGraw-Hill Higher Education.

–. 2013. "'How Do We Speak?' The Casting Out of the Canadian Arab Federation." *Targeted Transnationals: The State, the Media, and Arab Canadians*, edited by Jenna Hennebry and Bessma Momani, 197–220. Vancouver: UBC Press.

Hajjaj, Muslim b. *Sahih Muslim*. Sunnah.com. https://sunnah.com /muslim:2586a.

Hasham, Alyshah. 2021a. "Nine-Year-Old London Attack Survivor Now in Stable Condition in Hospital." *Toronto Star*, 11 June 2021. https://www .thestar.com/news/canada/2021/06/11/nine-year-old-london-attack -survivor-is-stable-receiving-cards-from-his-young-classmates.html.

–. 2021b. "Police Arrest Two after Toronto Mosque Staff Threatened." *Toronto Star*, 15 June 2021. https://www.thestar.com/news/gta/2021/06/15 /police-arrest-two-after-toronto-mosque-staff-threatened.html.

Hill, Marc Lamont, and Mitchell Plitnick. 2021. *Except for Palestine: The Limits of Progressive Politics*. New York: The New Press.

Jackson, Hannah. 2021. "'An Act of Evil': Trudeau Denounces Attack on London Ont., Muslim Family during Vigil." Global News. 8 June 2021. https://globalnews.ca/news/7932059/trudeau-islamophobia-london -attack/.

Jaffe-Walter, Reva, and Stacey J. Lee. 2018. "Engaging the Transnational Lives of Immigrant Youth in Public Schooling: Toward a Culturally Sustaining Pedagogy for Newcomer Immigrant Youth." *American Journal of Education* 124, no. 3 (May): 257–83. https://doi.org/10.1086/697070.

Kahana, Ariel. 2021. "'If I Win Elections, Canadian Embassy Will Be Moved to Jerusalem.'" *Israel Hayom*, 31 August 2021. https://www.israelhayom.com /2021/08/31/if-i-win-elections-canadian-embassy-will-be-moved-to -jerusalem/.

Kamboureli, Smaro. 2009. *Scandalous Bodies Diasporic Literature in English Canada*. 1st ed. Waterloo, ON: Wilfrid Laurier University Press.

Kashmeri, Zuhair. 1991. *The Gulf Within: Canadian Arabs, Racism, and the Gulf War*. Toronto: J. Lorimer.

Khalidi, R. 2020. *The Hundred Years' War on Palestine: A History of Settler Colonialism and Resistance, 1917–2017*. New York: Metropolitan Books.

Kingsley, Patrick. 2021. "Evictions in Jerusalem Become Focus of Israeli -Palestinian Conflict." *New York Times*, 2 November 2021. https://www .nytimes.com/2021/05/07/world/middleeast/evictions-jerusalem-israeli -palestinian-conflict-protest.html.

Lamoureux, Mack, and Ben Makuch. 2018. "Member of a Neo-Nazi Terror Group Appears to Be Former Canadian Soldier." Vice. 2 August 2018. https://www.vice.com/en/article/7xqe8z/member-of-a-neo-nazi-terror -group-appears-to-be-former-canadian-soldier.

Masalha, Nur. 1997. *A Land without a People: Israel, Transfer and the Palestinians, 1949–96*. London: Faber & Faber.

Mosleh, Omar. 2021. "As Muslim Women Are Attacked in Alberta, a Community Asks: Can Canada Face Its Islamophobia Problem?" *Toronto Star*, 4 July 2021. https://www.thestar.com/news/canada/2021/07/04 /they-only-call-it-a-hate-crime-after-you-get-killed-as-muslim-women -are-attacked-in-alberta-a-community-asks-can-canada-face-its -islamophobia-problem.html.

Mukbil, Huda. 2020. "Integrated National Security Efforts That Include More Stringent Security Screening Should Weed Out Violent White Supremacists in Canadian Military." *Hill Times*, 9 November 2020. https://www.hilltimes. com/2020/11/09/integrated-national-security-efforts-that-include-more -stringent-security-screening-should-weed-out-violent-white-supremacists -in-the-canadian-military/270485.

Nasser, Shanifa. 2018. "'In the Dark': Canadian Eyed by CSIS Blocked from Visiting Dying Father in U.S." CBC News. 16 January 2018. https://www .cbc.ca/news/canada/toronto/csis-muslim-u-s-border-refused-1.4483385.

–. 2019. "When CSIS Comes Knocking: Amid Reports of Muslim Students Contacted by Spy Agency, Hotline Aims to Help." CBC News. 7 August 2019. https://www.cbc.ca/news/canada/toronto/csis-students -university-muslim-campus-1.5229670.

–. 2021. "Canadians with Loved Ones in Gaza, Israel Watch with Heartbreak as Violence Unfolds." CBC News. 15 May 2021. https://www.cbc.ca/news /canada/toronto/gaza-strip-israel-canadians-violence-1.6027556.

Nixon, Rob. 2011. *Slow Violence and the Environmentalism of the Poor*. Cambridge, MA: Harvard University Press.

O'Toole, Erin. 2021. "Statement from Conservative Leader Erin O'Toole on Israel's Independence Day." Conservative Party of Canada. 14 April 2021. https://www.conservative.ca/statement-from-conservative-leader-erin- otoole-on-israels-independence-day/.

Pappé, Ilan. 2006. "The 1948 Ethnic Cleansing of Palestine." *Journal of Palestine Studies* 36, no. 1 (Fall): 6–20. https://doi.org/10.1525/jps.2006.36.1.6.

Patel, Raisa. 2021. "Canada Is Holding a National Summit on Islamophobia. Will It Kick-Start Real Change?" *Toronto Star*, 14 June 2021. https://www .thestar.com/politics/federal/2021/06/14/canada-is-holding-a-national -summit-on-islamophobia-will-it-kick-start-real-change.html.

Piller, Thomas. 2021. "Saskatoon Man Stabbed, Has Beard Cut in Alleged Targeted Attack." Global News. 25 June 2021. https://globalnews.ca /news/7982720/man-stabbed-beard-cut-targeted-attack-saskatoon/.

Razack, Sherene H. 1998. *Looking White People in the Eye: Gender, Race, and Culture in Courtrooms and Classrooms*. Toronto: University of Toronto Press.

–. 2008. *Casting Out: The Eviction of Muslims from Western Law and Politics*. Toronto: University of Toronto Press.

Reynolds, Christopher. 2021. "Two More Extreme Right-Wing Groups Join Proud Boys on Canada's Terror List." *Toronto Star*, 25 June 2021. https://www.thestar.com/politics/2021/06/25/two-more-extreme-right-wing-groups-join-proud-boys-on-canadas-terror-list.html.

Said, Edward W. 2000. *Out of Place: A Memoir*. New York: Vintage Books.

–. 2003. *Orientalism*. 25th anniversary ed. New York: Vintage Books.

Saleh, Muna, and Nada Aoudeh. 2021. "Schools Need to Step Up to Address Islamophobia." The Conversation. 29 November 2021. http://theconversation.com/schools-need-to-step-up-to-address-islamophobia-169937.

Shephard, Michelle, Ashley Mak, and Kim Kaschor. 2021. "White Hot Hate." CBC News. 10 November 2021. https://newsinteractives.cbc.ca/longform/undercover-investigation-patrick-mathews.

Shipley, Tyler. 2021. "Canada Hasn't Reckoned with Its Bloody Legacy in Afghanistan." The Breach. 17 August 2021. https://breachmedia.ca/canada-hasnt-reckoned-with-its-bloody-legacy-in-afghanistan/.

Smith, Robert C. 2006. *Mexican New York Transnational Lives of New Immigrants*. Oakland, CA: University of California Press.

Thobani, Sunera. 2007. *Exalted Subjects: Studies in the Making of Race and Nation in Canada*. Toronto: University of Toronto Press.

Toronto District School Board (TDSB). 2018. "2017 Student and Parent Census Overall Findings." November 2018. https://www.tdsb.on.ca/portals/0/research/docs/2017_Census.pdf.

Toronto District School Board (TDSB). n.d. "Building Critical Consciousness: Support for Developing Learning Resources and Well-Being Experiences: Equity, Anti-Racism and Anti-Oppression." Audio. https://www.tdsb.on.ca/Remote-Learning-Supports-and-Resources-for-Educators/Resources/Building-Critical-Consciousness.

Wills, Emily Regan, Jeremy Wildeman, Michael Bueckert, and Nadia Abu-Zahra, eds. 2022. *Advocating for Palestine in Canada: Histories, Movements, Action*. Halifax: Fernwood.

5 Fighting Anti-Semitism by Fomenting Islamophobia: The Palestine Trope, A Case Study

FAISAL A. BHABHA

Introduction

On the evening of 29 January 2017, a man walked into a busy mosque in Quebec City, pulled out a Glock semi-automatic pistol, and fired forty-eight rounds at the worshippers. In a span of just over two minutes, he murdered six men and injured nineteen more.[1] It was the most lethal attack on a place of worship in modern Canadian history (Mahrouse 2018).

The mosque massacre came after years of worsening social conditions for Canadian Muslims, who had grown distrustful and fearful of the country's national security agencies. The 11 September 2001 terrorist attacks in the United States had turned the security spotlight on Muslim communities, making them vulnerable to abuse and overreach (Lenard and Nagra 2016). Civil liberties groups documented how Muslims were subjected to unfair suspicion and profiling, blamed for international terrorism, and made to pay a higher price for national security at home (Bhabha 2018). Muslims complained about interference in their private and public lives caused by scrutiny and stigma perpetuated by biased government action (Lenard and Nagra 2016, 16). They faced persistent barriers to the free exercise of constitutionally protected activity. Even ordinary acts, like buying a book, boarding an airplane, meeting an acquaintance for coffee, or attending religious services, could be misconstrued as potentially incriminating (Lenard and Nagra 2016, 24).

The author has been acting as pro bono counsel to Imam Ayman Elkasrawy since 2017. The views expressed in this essay are the author's alone.
1 The murdered men were Ibrahima Barry, Mamadou Tanou Barry, Khaled Belkacemi, Aboubaker Thabti, Abdelkrim Hassane, and Azzedine Soufiane.

In addition to fearing being targeted by national security agencies, Canadian Muslims also came to face heightened vulnerability in society at the hands of fellow citizens. Official counter-terrorism discourse had legitimized and even encouraged anti-Muslim animus (Bhabha 2018, 189–94). Discriminatory acts against Muslims in public spaces and workplaces would spike whenever stories of global terrorism hit the headlines (Lenard and Nagra 2016, 24). Canadian Muslims had become the preferred scapegoat (Gaudet 2018, 8 chart 4; Leber 2017, 6 chart 3).[2]

In a climate of increasing hostility, many worried that violence against Muslims would only rise with the ascendancy of social media and the proliferation of online misinformation and hate. The mosque massacre was Canadian Muslims' worst nightmare realized. Alexandre Bissonnette, a white, French Canadian man, just twenty-seven years old at the time of the attack, had become radicalized on right-wing American websites: "His influencers were not obscure, underground hate sites, but rather well-known – albeit despicable – media figures. From Richard Spencer and Alex Jones to Donald Trump, the people who influenced Bissonnette were predominantly American, and white supremacists have always maintained cross-border relationships" (Moore 2018). The shooter told police that he was motivated by the prime minister's response to Donald Trump's travel restrictions on people from Muslim countries. Trudeau had tweeted: "To those fleeing persecution, terror & war, Canadians will welcome you, regardless of your faith" (Perreaux 2018). The deluded shooter sincerely believed that killing Muslims would protect his loved ones from a menacing threat (Perreaux 2018).

Given the challenges to addressing Islamophobia in general, it should not be surprising that laws designed to remedy discrimination have not been effective at protecting Muslims and Arabs from Islamophobia. Notwithstanding the well-documented experiences of Canadian Muslims since 9/11, there remain few if any reported human rights tribunal decisions in any Canadian jurisdiction finding discrimination based on Islamophobia (Bahdi 2017). Bahdi has carried out the only published study of Canadian human rights agencies' adjudication of allegations involving anti-Arab or anti-Muslim bias (Bahdi 2018). The article surveys thirteen cases[3] in multiple jurisdictions between 2002 and 2017 in

---

2 Comparing the 2016 statistics of hate crimes against Muslims to the 2014 data reveals a 40 per cent increase in just two years.

3 The thirteen cases were adjudicated by human rights tribunals in British Columbia, Ontario, Quebec, or Canada (federal) between 2002 and 2017.

which Arab or Muslim individuals turned to human rights law for a remedy following a perceived discriminatory event. Analysing the barriers to justice, Bahdi found that a "majority of the 13 claimants spent between two and 15 years pursuing a human rights claim, most did not secure the remedies they requested and many found their experiences minimized or misunderstood by adjudicators" (Bahdi 2018, 74–5). She concluded that, while human rights law "offers Arab and Muslim communities the possibility of redress and vindication for the significant discrimination they face in schools, workplaces, service counters, airports and other sites" the human rights system in practice appears to be failing those who need it "just when they need it the most" (Bahdi 2018, 74).

This essay presents a case study that highlights many noteworthy features of contemporary Islamophobia. Two weeks after the Quebec City mosque massacre, a prominent mosque in downtown Toronto became the target of Islamophobic incitement. On the surface, it appeared that the local community rallied behind the Muslims as politicians of all stripes condemned the targeting of the mosque. Beneath the surface, however, is the story of one individual Muslim scapegoat. It began with a spurious allegation of anti-Semitism against the mosque's imam based on the content of an Arabic-language prayer he had recited to a large congregation on a holy night many months before. The allegation turned out to be based on a fraudulent translation of the prayer. The translation exploited damaging stereotypes that cast Muslims as violent, terroristic, and intolerant. The truth, meanwhile, challenged the stereotypes and complicated a simple story. The truth was inconvenient and almost nobody was interested in it.

The presentation of the case study will illustrate how human rights fail to mitigate the impact or repair the damage caused by Islamophobia in circumstances when the perceived cost of addressing Islamophobia is likely to outweigh the perceived cost of ignoring it. The case study supports the hypothesis that meaningfully confronting Islamophobia has not been prioritized as a general matter and is actively de-prioritized when it is in tension with other interests, such as the struggle against anti-Semitism. In a context where fighting anti-Semitism is abused and weaponized against Palestinian human rights defenders (Nestel 2021), the fight against Islamophobia has actually been complicated and obstructed by the fight against anti-Semitism.

This essay's treatment of the case study centres on the troubling role that the pro-Israel lobby plays in perpetuating the global Islamophobia industry, stoking the fire of anti-Muslim bigotry in Canada and obstructing efforts to combat it. I proceed, in the sections that follow, to describe the background and context, present the case study, and analyse the implications for combating Islamophobia.

M-103: Studying and Combating Islamophobia

Canadian Muslim discontent with national security policy reached its high point as the 2015 federal election approached (Ahmad 2019). Canadian Muslims mobilized like never before to express opposition to Stephen Harper, who had been prime minister since 2006.[4] They took credit for helping secure the electoral defeat of the Conservative Party, ushering-in the Trudeau-led Liberal era of self-proclaimed "inclusive" politics, embodied in a racially diverse caucus that included ten Muslims (Grenier 2016).

About a year into the new government's term, a young, female, Pakistan-born, first-time backbench MP from Mississauga, Iqra Khalid, introduced a motion in the House of Commons warning of "the need quell the increasing public climate of hate and fear" (Levitz 2017). The motion, titled M-103, called on the government to "condemn Islamophobia" and to study the problems of racism and religious discrimination,includingIslamophobia,withaviewtodevelopinga"whole-of-government" approach while ensuring a "community-centred" focus (Parliament of Canada 2016). Khalid introduced her motion in the House in December 2016 with no idea that her chilling warning would become a reality in just six weeks' time. She also could have had no idea just how much public controversy would arise over her modest proposal.

After the mosque massacre, the government declared that combating Islamophobia was an urgent priority. The prime minister openly discussed how Canadian Muslims were "particularly vulnerable these days to intolerance and discrimination" when explaining the importance of doing the work that was called for in the motion (Harris 2017a). For a brief moment, it seemed, everyone in Canada could unite behind a clear and uncontroversial message against intolerance. Even a Conservative Party leadership contender, Michael Chong, defended M-103 with reference to the mosque massacre, stating, "it is appropriate and important that Canadian parliamentarians study the issue of anti-Muslim and anti-Islamic prejudice and discrimination" (Harris 2017b). The government scheduled the motion for debate on 15 February 2017, just two weeks after the mosque massacre.

---

4   Muslim voter turnout was 8 out of 10, significantly exceeding, for the first time in any
    election, Canada's overall voter turnout rate of 68.5 per cent (Environics Institute 2016, 12).

But then, real opposition began to build. It may have emanated from the right-wing fringe, but it quickly took hold in mainstream conservative circles. For example, Barbara Kay, a *National Post* columnist, questioned the need to combat Islamophobia at all, arguing that there were more hate crimes against Jews than Muslims, which was true at the time based on documented data (Harris 2017a).[5] The problem of undocumented data due to systemic underreporting of anti-Muslim incidents was one of the many things that M-103 was aimed at identifying and remedying. Writing for the *National Post*, Kay went on to worry about incursions on freedom of expression and warned of sharia creep (Kay 2017). She did not detail exactly how M-103 would accomplish this, and credible experts refuted characterizations of the motion being a Muslim "Trojan horse."

The Centre for Israel and Jewish Affairs (CIJA), the most influential Israel lobby group in the country, also opposed the motion. Its CEO, Shimon Fogel, testified that the term Islamophobia "has become a lightning rod for controversy, distracting from other important issues at hand" (Standing Committee on Canadian Heritage 2017). This was telling because the only "controversy" over M-103 was being fuelled by the same interests that feed anti-Muslim animus. Fogel invoked Islamophobic tropes to gaslight the motion's supporters, claiming that "extremism is a problem within parts of the Canadian Muslim community that must be addressed" (Standing Committee on Canadian Heritage 2017) and emphasizing that there are "elements or manifestations of Islam that are not only antithetical to Canadian values, but have been the basis of hatred towards and attacks on Jewish communities around the world" (Harris 2017b). He did not use the words "terrorists" or "anti-Semites" but the implication was clear.

M-103 was debated in the House of Commons on the scheduled day, 15 February 2017. During the debate, MP Khalid read aloud some of the demeaning tweets and death threats she had received after proposing the motion. The vote on the motion was put off to the following month, March 2017. In the days and weeks that followed, demonstrations would sprout up in cities across the country, and a large protest was held in Ottawa, as resistance to M-103 continued to swell (Kalvapalle 2017). Some incidents of violence were reported. Many incidents of discrimination and/or hate speech were reported. Canadian Islamophobia was coming out in the open for all to see.

---

5   There are many problems with the documented data about anti-Semitism in Canada (Nestel 2021).

Islamophobia out in the Open

Two days after the House debate, 17 February 2017, was a Friday, the day Muslims congregate for prayer. That Friday saw a prominent mosque in the heart of Toronto's downtown core, Masjid Toronto ("the mosque"), picketed by angry protesters (Miller 2017). It had been barely two weeks since the Quebec City mosque massacre. The mosque, with a capacity of around seven hundred, held three weekly, back-to-back, jam-packed afternoon prayer sessions, each lasting around forty-five minutes. The picketers remained positioned in front of the entrance throughout the afternoon, hurling insults and waving placards for hours. More than two thousand worshippers, including men, women, and children, pass though Masjid Toronto's doors on Fridays. That day, each one of them was called a terrorist, jihadist, suicide bomber, rapist, and paedophile.

Members of a far-right, pro-Israel group, Never Again Canada, posted photos of the picket to its Facebook page with a tag line stating: "No to M-103, no to wife-beating and no to child marriage. We will never be silenced. Stop Sharia, it's a crime in Canada" (Miller 2017). A 2019 investigation by the *Toronto Star* and *Buzzfeed* would find ties between Never Again Canada and the Jewish Defence League (JDL), which the FBI describes as a "violent extremist Jewish organization" and "right-wing terrorist group" (Oved et al. 2019). In 2017, Facebook had removed the JDL from its platform for continually violating community standards, calling it a "dangerous organization."[6] Never Again Canada appeared to pick up where JDL left off, using Masjid Toronto to attract attention and then to drive web traffic to anti-Muslim websites (Oved et al. 2019). On the street in front of the mosque, passers-by reported being genuinely put off by the tone and message of the picket, calling it "horrible, hateful" and "disgusting" (Miller 2017). There was a tremendous outpouring of support for Masjid Toronto from neighbours, local politicians, and members of other faith communities.

The day after the mosque picket, on Saturday, 18 February 2017, the first in a series of articles was posted online to a now-defunct website called CIJ News. Entitled, "Supplications at Masjid Toronto Mosque: 'Slay Them One by One and Spare Not One of Them,'" the article claimed to present a different side to Masjid Toronto.[7] The author,

---

6 Facebook had removed the JDL from its platform in 2017, according to the Canadian Jewish News, calling it a "dangerous organization" that violates its community standards (Oved et al. 2019).

7 The internet sites have been removed. Screenshots of the pages are held by the author.

Jonathan Halevi, referenced material obtained from the mosque's website. Masjid Toronto had begun posting unedited content to the internet in an effort to better serve the needs of its congregants. The posted material included video and audio recordings of special services and holy days. While the videos had been posted "publicly," enabling anyone to gain access, the materials were intended for an audience of the faithful. The content was entirely in Arabic and was not translated, dubbed, or subtitled.

Halevi is a well-known right-wing media figure and Rebel News blogger. Formerly the head of the Information Branch of the Israeli Defense Forces' (IDF) Spokesperson Unit from 2002 to 2003, he had also served as the head of the "Palestinian Research Branch" of the Israeli military in 1998–2002 (Zine 2022). The title of Halevi's lead CIJ News article referenced a recording of a prayer delivered some eight months earlier, in June 2016, during the Muslim holy month of Ramadan. Because the supplications were entirely in Arabic, the text needed translation to English, which Halevi undertook himself. He interpreted it to be advocating for "killing Jews" and calling for the "purification" of the Al-Aqsa mosque in Jerusalem "from the filth of the Jews."

The article was designed to leave the reader with only one option: conclude that Masjid Toronto, and the people who attend it, are intolerant and unworthy of public sympathy. If hundreds of Muslim congregants had prayed for the killing of Jews on the holiest night of the Muslim calendar, perhaps the things the picketers were saying about the mosque were true. Perhaps Muslims did not deserve sympathy and understanding. Perhaps the Quebec City shooter was correct; perhaps Muslims were a danger to society, and the concept of Islamophobia was a hoax.

The message of the CIJ News story was amplified as it was reproduced, without verification, by national news outlets, including the CBC (Nasser 2017a), and became the subject of endless commentary online. The prominent interfaith activist, Toronto Imam Hamid Slimi, was quoted in the press condemning the supplication based on the false translation. Instead of challenging the translation, which native Arabic speakers would know to be false, Slimi simply stated the obvious without casting judgment: "We must denounce any anti-Semitic act or statement whether in a sermon or a prayer" (Nasser 2017b). Meanwhile, the story received sustained attention in newspapers like the *Toronto Sun* (Warmington 2017a). No one disputed the translation or questioned the motives of those pushing the story.

Call and Response

On 21 February 2017, a few days after the mosque picket, B'nai Brith Canada, an aggressive pro-Israel advocacy group, wrote to the president of Toronto Metropolitan University (TMU, known at the time as Ryerson University), Mohamed Lachemi, referencing the "controversy surrounding the Masjid Toronto."[8] Media stories had reported that the imam who led the Ramadan prayer, Ayman Elkasrawy, was also a PhD student and part-time teaching assistant in TMU's engineering program. B'nai Brith demanded action by the university.

Lachemi, a practising Muslim who was born in Algeria (Gordon 2016), had just become university president four months earlier. He had already been asked to deal with multiple anti-Semitism allegations by B'nai Brith. The group's letter implied that Lachemi was not doing enough to take anti-Semitism seriously. It described Elkasrawy's supplication as "another episode in a pattern of anti-Semitic behaviour already demonstrated by another lecturer at Ryerson as well as numerous students, all of which we have pointed out to you." The letter went on: "It is totally unacceptable that someone who describes Jews as 'filth' should be allowed to deliver lectures or grade assignments at Ryerson ... I am sure that you will agree, it is particularly disappointing that Mr. Elkasrawy chose to spread this vile anti-Semitism under the guise of pious religious expression." The expectation was clear: Lachemi had to demonstrate decisive action to root out anti-Semitism. Jewish students had to believe they could feel safe in the classroom (Fishman, n.d.). Elkasrawy had to go. The letter ends with a request that B'nai Brith be updated "as soon as possible" about next steps.

At around the same time, a student activist, Aedan O'Connor, put up as many as one hundred posters across TMU's campus with Elkasrawy's photo, the mistranslated words, and a demand that he be fired. Several subsequent articles were published on the CIJ website that reinforced the pressure being applied to Lachemi. On 22 February 2017, Halevi wrote, "B'nai Brith notifies Ryerson U about anti-Jewish statements by teaching assistant."[9] Two days later, he published, "Students urge Ryerson administration to fire a teaching assistant over anti-Jewish statements."[10] Also on 22 February 2017, Toronto Police confirmed that the JDL had lodged a hate complaint against Masjid Toronto, which

---

8   Copy of letter on file with the author.
9   The website has been taken down. Copy of article on file with the author.
10   The website has been taken down. Copy of article on file with the author.

was under investigation (Warmington 2017b). Meir Weinstein, the head of the JDL, told the *Toronto Sun*: "We need to clarify what is going on at this mosque. Is this a den of worship or a den of hate?" (Warmington 2017c).

Facing immense public pressure, the Muslim Association of Canada (MAC), the group which operates Majid Toronto, announced on 22 February 2017 that it was suspending Elkasrawy from his Imam duties while the mosque investigated the allegations raised in the media. A mosque spokesperson stated: "We condemn all forms of discrimination and intolerance to any faith group … We take this incident very seriously and we are working to rectify it and ensure it doesn't happen at all in future" (Warmington 2017b). He went on to note that MAC had "also reached out to leaders in the Jewish community to express our sincere apology for this incident, and to continue the dialogue between our communities." According to Elkasrawy, the mosque leadership was terrified of backlash and losing goodwill in the broader society. In a first-person account of his ordeal, published in the *Toronto Star* several months later, this is how Elkasrawy explained the lack of support he received from the Muslim community:

> Our mosque and community leaders were afraid of aggravating the situation. No one would come to my aid. Few were even interested in my side of the story. I was radioactive – no one wanted to touch me. The damage was done. And the effects on my reputation and my life have been nothing short of devastating. (Elkasrawy 2017)

On February 27, 2017, TMU president Lachemi received further correspondence from B'nai Brith asking why the university had not issued a public statement or responded to B'nai Brith's previous letter, calling the lack of action "extremely disappointing." First thing the next morning, 28 February 2017, senior university officials met to determine next steps. They recommended terminating Elkasrawy's employment immediately. A few hours later, Elkasrawy received an email summoning him to a meeting with TMU's dean of the faculty of engineering and architectural science that day at 4:30 p.m. The email was marked "urgent" and stated that the purpose of the meeting was "to meet with the Dean to discuss an important issue relating to your employment contract with Ryerson."

Elkasrawy attended the meeting with a union representative believing he would be given an opportunity to present his side of the story. He told the dean that the words being attributed to him were not his. He said he was being falsely portrayed in the media, and his supplication had been mistranslated. He even brought a reliable English translation of the text of his supplication, which he said he had obtained from the president of the Canadian Council of Imams. He believed this evidence was exculpatory and could save his employment.

As it turned out, the university was not engaged in a search for the truth. It was in damage control mode, presumably due to the relentless pressure being applied by B'nai Brith. Elkasrawy's supplication constituted "off-duty conduct" that had an impact on the university because B'nai Brith were now saying that Jewish students could not feel safe being taught by Elkasrawy. The university determined it could not afford to maintain Elkasrawy's employment regardless of whether he was accurately or wrongly accused of anti-Semitism.[11] It was now a matter of protecting the institution's reputation and avoiding the negative attention B'nai Brith would be sure to generate in seeking to shame TMU and its first Muslim president for being soft on anti-Semitism.

Although Elkasrawy was given a chance to speak at the meeting with the dean, it was clear that what he said was not going to have any impact on the outcome, which had already been determined. After a short break, Elkasrawy was handed a lengthy dismissal letter that ignored his credible claim that his words were, at best, wrongly understood and, at worst, deliberately maligned. The termination letter appeared to have been substantially, if not entirely, drafted before the meeting even took place – well before Elkasrawy had a chance to meaningfully address the allegations. The university even offered him, without admitting liability, a financial payment to settle the claim quietly. His union representative advised him to take the offer, but he declined.

About an hour after Elkasrawy was handed the termination letter, Lachemi wrote to B'nai Brith stating that Elkasrawy was "no longer employed by the university" and that "we remain actively engaged in addressing anti-Semitism in our community."[12] The next day, on the morning of 1 March 2017, the student activist, Aedan O'Connor, took to social media to thank president Lachemi personally for his "decisive action" and to claim credit for getting Elkasrawy fired. B'nai Brith also published a press release suggesting that its pressure campaign had worked (Fishman, n.d.). Lachemi himself did not address the issue publicly until later that day, posting a statement that "a teaching assistant made disturbing, anti-Semitic comments off-campus in the summer of

---

11 His status as a student was not affected. He continued to attend the university and successfully defended his PhD several years later without interruption.

12 Document on file with the author.

2016" and that "the university has taken appropriate action" (Hudes 2017). No Canadian Muslim leader or organization spoke publicly to cast doubt on Lachemi's assertions about Elkasrawy. No one spoke-up to call-out or correct Halevi's mistranslation or to clear-up the false impression that Elkasrawy had said what he was accused of saying.

Despite losing his employment and being publicly condemned by the university president, all the while maintaining his innocence, Elkasrawy decided to voluntarily undertake cultural sensitivity and anti-racism training, involving five specially tailored workshops, which included visiting a synagogue and meeting with rabbis. The program was organized with the help of a prominent Jewish community activist and former head of the Canadian Jewish Congress, Bernie Farber, who had once helped rehabilitate a repentant neo-Nazi. It quickly became clear to him that Elkasrawy did not need rehabilitation. Farber told the *Toronto Sun*: "In my experience I can tell who's an anti-Semite and Mr. Elkasrawy is not one. He is a fine young man" (Warmington 2017a).

A Journalist Investigates

There was an intrepid journalist who took an interest in Elkasrawy. Jennifer Yang, a *Toronto Star* reporter writing on identity and inequality, broke through with Elkasrawy's story. After seven months of investigation, her article appeared on the front page of the *Sunday Star* (Yang 2017). The 5,000-word feature painted a very different picture of the man and the events surrounding him than had been previously reported. The *Star* story set Elkasrawy's ordeal in the broader context of Islamophobia and unveiled the spurious smear. Yang contacted five separate, world-renowned Arabic-language experts to independently analyse the impugned supplication. They all concluded it had been translated in a misleading way.

The video in question captured the holiest night of Ramadan. Masjid Toronto was filled to capacity, with around six hundred people engaged in supplementary prayers extending late into the night. Elkasrawy, the part-time Imam, was leading the congregation. At a key point, Elkasrawy engaged in a lengthy, emotional supplication for relief. He prayed to protect the world's suffering people. He condemned violence and injustice. The key allegations, based on Halevi's false translation, were that Elkasrawy had called for "killing Jews" and prayed for the "purification" of the Al-Aqsa mosque in Jerusalem from the "filth of the Jews."

The *Star*'s experts showed how the video had been digitally re-sequenced ("spliced") in a way to deliberately distort Elkasrawy's words, give them a sinister meaning, and make it sound like he was talking about Jews when he was not. Elkasrawy had in fact prayed to protect the Al-Aqsa mosque from desecration. The timing was significant, and emphasizes the transnational dimensions of Islamophobia in Canada, as addressed by Hasan, Z. Khan, and Smith in this volume: in 2016, Israeli settlers and soldiers had been storming the Al-Aqsa compound, as they had done in previous years during Ramadan (Shalabi 2022), with increasing frequency and ferocity. In June 2016, during the last ten days of the Muslim holy month, soldiers entered the Al-Aqsa mosque and beat Palestinian worshippers (News Agencies 2016). These provocations were upsetting not only to Palestinians but to Muslims everywhere. At the same time, in Syria, the population were enduring violence and grave suffering in a brutal civil war. Elkasrawy's supplications focused on the respective plights of the Syrian and Palestinian people.

Lost in Translation

For Elkasrawy's detractors, the *Star* story changed nothing. If anything, those who had demanded Elkasrawy's dismissal doubled down and intensified the online pillorying of his reputation. B'nai Brith rejected the opinions of the five consulted experts and raised the spectre of bias, without any evidence (Yang 2017). One of the experts, University of Toronto faculty member Atiqa Hachimi, described in a public lecture venomous Islamophobic hate mail she received after being featured in the story (Hachimi 2018). B'nai Brith's CEO, Michael Mostyn, told Yang that Elkasrawy's "message at the mosque was irrefutably offensive and anti-Semitic" (Yang 2017). He claimed that B'nai Brith had verified the translation before pressuring TMU to fire Elkasrawy, though Mostyn would not disclose who had been consulted. Instead, he pointed the *Star* to Mordechai Kedar, an Arabic-language professor at Israel's Bar-Ilan University, who not only defended Halevi's original translation but described Elkasrawy's supplication as a form of "terrorism" (Yang 2017). Kedar is a former Israeli military officer and has been associated with various Islamophobic organizations (Yang 2017). Referring to Muslims like Elkasrawy, Kedar told the *Star*, "[They want] to make the mainstream media in the free world believe them that they are the targets, when they are the problem in the whole world" (Yang 2017).

Meanwhile, on 23 October 2017, two days after the publication of the *Star* article, the American anti-Muslim writer, Robert Spencer, published an article on his website, Jihad Watch, criticizing Yang's piece as a "con job" (Spencer 2017). For Spencer, the purpose of the article was another effort to build false sympathy for Muslims: "So now we come to the real point of the Toronto Star article: when a Muslim prays for the killing of the Jews, it is Muslims who are the victims. As always" (Spencer 2017).

There is a real question of what justice can possibly look like for someone in Elkasrawy's position, where there is relentless reputational assault based on a false allegation. Like defamation, discriminatory smearing casts a negative cloud over a person's reputation regardless of mitigation efforts. Repairing the damage can be hopeless, especially where the smeared person is a member of a vulnerable minority group. Even where a retraction or correction is issued, the internet ensures it will never go away. Smearing, it turns out, is a highly effective way to discredit one's less powerful opponents. In a climate of entrenched Islamophobia, a Muslim seeking to refute a scurrilous allegation that aligns with a negative stereotype faces an uphill, if not impossible, challenge.

The fact that smearing works might explain why what happened to Elkasrawy is not that unusual. There is a (mis)translation industry that is part of the global Islamophobia network (Zine 2022). One of the experts consulted by the *Toronto Star* referred to the work of people like Halevi as "propaganda translation" (Yang 2017). Scholars of language note that the work of translation is not just about reproducing the meaning of words; it is about producing something new. Understood this way, translation is "a deliberate and conscious act of selection, assemblage, structuring, and fabrication – and even, in some cases, of falsification, refusal of information, counterfeiting, and the creation of secret codes. In these ways translators, as much as creative writers and politicians, participate in the powerful acts that create knowledge and shape culture" (Tymoczko and Gentzler 2002, xxi).

Researchers have noted that the mistranslation of Arabic text is a tactic used by anti-Muslim writers to reinforce stereotypes about Muslims and Islam as violent and intolerant. Zine refers to this as the "weaponization of the Qur'an" (Zine 2022), while Hachimi dubs it the "war on translation" (Hachimi 2018). In its report on the Islamophobia network, titled *Fear Inc.* (Ali et al. 2011), the Center for American Progress identified the Middle East Media and Research Institute (MEMRI) as "the Islamophobia network's go-to place for selective translations of Islamist rhetoric abroad" (Ali et al. 2011, 94). MEMRI is a press monitoring agency created by retired members of the Israeli military. It produces free Arabic-English translations of Middle Eastern press stories for the purpose of informing the debate over American policy in the Middle East. However, its translations have been criticized as "cherry picking," "highly partisan," and "propagandist" (Ali et al. 2011, 94–5). The only

people who regularly cite MEMRI are members of the Islamophobia
network itself, including Daniel Pipes and Steve Emerson. *Fear Inc.*
notes that the Norwegian right-wing terrorist, Anders Breivik, cited
MEMRI more than a dozen times in his manifesto.

Questions of Law

Shortly after he was dismissed from his TA job, Elkasrawy filed an application with the Human Rights Tribunal of Ontario (HRTO), alleging
discrimination against the university for its rush to judgment in terminating his employment. The case raised numerous important questions. How is anti-Semitism defined under the Human Rights Code?
What is a university to do when an allegation of off-campus anti-
Semitism is raised? What if the person against whom the allegation is
made responds that the complaint itself is spurious, malicious, and discriminatory? Does the employer have a duty to investigate the truth
or does an employer's right to protect its reputation trump the search
for truth? Does the discrimination analysis differ if the party being accused of anti-Semitism belongs to a vulnerable group and that group
has been tarred by stereotypes that align with the allegation? What if
the anti-Semitism charge itself is rooted in bias and negative stereotyping about Muslims?

Elkasrawy's case also raised a key systemic question: what good is
anti-discrimination law if it does not require a public institution, like
a university, to investigate an allegation of Islamophobia when a questionable allegation of anti-Semitism has been made? Strictly speaking,
the university was correct to say it had no legal obligation to investigate
whether Elkasrawy had been treated fairly in the media. It is not an
employer's general responsibility to proactively defend an employee's
reputation. At the same time, pursuant to human rights law, the university had a duty to not participate in any conduct that could disadvantage or harm Elkasrawy's dignity in a way related to a protected
ground. Elkasrawy asked the hearing to find that the university could
not rely on management rights to tend to its reputation while paying no
heed to the impact on Elkasrawy's dignity, reputation, and status. He
argued that a public institution should be expected to fully investigate
allegations of discrimination and to seek out the truth.

An obvious question emerges when the facts of Elkasrawy's case are
brought to light: How does a university protect its brand by firing an
imam? Relatedly, why would a university president who is Muslim allow himself to be manipulated by an outside organization to legitimize
an Islamophobic smear? Should he be expected to know better?

The question, in terms of the law, is how to identify Islamophobia, understood as discrimination on the basis of actual or perceived Muslim identity, in complex social settings. This, I suggest, is an essential question. As highlighted at the outset, Bahdi (2018) found that the HRTO is ineffective at remedying Islamophobia in the social areas covered by the Code, which creates an effective rights vacuum and, arguably, a rule of law deficiency. One explanation for the fact that the HRTO is not effective in addressing Islamophobia could be that the tribunal, and the lawyers and individuals appearing before it, do not have the tools and experience to properly identify Islamophobia. These are problems of education and training, which are exactly what M-103 proposed to improve, and precisely what the Israel lobby sought to stymie.

How the law of discrimination interprets Islamophobia remains to be seen. Islamophobia falls under statutory human rights, which guarantee freedom from discrimination in employment, the receipt of goods and services, in housing, and in vocational associations. The Code is incorporated into university policies, which means the right to be free from discrimination enjoys robust protection on post-secondary campuses. In fact, this is one of the primary reasons TMU gave to *justify* its decision to terminate Elkasrawy: that providing a discrimination-free space for Jewish students was a legal obligation. What the university was unable or unwilling to consider was the discriminatory foundation and exclusionary impact of Elkasrawy's termination, the likely effect being a hostile environment for Palestinian, Arab, and Muslim students.

Elkasrawy alleged that the university had essentially cooperated in an act of discrimination perpetrated by third parties; namely, Halevi, CIJ News, and B'nai Brith, among others. Human rights jurisprudence establishes that intentions are not determinative: discrimination need only be a factor, even a small factor, in an otherwise lawful decision, to have the effect of invalidating the entire decision as discriminatory.

In terms of the legal test for discrimination, a tribunal would not require Elkasrawy to prove that the stereotypes contained in the smear played an intentional or even conscious role in the university's decision to terminate. In *Pieters*, the Ontario Court of Appeal upheld the HRTO's finding that there need be no direct evidence of discrimination (*Peel Law Association v. Pieters*, 2013 ONCA 396, para. 111). Discrimination of this sort will more often be proved by circumstantial evidence and inference because racial stereotyping is usually the result of subtle unconscious beliefs, biases, and prejudices. In Elkasrawy's case, the unstated biases emanated from the mistranslation, which was designed to accentuate obvious tropes. The mistranslation also aligned with the things that the picketers were saying about Muslims in front of Masjid Toronto the day before the article was published: Muslims are intolerant, violent, and untrustworthy. Additionally, a powerful lobby group was seizing upon the opportunity to impugn defenders of Palestinian rights in a way which reinforces the Islamophobic notion that Islam and Muslims are generally anti-Semitic.

Countering False Anti-Semitism

In recent years, the fight against anti-Semitism has been instrumentalized by the Israeli government and its supporters to delegitimize the Palestinian cause and to silence defenders of Palestinian rights. In May 2016, the International Holocaust Remembrance Association (IHRA) adopted a definition of anti-Semitism.[13] It was accompanied by a list of eleven "contemporary examples" of potentially anti-Semitic statements or behaviours, which include seven that refer to the state of Israel. Some of the examples of potential anti-Semitism include the application of "double standards" to Israel, comparing "contemporary Israeli policy to that of the Nazis," or calling Israel "a racist endeavour."

Since 2016, the pro-Israel lobby has been advocating to all levels of government across Canada the adoption of the IHRA definition of anti-Semitism. Civil liberties groups began opposition campaigns, warning governments that adopting the IHRA definition will undermine both democracy and the fight against anti-Semitism. That has not stopped governments and universities around the world from adopting the IHRA. Starting in 2017, evidence began to emerge that the enforcement of the IHRA definition was having a chilling effect on campuses and was being used aggressively to police expressions of solidarity with the Palestinians (Sachs 2019).

While Israel uses anti-Semitism to repel criticism of its policy and actions, much of Israel's justification for its treatment of the Palestinians is steeped in Islamophobic tropes. Official policy in many countries, including Canada, recognizes that Palestinians are a people living under illegal occupation and who have rights of national self-determination that have not been realized for nearly seventy-five years since the creation of Israel. In recent history, successive Israeli governments have adopted increasingly illiberal policies, tightening Israel's grip on the Palestinian territories, and diminishing the

---

13   International Holocaust Remembrance Alliance: https://www.holocaustremembrance
.com/resources/working-definitions-charters/working-definition-antisemitism.

likelihood of a negotiated two-state solution. Consequently, there is a growing global consensus that Israel is committing apartheid, as understood under international law (Human Rights Watch 2021; Amnesty International 2022). This conclusion is shared by Israel's own leading and most respected human rights organizations (B'Tselem 2021, Yesh Din 2020).

The charge of Israeli apartheid coincided with the 2020 murder of African American George Floyd by a white police officer, which triggered an enormous wave of civic action for racial justice in the US and around the world. It also induced renewed interest in the plight of the Palestinians. This has opened space for scholars, writers, and policy makers to consider the concept of anti-Palestinian racism (Abu-Laban and Bakan 2021), as a subset of "racism" and a concept related to, though distinct from, "Islamophobia" (Bahdi and Kanji 2018). Unfortunately for Elkasrawy, in 2017, space for this kind of understanding had not yet opened-up.

In seeking to defend himself against the unfair charge of anti-Semitism, Elkasrawy tried to raise Islamophobia as an explanation for how his words came to be so misconstrued from their intended meaning. However, that failed to prompt appropriate action by the university. With its extensive resources and experts, not to mention an academic mission to pursue truth, TMU did nothing to meaningfully investigate Elkasrawy's allegation that he was discriminatorily targeted. The false accusation stood comfortably on its own, converging with anti-Muslim stereotypes. Elkasrawy had virtually no defenders within the Arab or Muslim communities. Masjid Toronto issued a public statement distancing the mosque from Elkasrawy. Members of the congregation and mosque administration all expressed sympathy and support to him, privately. When the mosque's internal investigation was complete, Elkasrawy was brought back to work at the mosque, facing no sanction or discipline.

After the *Toronto Star* article was published, TMU not only refused to reconsider its decision, but it would also not even acknowledge that new facts had entered the public realm. This bolstered the concern that the university was hiding from the truth. It also illustrated how a facially plausible concern about Islamophobia was not treated with the same seriousness as the initial concern expressed about anti-Semitism. In fact, it became clear that President Lachemi himself was actively seeking to suppress the Islamophobia allegation. Internal communications revealed that the president decided on a public relations strategy of total non-cooperation with the media. Not one university official agreed to be interviewed for the *Star* story. At the time of writing, more than five years after the incident, the university continues to refuse to retract President Lachemi's public statement describing Elkasrawy's prayer as anti-Semitic.

It is hard to conclude, based on TMU's handling of the Elkasrawy affair, that the university equally prioritizes combating Islamophobia and combating anti-Semitism. Given that it doubled down on an anti-Semitism smear at precisely the time that it was confronted with a compelling allegation of Islamophobia, it appears public relations more than principle are driving the university's equity, diversity, and inclusion (EDI) agenda. Pro-Israel organizations weaponize feelings of hurt experienced by some members of the Canadian Jewish community when informed about alleged anti-Jewish speech or action. Meanwhile, groups like Independent Jewish Voices (IJV) seek to correct misinformation and offer a Canadian Jewish perspective on the Israeli-Palestinian conflict that aligns with fundamental human rights and universal values. However, such mitigation efforts cannot undo the harm perpetrated by groups like B'nai Brith, which are particularly deft at deploying misinformation to mobilize mostly unsuspecting members of their community to participate in Islamophobic smears. The pressure that B'nai Brith applied in private communications to TMU's president was coupled with a public letter-writing campaign that proved effective at achieving Elkasrawy's dismissal.

The pursuit of truth is central to the university's mission and requires ongoing effort. Contested facts can only be resolved through thorough investigation. When a post-secondary institution succumbs to outside pressure to cancel someone, it may achieve some short-term benefit, but in the long run it does damage to the institution itself. University leaders who wish to be seen as committed to EDI must be willing to confront the tough issues if EDI commitments are to mean anything. At minimum, post-secondary leaders should be committed to the pursuit of truth regardless of the consequences. Deference to the most aggressive and well-resourced voices in the community is almost certain to produce unjustifiably unequal outcomes and to obstruct efforts to mitigate the impact of Islamophobia.

Conclusion

Public controversy about the Israeli-Palestinian conflict abounds. Cases rarely benefit from the kind of thorough investigation that the *Toronto Star* carried out in the Masjid Toronto case. The case study illustrates how Palestine serves as a trope for systemic Islamophobia. It also highlights the uncomfortable tension that arises from political

Photo: Masjid Toronto, Toronto, Canada, 17 February 2017
Source: Faisal Bhabha

commitments to combating anti-Semitism when overbroad definitions of that term tend to reinforce and reproduce Islamophobia. While the Palestinian struggle is fundamentally political, it has distinct religious dimensions. This not only has to do with the fact that the holy city of Jerusalem lies at the centre of the conflict. It is also at least partly due to the fact that the dominant political ideology, Zionism, which operates as an obstacle to Palestinians' liberation, is itself deeply entwined with conceptions of Jewish identity and religion. Attempts to confront Zionism or the facts of Israeli apartheid are bound to trigger objections rooted in individuals' hurt feelings about associating Jewish politics with oppression. For those who believe Israel is the only bulwark against another Holocaust, it can be very difficult to hear Israel portrayed not as a protector of the Jews but as the violator of another people's rights.

It is now well understood that gaslighting is a technique used to cause a person to question their own reality, especially when that reality involves an experience of harm. It tells victims of abuse that they are wrong to feel aggrieved. The Palestinian experience is systematically gaslit as efforts to confront injustice and oppression are cast as expressions of hostility, intolerance, and even terrorism. Expressing the sentiments "free Palestine," "from the river the sea, Palestine will be free," or "viva Intifada" are portrayed as calling for the killing of Jews. Palestinian art and music, religious expression, cultural heritage, and more face the persistent risk of being presumptively classified as anti-Semitic due to overbroad and intentionally stifling definitions of anti-Semitism. The Palestine trope exists as a distinctive dimension of Islamophobia, yet it also remains a difficult truth to confront. Some of the reasons for this are illustrated in the case study contained in this essay. It is inescapable that if we are to take the struggle for equity, diversity, and inclusion seriously, the Palestine trope can no longer be ignored or concealed.

WORKS CITED

Abu-Laban, Yasmeen, and Abigail B. Bakan. 2021. "Anti-Palestinian Racism: Analyzing the Unnamed and Suppressed Reality." Project on Middle East Political Science, POMEPS Studies 44 – Racial Formations in Africa and the Middle East: A Transregional Approach. https://pomeps.org/anti -palestinian-racism-analyzing-the-unnamed-and-suppressed-reality.

Ahmad, Fahad. 2019. *Securitization and the Muslim Community in Canada.* Broadbent Institute. 17 July 2019. https://www.broadbentinstitute.ca /atlast_atweet/securitization_and_the_muslim_community_in_canada.

Ali, Wajahat, Eli Clifton, Matthew Duss, Lee Fang, Scott Keyes, and Faiz Shakir. 2011. *Fear, Inc.: The Roots of the Islamophobia Network in America.* Center for American Progress. https://www.americanprogress.org/article /fear-inc/.

Amnesty International. 2022. *Israel's Apartheid against Palestinians.* Amnesty International. 1 February 2022. https://www.amnesty.org/en/latest /news/2022/02/israels-apartheid-against-palestinians-a-cruel-system -of-domination-and-a-crime-against-humanity/.

Bahdi, Reem. 2017. "Human Rights Tribunals May Be Failing Arab, Muslim Workers Post-9/11." Lawyer's Daily. 17 October 2017. https://www .thelawyersdaily.ca/articles/4746/human-rights-tribunals-may-be-failing -arab-muslim-workers-post-9-11.

Bahdi, Reem. 2018. "Arabs, Muslims, Human Rights, Access to Justice and Institutional Trustworthiness: Insights from Thirteen Legal Narratives." *Canadian Bar Review* 96 no. 1: 72–119. https://cbr.cba.org/index.php/cbr /article/view/4450.

Bahdi, Reem, and Azeezah Kanji. 2018. "What Is Islamophobia?" *University of New Brunswick Law Journal* 69: 322–60. https://journals.lib.unb.ca/index .php/unblj/article/view/29035.

Bhabha, Faisal. 2018. "The Spies Who Hate Us: Official Misdeeds and Sowing Distrust in Canadian National Security." *University of New Brunswick Law Journal* 69: 160–97. https://www.academia.edu/en/37650836/The_Spies _Who_Hate_Us_Official_Misdeeds_and_Sowing_Distrust_in_Canadian _National_Security.

B'Tselem. 2021. "A Regime of Jewish Supremacy from the Jordan River to the Mediterranean Sea: This is Apartheid." 12 January 2021. https://www .btselem.org/publications/fulltext/202101_this_is_apartheid.

Centre for Israel and Jewish Affairs. 2018. "CIJA Testimony to the House of Commons Standing Committee on Canadian Heritage with Regard to M-103: 'Islamophobia,' Racism and Religious Discrimination." CIJA. 18 October 2018. Page no longer available.

Elkasrawy, Ayman. 2017. "I Never Prayed for the Killing of Jews: Elkasrawy." *Toronto Star*, 30 October 2017. https://www.thestar.com/opinion /commentary/2017/10/30/i-never-prayed-for-the-killing-of-jews -elkasrawy.html.

Environics Institute. 2016. *Survey of Muslims in Canada 2016: Final Report*. April 2016. https://www.environicsinstitute.org/docs/default-source /project-documents/survey-of-muslims-in-canada-2016/final-report .pdf?sfvrsn=fbb85533_2.

Fishman, Aidan. n.d. "Teaching Assistant Who Led Antisemitic Prayer Fired by Ryerson University." B'nai Brith Canada. https://www.bnaibrith .ca/teaching_assistant_who_led_antisemitic_prayer_fired_by_ryerson _university/.

Gaudet, Maxime. 2018. "Police-Reported Hate Crime in Canada, 2016." Statistics Canada. 25 April 2018. https://www150.statcan.gc.ca/n1 /pub/85-002-x/2018001/article/54915-eng.htm.

Gordon, Andrea. 2016. "From an Algerian Earthquake to Head of Ryerson." *Toronto Star*, 23 October 2016. https://www.thestar.com/news/insight /2016/10/23/from-an-algerian-earthquake-to-head-of-ryerson.html.

Grenier, Eric. 2016. "Liberals Won Over Muslims by Huge Margin in 2015, Poll Suggests." CBC News. 29 April 2016. https://www.cbc.ca/news/politics /grenier-environics-muslims-politics-1.3555216.

Hachimi, Atiqa. 2018. "The War on Translation: Arabic and the Production of Islamophobia." Snider Speaker's Series. 1 May 2018. University of Toronto Scarborough.

Harris, Kathleen. 2017a. "Liberal MP's Anti-Islamophobia Motion Set for Debate on Wednesday." CBC News. 9 February 2017. https://www.cbc.ca /news/politics/m103-islamophobia-khalid-motion-1.3972194.

–. 2017b. "Conservatives Wrestle over Liberal MP's Anti-Islamophobia Motion." CBC News. 14 February 2017. https://www.cbc.ca/news/politics /islamophobia-m103-khalid-motion-1.3982013.

Hudes, Sammy. 2017. "Ryerson Fires Teaching Assistant Accused of Making Anti-Semitic Comments." *Toronto Star*, 1 March 2017. https://www.thestar .com/news/gta/2017/03/01/ryerson-fires-teaching-assistant-over-alleged -anti-semitic-comments.html.

Human Rights Watch. 2021. *A Threshold Crossed: Israeli Authorities and the Crimes of Apartheid and Per*secution. Human Rights Watch. 27 April 2021. https://www.hrw.org/report/2021/04/27/threshold-crossed/israeli -authorities-and-crimes-apartheid-and-persecution#.

Kalvapalle, Rahul. 2017. "Anti-Islamophobia Motion Provokes Protests, Counter-Protests across Canada." Global News. 4 March 2017. https:// globalnews.ca/news/3288205/anti-islamophobia-motion-protests-m103/.

Kay, Barbara. 2017. "Actually, One Needn't Be a Hysterical Bigot to Have Concerns with M-103." *National Post*, 21 February 2017. https:// nationalpost.com/opinion/barbara-kay-actually-one-neednt-be-a-hysterical -bigot-to-have-concerns-with-m-103.

Leber, Ben. 2017. "Police-Reported Hate Crime in Canada, 2015." Statistics Canada. 14 June 2017. https://www150.statcan.gc.ca/n1/pub/85-002-x /2017001/article/14832-eng.htm.

Lenard, Patti Tamara, and Baljit Nagra. 2016. "Public Safety Report: Muslim Community Concerns and Experiences Regarding Counter-Terrorism Legislation in Canada." In *Securitizing Minority/Muslim Canadians: Evaluating the Impact of Counter-Terrorism, National Security and Immigration Policies since 9/11*, edited by Kanishka Research Team. Ottawa: University of Ottawa.

Levitz, Stephanie. 2017. "Iqra Khalid Urges Fellow MPs to Take Unified Approach in Islamophobia Study." CTV News. 18 September 2017. https:// www.ctvnews.ca/politics/iqra-khalid-urges-fellow-mps-to-take-unified -approach-in-islamophobia-study-1.3593916?cache=ncyvrizdfixvnk.

Mahrouse, Gada. 2018. "Minimizing and Denying Racial Violence: Insights from the Québec Mosque Shooting." *Canadian Journal of Women & the Law* 30, no. 3: 471–93. https://doi.org/10.3138/cjwl.30.3.006.

Miller, Adam. 2017. "'Anti-Islamic' Protesters Demonstrate outside Toronto Mosque Calling for Ban on Islam." Global News. 17 February 2017. https:// globalnews.ca/news/3257296/anti-islamic-protesters-demonstrate-outside -toronto-mosque-calling-for-ban-on-islam/.

Moore, Elizabeth. 2018. "Alexandre Bissonnette's Loved Ones Missed the Signs. We Can't Make That Mistake Again." *Maclean's*, 20 April 2018. https://www.macleans.ca/opinion/alexandre-bissonnettes-loved-ones -missed-the-signs-we-cant-make-that-mistake-again/.

Nasser, Shanifa. 2017a. "Police Investigate Anti-Muslim Rally outside Toronto Mosque and Allege Hate Speech Inside." CBC News. 22 February 2017.

https://www.cbc.ca/news/canada/toronto/police-investigate-anti-muslim-rally-outside-toronto-mosque-and-alleged-hate-speech-inside-1.3995132.

–. 2017b. "Ryerson University Fires TA over Alleged Anti-Semitic Statements at Toronto Mosque." CBC News. 1March 2017. https://www.cbc.ca/news/canada/toronto/ryerson-university-fires-ta-over-alleged-anti-semitic-statements-at-toronto-mosque-1.4004937.

Nestel, Sheryl. 2021. *The Use and Misuse of Antisemitism Statistics in Canada.* Independent Jewish Voices-Canada. 1 April 2021. https://www.ijvcanada.org/wp-content/uploads/2021/04/Sheryl-Nestel_Use-and-Misuse-of-Antisemitism-Statistics.pdf.

News Agencies. 2016. "Palestinians Injured in Clashes at Jerusalem's al-Aqsa" Al Jazeera English. 26 June 2016. https://www.aljazeera.com/news/2016/6/26/palestinians-injured-in-clashes-at-jerusalems-al-aqsa.

Oved, Marco Chown, Alex Boutilier, Jane Lytvynenko, and Craig Silverman. 2019. "You Can't Be Sure What You're Clicking on When Visiting This Facebook Page." *Toronto Star*, 12 April 2019. https://www.thestar.com/news/canada/2019/04/12/you-cant-be-sure-what-youre-clicking-on-when-visiting-this-facebook-page.html.

Parliament of Canada. 2016. M-103: Systemic Racism and Religious Discrimination. 42nd Parliament, 1st Session. Ottawa: House of Commons. https://www.ourcommons.ca/members/en/88849/motions/8661986.

Perreaux, Les. 2018. "Quebec Mosque Shooter Told Police He Was Motivated by Canada's Immigration Policies." *Globe and Mail*, 13 April 2018. https://www.theglobeandmail.com/canada/article-mosque-shooter-told-police-he-was-motivated-by-canadas-immigration/.

Sachs, Jeffrey. 2019. "Canada's New Definition of Anti-Semitism Is a Threat to Campus Free Speech." University Affairs. 10 September 2019. https://www.universityaffairs.ca/opinion/in-my-opinion/canadas-new-definition-of-anti-semitism-is-a-threat-to-campus-free-speech/.

Shalabi, Malak. 2022. "22 Years of Unbreakable Palestinian Resistance in Ramadan." Muslim Matters. 19 April 2022. https://muslimmatters.org/2022/04/19/palestine-attacks-in-ramadan/?s=04&fbclid=IwAR0RUWcF7SBLqYduIanSuhhnMNCXXXjD9RXSvIhqOelEyESxfpvHpuE_FAU.

Spencer, Robert. 2017. "Toronto: Imam Prays for the Killing of the Jews, Toronto Star Explains He Didn't Really Mean It." Jihad Watch. 23 October 2017. https://robertspencer.org/2017/10/toronto-imam-prays-for-the-killing-of-the-jews-toronto-star-explains-he-didnt-really-mean-it.

Standing Committee on Canadian Heritage. 2017. *Centre for Israel and Jewish Affairs Testimony to the House of Commons Standing Committee on Canadian Heritage with Regard to M-103: 'Islamophobia,' Racism and Religious Discrimination.* Meeting 78, 1st Session, 42nd Parliament. 18 October 2017.

https://www.ourcommons.ca/DocumentViewer/en/42-1/CHPC/meeting
-78/evidence.

Tymoczko, Maria, and Edwin Gentzler, eds. 2002. *Translation and Power*.
Amherst: University of Massachusetts Press.

Warmington, Joe. 2017a. "Imam Accused of Spewing Hate at a Toronto
Mosque...Again." *Toronto Sun*, 5 November 2017. https://torontosun.com
/news/local-news/warmington-imam-accused-of-spewing-hate-at-a
-toronto-mosque-again.

–. 2017b. "Police Probe Imams' Sermons." *Toronto Sun*, 22 February 2017.
https://torontosun.com/2017/02/22/police-probe-imans-sermons.

–. 2017c. "Jewish Defence League Alleges Hate Crime." *Toronto Sun*, 20
February 2017. https://torontosun.com/2017/02/20/jewish-defence
-league-alleges-hate-crime.

Yang, Jennifer. 2017. "A Toronto Imam Was Accused of Hate-Preaching against
Jews. But That Wasn't the Whole Story." *Toronto Star*, 22 October 2017.
https://www.thestar.com/news/gta/2017/10/22/a-toronto-imam-was
-accused-of-hate-preaching-against-jews-but-that-wasnt-the-whole-story
.html.

Yesh Din. 2020. "The Occupation of the West Bank and the Crime of
Apartheid." 9 July 2020. https://www.yesh-din.org/en/the-occupation
-of-the-west-bank-and-the-crime-of-apartheid-legal-opinion.

Zine, Jasmin. 2022. *The Canadian Islamophobia Industry: Unmasking the Networks
of Bigotry and Hate*. Islamophobia Research and Documentation Project
(IRDP), University of California at Berkeley (forthcoming).

6 Contesting Islamophobia, Reimagining Muslims: Shifting Representations and Narratives of Muslims in News Media

ZEINAB FAROKHI AND YASMIN JIWANI

Introduction: Templates of Terror

In a practice that precedes even the 9/11 attacks, Western media outlets have consistently perpetuated unbalanced, prejudicial, and unfair reporting on Muslims, which has largely contributed to the legitimization of Islamophobia. Scholars have demonstrated how Western media has played an important role in depicting Muslims as a largely homogeneous "terrorist" group, helpless and abject women and refugees, and as backward, tribalistic, and animalistic Others (Alghamdi 2015; Khan and Eid 2011; Bin Haji Ishak and Solihin 2012; Perigoe and Eid 2014). As Yasmin Jiwani (2017, 202) has argued, a "terror template" underpins the media coverage of Muslims. Anchored in Orientalism, this template operates as a shorthand discursive device in framing Muslims, predicated on interpretative schemas in which Muslims are framed as inferior and barbaric (Karim and Eid 2012), prone to violence, untrustworthy (Bahdi 2019; Bahdi 2003), ultra-patriarchal (Sensoy and DiAngelo 2006), and above all, "lethal" (Bhattacharyya 2008; Dossa 2009).

In this chapter we identify several trends and problems with the ways in which Muslims have been depicted in Western media and provide alternatives that can contribute to better and more constructive coverage on Muslim communities. We identify three major problematic depictions or tropes concerning Muslims in mainstream media: (1) Muslims as terrorists, (2) Muslim refugees as terrorists, and (3) Muslim

We acknowledge the financial support of the Government of Canada. We would also like to acknowledge Marie Bernard-Brind'Amour and David Anderson for their careful reading and feedback on this chapter.

women as oppressed and passive victims. Our focus is on North American and European media because of their global significance and ideological weight. We do not offer here an exhaustive analysis of these representations but rather aim to generate reflection on how to improve the diversity and quality of reporting on Muslim communities.

Racist Fears of Racialized Terror

The predominant template that organizes other related discursive frames of Muslims hinges on their depictions as terrorists. The link of Muslims with terrorism was already formed in the collective imagination prior to 9/11, but it was solidified as a result of those attacks. Central to the discourse on terrorism is the *racialization of terrorists*, a phenomenon that emerged in the 1970s and is inextricably linked to the political and socio-economic conditions of US empire building (Kumar 2020). In racializing Muslims, the media often focuses on their cultural attributes, which are then understood as characteristics of Islam.

Two coexisting narratives – "all terrorists are Muslims" and "no white Christian people are terrorists" – have been widely circulated in public discourse (Corbin 2017, 455). Such discourses not only jeopardize the safety and security of Muslims (or anyone who might be perceived as Muslim), but also result in overlooking the danger posed by radical white Christians. An instructive example is the US media coverage of the 2017 massacre at Grand Mosque in Quebec City, where Alexandre Bissonnette, a twenty-seven-year-old white male, shot six men and left nineteen injured. In the immediate aftermath of the killings, Fox News tweeted that the attacker was a Moroccan man: "Suspect in Quebec Mosque terrorist attack was of Moroccan origin" (Selk 2017). In fact, the killer was a young White French Canadian; the Moroccan-born man was one of the witnesses who had called the police to find help. After his identity was confirmed, Bissonnette was framed around usual narratives of a "lone wolf" attacker suffering from mental illness. While political leaders, federal and provincial, called it an act of terror, Bissonnette was not convicted of terrorism (Roach 2018; Jiwani and Al-Rawi 2020).

This was not the first time that white Christian perpetrators were framed as lone and anomalous exceptions. For example, Nathaniel Veltman, a young Christian white man, attacked a Muslim family, killing four and injuring a nine-year-old boy in London, Ontario in 2021. After the heinous act of violence against the Muslim family, the only picture of Nathaniel Veltman that was released by the media was one that showed him running a marathon instead of his mugshot. Veltman was portrayed as "an introverted man" (Juha et al. 2021) and "very quiet and very sad and he didn't talk much" in the London Free Press. This coverage demonstrates how white privilege, that is to say, "an invisible package of unearned assets" that can be cashed in anytime, serves to reinforce the image of white people as "never terrorists." (Corbin 2017, 455). This stands in contrast to how Muslims are portrayed.

Terrorist attacks perpetrated by Muslims are sensationalized and receive a disproportionate amount of news coverage, while those perpetrated by white Christians receive little to no media attention (Alsultany 2012; Gottschalk and Greenberg 2008; Park, Felix, and Lee 2007; Yurkadul and Korteweg 2021). Kearns, Betus, and Lemieux's analysis (2019) of news media coverage of terrorism shows that attacks by Muslim perpetrators received, on average, 357 per cent more coverage than other attacks. Dixon and Williams' analysis (2015) of 146 cable and network news programs broadcast between 2008 and 2012 also reveals that Muslims were greatly overrepresented as terrorists. Similarly, West and Lloyd (2017) found that any violent acts committed by Muslims were more likely to be labelled as terroristic and were also judged more negatively. The media's selective coverage of acts of terror based on the religion of perpetrators plays an important role in exceptionalizing certain attacks while generalizing and demonizing Others. In other words, the media amplifies incidents involving Muslims and influences anti-Muslim, Islamophobic opinions of audiences, which in turn shape how the public views certain individuals and particular communities (i.e., Muslim attacker = Terrorist = Bad; White attacker = Sick = Pitiful). These trends are alarming in the age of digital media in which people not only develop strong opinions and take public stands on rapid streams of news content, but also share, like, and discuss such content constantly.

The implication of the terror templates that underpins such coverage is that it often leads to media reproducing and legitimating inaccurate news content (King, Scheer, and White 2017). For example, in the wake of the Muslim ban[1] issued by the Trump administration, the hashtags #Muslimban and #BanMuslim were deployed by supporters of the ban on social media. The most prominent discourse within these

---

1 A week after his swearing in, Trump issued Executive Order 13769, titled "Protecting the Nation from Foreign Terrorist Entry into the United States." The original ban barred nationals from Iran, Iraq, Libya, Somalia, Sudan, Syria, and Yemen, where the majority of the population is Muslim, from entering the US. The ban also reduced the number of admitted refugees and suspended the entry of Syrian refugees indefinitely. The Muslim ban was revoked by President Joe Biden in January 2021.

posts positions Muslims as terrorists, as violent, and as deviant Others (among a variety of undesirable stereotypes). For most of the users engaged in the dissemination of these hashtags, the Muslim ban was understood as entirely justified. Islam was for these users a religion of violence, which led to the conclusion that all Muslims are violent, and therefore no Muslim should be allowed to enter the US (Farokhi 2021).

False narratives about Muslims propagated by mainstream media outlets inevitably lead to the wider population advancing the same false storylines. Reporting inaccurate news also heightens readers' acceptance of these unfounded truths as absolute truths because of their continued repetition. This is especially the case on social media platforms and in online news where commentators can repetitively post these inaccuracies and toxic comments. Surrounded by the repetition of flattening, sensational, and fearmongering lies, even the most neutral or critical reader becomes hard pressed not to be swayed by the sheer volume of such false narratives.

Terrorizing Refugees, Refugees as Terrorists

Another common figure in the anti-Muslim news media landscape ecology is the *refugee as terrorist*. This template attributes refugees with underlying motives – namely, to infiltrate the countries that have accepted them in order to carry out terrorist attacks. While not a single refugee has been responsible for any terrorist attack in the United States (Newland 2015), refugees are inordinately framed as potential terrorist threats in the media, and during public, political, and policy debates (Berry, Garcia-Blanco, and Moore 2015).[2] For example, the terror attacks that occurred in Paris on 13 November 2015 were immediately linked to Syrian refugees in the French nationalist imaginary. Although the attacks were perpetuated by European citizens, the blame was placed on the lack of border security and the perceived "flood" of migrants (Nail 2016). The Munich mass shooting on 22 July 2016 is another example in which the media held refugees accountable. Even though the perpetrator was a German-born citizen inclined towards right-wing extremism, a Bild headline posed this rather sensational and rhetorically

---

2   It is worth noting that in the context of the United States, out of the 784,000 refugees admitted to the United States since 2001, only three refugees have been accused of plotting terrorist activities, two of whom were planning terrorist activities in Iraq rather than the US. Even more notably, the third person accused of planning terrorism was described as "barely credible" (Newland 2015).

anti-refugee question: "After Bloody Week in Germany, How Are Refugees Monitored?" (Ethical Journalism Network 2019). Such headlines reinforce the idea that all refugees, many of them Muslim, are potential terrorists who pose a threat to the nation that admitted them (Ethical Journalism Network 2019). These types of narratives result in hostile immigration policies among EU member states. For example, the Hungarian prime minister announced plans to build a fortified fence along the Serbian border to keep out migrants (CTV News 2015). Similarly, Denmark suspended all rail links with Germany, claiming migrants were refusing to leave their trains because they did not want to be registered in Denmark (BBC News 2015).

Since the collapse of the Afghan government and the Taliban takeover of the country in August 2021, there has also been an increased public conversation about Afghan refugees as a potential threat to the West. These narratives intensify the debate over domestic security and whether or not to accept refugees. Afghan refugees have come to be seen not only as a threat simply because they are Muslim but also because they are racialized and thus perceived as more likely to become Democratic voters (Weigel 2021). For instance, Fox News anchor Tucker Carlson warned against allowing "thousands of potentially unvetted refugees" onto American soil, calling it an "invasion" (Gopal and Ojeda 2021). Similarly in Canada, the false connection between refugees and terrorists has become intertwined in public discourse. For example, the editor of the right-wing Rebel News, Ezra Levant, stated:

> I'm open to examining Afghans who helped the West, after they're vetted to make sure they are indeed not terrorists themselves, not double agents, not just opportunists. I'm open to Canada accepting some genuine refugees [fleeing] from the Taliban. (Rebel News 2021)

Using terms like "terrorist," "double agent," and "opportunists" creates *sensational probes* – condensed, affectively charged references to pre-existing social narratives. More specifically, placing the words "terrorist," "double agent," and "opportunists" alongside "Afghan" refugees in the above statement not only equates Muslimness with terrorism but also serves to fuel anti-Muslim sentiments which empower far-right actors to depict Muslims as unwanted, dangerous Others (Abbas 2004). Such sensational probes enabled Fox News and Rebel News to swiftly define Afghan refugees as terrorist threats in public discourse. These sorts of affective narratives of Muslim Others present Canada, the US, and other Western nations "as the injured party; the one that is 'hurt' or damaged by the 'invasion' of others" (Ahmed 2014, 49). Consequently, these discourses pathologize and demonize Muslims by presenting them as a "problem" that needs to be "dealt with" – often through violence. The disproportionate and biased media coverage of Afghan refugees showcases the ways in which terrorism and the figure of refugees are linked together. These narratives, mediated through images, text, and the use of negatively charged words, help narrowly define who terrorists are, promoting in the process an Orientalist conception of the Other that instils pervasive and unfounded public fear about Muslims. While some Western media have pinpointed the ways in which terrorists reference Islam to justify their violence, biased media reporting on the linking of terrorism with Muslim communities has overwhelmingly resulted in increased demonization of the Muslim Other.

"Saving" Muslim Women from Muslim Men: Oppressive Media Depictions of "Oppressed" Muslim Women

Post 9/11, the objectification, demonization, and re-appropriation of Muslim women in the West has reached the level of "hypervisibility" in Western media discourses. Archetypal representations of oppressed burqa-clad women were circulated widely in the news media in the years immediately following 9/11. Such representations not only fix Muslim women's status as oppressed Others who lack agency, but also serve to demonize the burqa as an inherent source of oppression (Cloud 2004; Macdonald 2006; Scott 2007; Zine 2009). The rhetorical construction of Muslim women as unable to liberate themselves from the oppression of Islam has been used to falsely legitimize violent military interventions by the US in Afghanistan and Iraq (Ayotte and Husain 2005). In this way, the body of the Muslim woman as a gendered being has been mobilized for political gain (Jiwani 2010). While the motif of "rescuing" Muslim women from "dangerous" Muslim men was previously mobilized to justify the invasion of other countries, it is now regularly employed to justify the exclusion and elimination of the "enemy" inside Western nations (Ayotte and Husain 2005; Gidaris 2018).

The figuration of the body of the Muslim woman continues to be exploited to meet current political ends. During Trump's presidency, although US troops were initially slated to be removed from Afghanistan, additional troops were dispatched. One of the main reasons given for Trump's decision to stay in Afghanistan was a black-and-white snapshot of an unveiled Afghan woman presented to him by his national security adviser, H.R. McMaster (Rucker and Costa 2017). The photo – from 1972 – depicts three cheerful, unveiled Afghan women in miniskirts walking in Kabul. Trump and his advisers propagandized this imagery to invoke a sense of optimism that Western norms had existed earlier and hence could be restored in Afghanistan. Critically, this line of rhetoric argued that Afghanistan was not a "hopeless place" so long as the US military was on the ground, "protecting" Afghan women and bringing them back to the "modernity" they previously enjoyed before the repressive Taliban came to power. In other words, the photo provided the necessary justification and rationalization that only US troops stationed in Afghanistan could "liberate" Afghan women as they were prior to the Taliban coming to power. This photo of joyous, Westernized Afghan women has been widely circulated on far-right social media platforms to illustrate that Islam has oppressed women and that only Trump can "save" Muslim women from their barbaric culture (Warren 2017). It is pertinent to mention that despite the invasion of Afghanistan being justified and legitimized under the pretext of "saving" Afghan women, in the "post-war" period the plight of Afghan women has deeply worsened. The invasion of Afghanistan provided fertile ground for the production of hyper-militarized masculinities that resulted in the manifestation of profound violence in the domestic sphere. In the post-war setting, due to successive armed conflicts, not only has violence against women increased, but Afghan women now also face new forms of violence (e.g., forced prostitution) that were not widely prevalent before the invasion – putting them at even higher and increased forms of risk and bodily peril (Ahmad and Anctil Avoine 2018).

Shifting Templates: Improving the Coverage of Muslims and Islam

Stereotypical and biased coverage in the news has led to increased discussion concerning how journalists should cover terrorist attacks in both the United States and Europe (e.g., Beckett 2021; Marthoz 2017). Scholars have offered important recommendations for such coverage (Beckett 2021) and have suggested measures that, should they be taken up by the media, would reduce false representations of terrorist acts that far-right media and actors often use to advance their political agendas (Frey and Luechinger 2008; Rohner and Frey 2007). Although some Western media have put effort into providing more fair and objective depictions of Muslim communities, "the dominant portrayals tend to be negative" (Eid 2014, 99).

In the Appendix to this chapter we have outlined recommendations for change. Here, we summarize the most critical points of intervention required in order to fundamentally shift and improve the current false, negative, and misleading coverage of Muslims and Islam. Some of the most immediate changes that can be implemented include but are not limited to the following: (1) *avoiding the use of negative and otherwise loaded discourse and dehumanizing language* such as "terrorist," "double agent," and "opportunists," among others (as can be noticed in the Rebel News coverage) in conjunction with the words "Islam," "Muslim," and "refugees." The deployment of such affectively and negatively loaded phrases embedded in prevalent narratives not only risks normalizing and desensitizing people to harmful views (Farokhi 2021), but also lends undue credence to false narratives about Muslim communities in general and refugees in particular. (2) *News organizations need to increase diversity within their newsrooms.* This is imperative not only to address the wider issues of equity and inclusion, but also to ensure that Muslim perspectives are present in the organizations generating media narratives. In line with this, journalists should reach out to diverse Muslim communities and seek out the views of those who are actively working to combat Islamophobia and violent extremism. (3) *Journalists and editors should avoid reproducing negative stereotypes and other oppressive and other dehumanizing expressions when referring to the ethnicity or religious orientation of refugees that perpetuate sexist and racist discourses about them.* Instead of framing refugees as "Others" whose values are in contrast with "our" traditions and culture, journalists and editors should portray a sympathetic image of the displaced (Trilling 2019). In addition, when covering news of refugees, journalists and editors should ensure that their information and resources are accurate and that their journalism contextualizes contemporary accounts within wider, systemic perspectives. Not only should they critically analyse statements provided to them by authoritative voices and elite spokespeople, but media organizations should also hold such authorities accountable while challenging the intolerance of any political rhetoric (Jiwani 2017).

As well, the victimization and oversimplification of refugee narratives should be avoided in media coverage. Refugees are mainly perceived as either victims or perpetrators in current public discourse and across social media ecologies. Journalists and editors, however, can challenge such portrayals by sharing diverse stories of displacement and by foregrounding the perspectives of refugees themselves (International Organization for Migration 2019). Media organizations should privilege specific, contextualized, and diverse information about refugees while flattening false and contested conversations about them (Georgiou and Zaborowski 2017). Finally, journalists and editors should be trained more thoroughly in journalism ethics and should also actively educate the public through their coverage in order to contribute to a deeper and more compassionate understanding of refugees and displacement (International Organization for Migration 2019).

News media sites should also install more vigorous processes of control and moderation if they are to continue encouraging public commentary; if that cannot be done, there should be the creation of an association that monitors online hate and works to curb both its explicit and implicit expression. Similarly, in the case of digital platforms, news media sites should identify false, bigoted, and manipulative sources' statements by providing historical and ideological contexts, and editors and journalists should intervene to dislodge falsehoods about Muslim communities. In addition to being cautious about not reproducing stories that originate from social media platforms that may cause harm, journalists and editors should also explicitly and strenuously object to amplifying racist and sexist rhetoric. Given that every individual who has access to social media can potentially contribute to producing negative stereotypes, increased education in digital media literacy strategies is sorely needed in order to better recognize and resist networked manipulation campaigns. Equally important, social media companies should bear the responsibility for how the design and politics of their platforms have become dangerous tools in the hands of extremist, right-wing, and other hate-filled radicals who seek to sow confusion, disseminate fake news, and manufacture false and all-too-often violent "truths" against Muslim communities. By the same token, governments must also intervene and define the responsibilities of social media companies and pass laws governing fake news, hate speech, and conspiracy theories among other problematic trends. Until these essential alterations in mainstream news media and related social media ecologies transpire, Islamophobia will continue to increase in intensity and in violent rhetoric and will continue to proliferate throughout media landscapes, producing injurious impacts online and offline.

Conclusion

Evidence presented in this chapter clearly demonstrates that mainstream Western media outlets are implicated in negatively representing Muslims and Islam. But this does not mean that media and journalists should cease coverage of breaking news stories pertaining to terrorism and refugees and/or stop reporting on important events of obvious value about Muslim communities. Rather, media outlets should resist employing sensational probes and other lurid and graphic depictions about Muslim communities. Equally important, journalists must offer properly contextualized coverage of Muslim communities and their positive contributions to the West, including their efforts to combat extremism in its various guises. More critically, journalists and reporters must become better aware that the values or interpretations of Islam held by extremists do not reflect those of the whole community (Stone 2017). In the context of reporting on Muslims, journalists must take extra care not to feed narratives that produce and reinforce ideologies and a rhetoric of "us vs. them." Not only should the media commit to the creation of narratives concerning Muslims in ways that are accurate, intelligible, and socially responsible, but they should also take responsibility to produce journalism that exposes fake news and extremist propaganda about Muslims while also working to enhance meaningful and respectful communication between Muslim and non-Muslim communities. Fundamentally, journalists should recognize how the currently unbalanced coverage of Muslims in the news contributes to and amplifies the rhetoric of various dangerous key players (i.e., far-right politicians and news outlets) who seek to exploit such narratives in order to perpetuate the idea that the West and Islam are inherently incompatible and are at the brink of a "necessary" or otherwise justifiable war.

In the age of digital media, anti-Muslim sentiment has seeped widely and deeply throughout social media ecologies, establishing echo chambers filled with hate which often produce offline crime and violence against Muslims. Online platforms are utilized to reshape the information landscape, leading to the emergence of new forms of power. Journalists must become fully aware of their responsibility for contributing to these power dynamics and resulting media manipulation in conventional information settings. Journalists must make better choices in covering news about Muslims because what they cover and how they cover such media stories play a crucial role in amplifying the already existing and increasingly negative and oppressive falsehoods and myths about Muslims circulating in contemporary media ecologies. To avoid framing Muslim communities in a negative light, journalists need to not only *challenge* the manipulation of news that is prevalent online, but also *identify* the hidden circumstances that result in reporting false and misleading narratives. Such misinformation increases the vulnerability of Muslim communities to vilification and stereotyping that, harnessed by extremism and hate, confusion and discord, ultimately leads to violence.

APPENDIX: RECOMMENDATIONS FOR CHANGE

Considering the persistence of the terror template and the frames that are active within it, how can the quality of reporting on Muslim communities be improved? What are the ways through which the media can construct and circulate more accurate and diverse representations of Muslim communities? Below, we present a synthesis of recommendations from previous critical work that outlines how more ethical coverage of Muslims can be achieved.[3] These guidelines are specifically tailored towards journalists, government actors, as well as social media companies.

1 Journalists should desist in the employment of all derogatory and stereotypical language and depictions of members of Muslim communities which fundamentally constitute incitement to hatred and violence against them.

2 Schools of journalism and media training institutes should introduce curricula and other active training programmes with a view to developing a sense of professional ethics which are sensitive to reporting on Muslim communities and other racialized minorities.

3 Schools of journalism and media training institutes should organize periodic publicity campaigns to (a) expose media discrimination against Muslim communities, and (b) increase public awareness of media that negatively depicts Muslim communities, that is inflammatory in nature, and that would likely incite violence.

4 News organizations and media support groups should develop more elaborate professional recommendations and guidelines for the coverage of Muslim communities that directly address issues of discrimination and intolerance regarding Muslim communities.

5 News media organizations should foster an internal culture that actively supports non-discriminatory reporting towards Muslim communities and other racialized minorities.

6 Journalists should make every effort to report factually and accurately concerning news stories related to Muslims given the deeply rooted fears and anxieties regarding Muslims that already exist within many societies, especially in the West. Journalists should ask themselves whether or not it is necessary to mention that a perpetrator is Muslim.

7 Journalists need to provide more context-based accounts when reporting on Muslims.

8 Media organizations should organize seminars and workshops for journalists on how to identify and confront stereotypes about Muslims and how to communicate with and report on diverse Muslim communities.

---

3 These recommendations were inspired by the work of Whitney Phillips, particularly her chapter "Tips for Reporting on Specific Manipulators, Bigots, and Abusers" in her 2018 book *The Oxygen of Amplification: Better Practices for Reporting on Extremists, Antagonists, and Manipulators.*

9 News organizations must employ people from Muslim backgrounds. This would improve factual reporting, ethical coverage,
professionalism, and performance, and increase the diversity of
perspectives.

10 Journalists should carefully assess the newsworthiness of information about Muslim communities and avoid breaking negative
stories about Muslims without careful contextualization, a commitment to factuality, and an awareness and feeling of responsibility to the possible production of stereotypes (and resulting
violence) due to their reporting.

11 Journalists should be transparent about the origins of their information and its broader context, carefully contextualizing it and
responding impartially and objectively to it (Phillips 2018), especially when quoting extremist viewpoints. Journalists should make
every effort to identify fake news, false narratives, and disinformation about Muslims and absolutely avoid quoting and legitimizing
such false rhetoric.

12 When reporting on accounts concerning Muslims or their communities that might be negative in nature, journalists should first
wait to ensure that their information of the story is accurate and
well contextualized. Journalists should ensure that audiences are
fully aware of who is actually responsible for violent attacks and
actively discourage suspicion, speculation, and sensationalism.

13 Following a violent tragedy, journalists should minimize publicizing information regarding the ethnic backgrounds that are
involved in such actions (Phillips 2018). For instance, reporting
on a femicide committed by a Muslim without factual, detailed,
and meaningful context does not enhance the importance of a
story about violence against women, but instead simply contributes, in the hyper-virulent context of Islamophobia, to the idea
that *all* Muslims actively participate in gender-based violence as a
community.

14 When broadcasting breaking stories about violence carried out by
Muslim individuals or communities, journalists should foreground
and directly quote the opinions and perspectives of Muslim community members, intellectuals, and other relevant authorities,
especially those who have been working to combat such actions in
and outside of their communities.

15 New media organizations should either curtail or responsibly
moderate open comment sections on news articles about Muslims
as these are little more than echo chambers for toxic discourse
against Muslims and their communities.

16 Journalists should avoid reproducing negative narratives and disinformation originating from (especially dubious) social media platforms that may run the risk of eliciting violence against Muslims. Opinions should be solicited from experts, authorities, and activists who work for more peaceable relations, not those who wish to foment discord and hate.

17 Journalists should be encouraged to build communication networks with, elicit stories and responses from, and report on the diverse communities that adhere to Islam. This would avoid reports that present Muslims in flattened, mono-cultural terms or that portray Muslim communities as homogeneous and thus easier to stereotype. Journalists should also, in the interest of fair coverage, produce news which highlights the celebrations, achievements, and contributions of Muslim individuals and communities.

18 Governments should develop laws and regulations that prohibit the dissemination of Islamophobic materials and the distribution of information that incites animosity against Muslim communities.

19 Governments must intervene by defining and demanding the application of social and political responsibilities of social media companies and pass strong laws with meaningful penalties governing the inability or refusal of such companies to limit, contain, and prevent the spread of disinformation, conspiracy theories, violent rhetoric, and fake news, among others.

20 Social media companies should take full responsibility for combating hate and disinformation against Muslim communities. While companies may use reactionary tactics, such as censoring Islamophobic content and using artificial intelligence to identify and detect false information, they should primarily invest in proactive tactics, such as producing alternative information about Muslim communities that not only exposes disinformation about them but also provides accurate information (Yaraghi 2019).

WORKS CITED

Abbas, Tahir. 2004. "After 9/11: British South Asian Muslims, Islamophobia, Multiculturalism, and the State." *American Journalism of Islam & Society* 21, no. 3: 26–38. https://doi.org/10.35632/ajis.v21i3.506.

Ahmad, Lida, and Priscyll Anctil Avoine. 2018. "Misogyny in 'Post-War' Afghanistan: The Changing Frames of Sexual and Gender-Based Violence." *Journal of Gender Studies* 27, no. 1: 86–101. https://doi.org/10.1080/09589236.2016.1210002.

Ahmed, Sara. 2014. *The Cultural Politics of Emotion.* 2nd ed. Edinburgh: Edinburgh University Press.

Alghamdi, Emad A. 2015. "The Representation of Islam in Western Media: The Coverage of Norway Terrorist Attacks." *International Journal of Applied Linguistics & English Literature* 4, no. 3: 198–204. https://doi.org/10.7575/aiac.ijalel.v.4n.3p.198.

Alsultany, Evelyn. 2012. *Arabs and Muslims in the Media: Race and Representation after 9/11.* New York: New York University Press.

Ayotte, Kevin K., and Mary E. Husain. 2005. "Securing Afghan Women: Neocolonialism, Epistemic Violence, and the Rhetoric of the Veil." *NWSA Journal* 17, no. 4: 112–33. http://hdl.handle.net/10211.3/194526.

Bahdi, Reem. 2003. "No Exit: Racial Profiling and Canada's War against Terrorism." *Osgoode Hall Law Journal* 41, no. 2/3: 293–316. https://ssrn.com/abstract=1716893.

–. 2019. "'All Arabs Are Liars': Arab and Muslim Stereotypes in Canadian Human Rights Law." *Journal of Law and Social Policy* 31: 92–123. https://digitalcommons.osgoode.yorku.ca/jlsp/vol31/iss1/5/.

BBC News. 2015. "Migrant Crisis: Denmark-Germany Rail Links Suspended." 9 September 2015. https://www.bbc.com/news/world-europe-34203366.

Beckett, Charlie. 2021. "Fanning the Flames: Reporting on Terror in a Networked World." *Columbia Journalism Review,* 6 November 2021. https://www.cjr.org/tow_center_reports/coverage_terrorism_social_media.php.

Berry, Mike, Inaki Garcia-Blanco, and Kerry Moore. 2015. *Press Coverage of the Refugee and Migrant Crisis in the EU: A Content Analysis of Five European Countries.* UNHCR, December 2015. https://www.unhcr.org/56bb369c9.pdf.

Bhattacharyya, Gargi. 2008. *Dangerous Brown Men: Exploiting Sex, Violence and Feminism in the War on Terror.* London: Zed Books.

Bin Haji Ishak, Mohd. Shuhaimi, and Sohirin Mohammad Solihin. 2012."Islam and Media." *Asian Social Science* 8, no. 7: 263–9. https://doi.org/10.5539/ass.v8n7p263.

Cloud, Dana L. 2004. "'To Veil the Threat of Terror': Afghan Women and the Clash of Civilizations in the Imagery of the U.S. War on Terrorism." *The Quarterly Journal of Speech* 90, no. 3: 285–306. https://doi.org/10.1080/0033563042000270726.

Corbin, Caroline M. 2017. "Terrorists Are Always Muslim but Never White: At the Intersection of Critical Race Theory and Propaganda." *Fordham Law Review* 86, no. 2: 455–85. https://ssrn.com/abstract=3020330.

CTV News. 2015. "Hungary's PM Defends Plan to Build Fences to Keep Out Migrants." 19 June 2015. https://www.ctvnews.ca/world/hungary-s-pm-defends-plan-to-build-fences-to-keep-out-migrants-1.2430697.

Dixon, Travis L., and Charlotte L. Williams. 2015. "The Changing Misrepresentation of Race and Crime on Network and Cable News." *Journal of Communication* 65, no. 1: 24–39. https://doi.org/10.1111/jcom.12133.

Dossa, Shiraz. 2009. "Lethal Muslims: White-Trashing Islam and the Arabs." *Journal of Muslim Minority Affairs* 28, no. 2: 225–36. https://doi.org/10.1080/13602000802303169.

Eid, Mahmoud. 2014. "Perceptions about Muslims in Western Societies." In *Re-Imagining the Other: Culture, Media, and Western-Muslim Intersections*, edited by Mahmoud Eid and Karim H. Karim, 99–119. New York: Palgrave Macmillan.

Ethical Journalism Network. 2019. "Muslims in the Media: Bias in the News: Reporting Terrorism." https://ethicaljournalismnetwork.org/bias-news-reporting-terrorism.

Farokhi, Zeinab. 2021. "Hindu Nationalism, News Channels, and 'Post-Truth' Twitter." *Affective Politics of Digital Media: Propaganda by Other Means*, edited by Megan Boler and Elizabeth Davis, 226–44. New York: Routledge.

–. 2021. "Cyber Homo Sacer: A Critical Analysis of Cyber Islamophobia in the Wake of the Muslim Ban." *Islamophobia Studies Journal* 6, no. 1: 14–32. https://doi.org/10.13169/islastudj.6.1.0014.

Frey, Bruno S., and Simon Luechinger. 2008. "Three Strategies to Deal with Terrorism." *Economic Papers: A Journal of Applied Economics and Policy* 27, no. 2: 107–14. https://doi.org/10.1111/j.1759-3441.2008.tb01030.x.

Georgiou, Myria, and Rafal Zaborowski. 2017. "Media Coverage of the 'Refugee Crisis': A Cross-European Perspective." Council of Europe Report, DG1(2017)03. https://rm.coe.int/1680706b00.

Gidaris, Constantine. 2018. "Victims, Terrorists, Scapegoats: Veiled Muslim Women and the Embodied Threat of Terror." *Postcolonial Text* 13, no. 1: 18. https://www.researchgate.net/publication/324017434_Victims_Terrorists_Scapegoats_Veiled_Muslim_Women_and_the_Embodied_Threat_of_Terror.

Gopal, Anand, and Ojeda, Richard. 2021. "On Afghanistan." Intercept. 21 August 2021. https://theintercept.com/2021/08/21/deconstructed-afghanistan-richard-ojeda-anand-gopal/.

Gottschalk, Peter, and Gabriel Greenberg. 2008. *Islamophobia: Making Muslims the Enemy.* Lanham, MD: Rowman & Littlefield.

International Organization for Migration. 2019. "How to Cover Migration in Media? 7 Recommendations for Journalists." 13 September 2019. https://rosanjose.iom.int/en/blogs/how-cover-migration-media-7-recommendations-journalists.

Jiwani, Yasmin. 2010. "Doubling Discourses and the Veiled Other: Mediations of Race and Gender in Canadian Media." *States of Race: Critical Race*

Feminism for the 21st Century, edited by Sunera Thobani, Sherene H. Razack, and Malinda S. Smith, 59–86. Toronto: Between the Lines Press.

–. 2017. "Racism and Sexism in Canadian News Coverage" *Introduction to Journalism*, edited by Bruce Gillespie, 198–206. Oxford: Oxford University Press.

Jiwani, Yasmin, and Ahmed Al-Rawi. 2020. "Hashtagging the Quebec Mosque Shooting: The Twitter Discourse of Mourning, Nationalism and Resistance." In *Affect, Algorithms and Propaganda: Interdisciplinary Research for the Age of Post-Truth*, edited by Megan Boler and Elizabeth Davis, 204–25. New York: Routledge.

Juha, Jonathan, Terry Bridge, Jane Sims, and Calvi Leon. 2021. "'Isolated,' 'Estranged', 'Angry': Who Is Accused Mass Killer Nathaniel Veltman?" *London Free Press*, 11 June 2021. https://lfpress.com/news/local-news/isolated-and-estranged-who-is-accused-mass-killer-nathaniel-veltman.

Karim, Karim H., and Mahmoud Eid. 2012. "Clash of Ignorance." *Global Media Journal Canadian Edition* 5, no. 1: 7–27. http://gmj-canadianedition.ca/current-issue/2012-volume-5-issue-1/v5i1pp7-27/.

Kearns, Erin M., Allison E. Betus, and Anthony F. Lemieux . 2019. "Why Do Some Terrorist Attacks Receive More Media Attention than Others?" *Justice Quarterly* 36, no. 6: 985–1022. https://doi.org/10.1080/07418825.2018.1524507.

Khan, Sarah, and Mahmoud Eid. 2011. "A New-Look for Muslim Women in the Canadian Media: CBC's Little Mosque on the Prairie." *Middle East Journal of Culture and Communication* 4, no. 2: 184–202. https://doi.org/10.1163/187398611X571355.

King, Gary, Benjamin Scheer, and Ariel White. 2017. "How the News Media Activate Public Expression and Influence National Agendas." *Science* 358, no. 6364: 776–80. https://doi.org/10.1126/science.aao1100.

Kumar, Deepa. 2020. "Terrorcraft: Empire and the Making of the Racialised Terrorist Threat." *Race & Class* 62, no. 2: 34–60. https://doi.org/10.1177/0306396820930523.

Macdonald, Myra. 2006. "Muslim Women and the Veil: Problems of Image and Voice in Media Representations." *Feminist Media Studies* 6, no. 1: 7–23. https://doi.org/10.1080/14680770500471004.

Marthoz, Jean Paul. 2017. *Terrorism and the Media: A Handbook for Journalists*. United Nations Educational, Scientific and Cultural Organization (UNESCO), Paris.

Nail, Thomas. 2016. "A Tale of Two Crises: Migration and Terrorism After the Paris Attacks." *Studies in Ethnicity and Nationalism* 16, no. 1: 158–67. https://doi.org/10.1111/sena.12168.

Newland, Kathleen. 2015. "The U.S. Record Shows Refugees Are Not a Threat." Migration Policy Institute. 7 October 2015. https://www.migrationpolicy.org/news/us-record-shows-refugees-are-not-threat.

Park, Jaihyun, Karla Felix, and Grace Lee. 2007. "Implicit Attitudes toward Arab-Muslims and the Moderating Effects of Social Information." *Basic and Applied Social Psychology* 29, no. 1: 35–45. https://doi.org/10.1080 /01973530701330942.

Perigoe, Ross, and Mahmoud Eid. 2014. *Mission Invisible: Race, Religion, and News at the Dawn of the 9/11 Era.* Vancouver: UBC Press.

Phillips, Whitney. 2018. "The Oxygen of Amplification: Better Practices for Reporting on Extremists, Antagonists, and Manipulators." Data & Society. 22 May 2018. https://datasociety.net/library/oxygen-of -amplification/.

Rebel News. 2021. "Canada Accepting 5,000 Afghan Refugees while 1,250 Canadians Stranded in Afghanistan." 1 September 2021. https://www .rebelnews.com/canada_accepting_5000_afghan_refugees_while_1250 _canadians_stranded.

Roach, Kent. 2018. "Why the Quebec Mosque Shooting Was Terrorism." *Globe and Mail*, 19 April 2018. https://www.theglobeandmail.com/opinion /article-why-the-quebec-city-mosque-shooting-was-terrorism/.

Rohner, Dominic, and Bruno S. Frey. 2007. "Blood and Ink! the Common-Interest-Game between Terrorists and the Media." *Public Choice* 133, no. 1/2: 129–45. https://doi.org/10.1007/s11127-007-9182-9.

Rucker, Philip, and Robert Costa. 2017. "'It's a Hard Problem': Inside Trump's Decision to Send More Troops to Afghanistan." *Washington Post*, 21 August 2017. https://www.washingtonpost.com/politics/its-a-hard -problem-inside-trumps-decision-to-send-more-troops-to-afghanistan /2017/08/21/14dcb126-868b-11e7-a94f-3139abce39f5_story.html.

Scott, Joan W. 2007. *The Politics of the Veil.* Princeton, NJ: Princeton University Press

Selk, Avi. 2017. "Fox News Falsely Reported that the Quebec Terrorism Suspect Was Moroccan. Then Canada Got Mad." *Washington Post*, 1 February 2017. https://www.proquest.com/docview/1863541458?pq-origsi te=primo&accountid=14771.

Sensoy, Özlem, and Robin DiAngelo. 2006. "'I Wouldn't Want to Be a Woman in the Middle East': White Female Student Teachers and the Narrative of the Oppressed Muslim Woman." *Radical Pedagogy* 8, no. 1. https:// radicalpedagogy.icaap.org/content/issue8_1/sensoy.html.

Stone, Meighan. 2017. "Snake and Stranger: Media Coverage of Muslims and Refugee Policy." Shorenstein Center on Media, Politics, and Public Policy. 22 June 2017. https://shorensteincenter.org/media-coverage-muslims -refugee-policy/.

Trilling, Daniel. 2019. "How the Media Contributed to the Migrant Crisis." *Guardian*, 1 August 2019. https://www.theguardian.com/news/2019 /aug/01/media-framed-migrant-crisis-disaster-reporting.

–. 2021. "Fear of Refugees Must Not Shape the Response to Afghanistan's Crisis." *Guardian*, 18 August 2021. https://www.theguardian.com /commentisfree/2021/aug/18/fear-refugees-afghan-crisis-taliban.

Warren, Rossalyn. 2017. "Are Old Photos of 'Westernized' Afghan Women Driving Trump's Foreign Policy?" *Guardian*, 23 August 2017. https://www .theguardian.com/commentisfree/2017/aug/23/photos-afghan-women -foreign-policy-trump-womens-rights.

Weigel, David. 2021. "The Trailer: 'An American Dream': Afghans in the U.S. Confront Post-withdrawal Politics." *Washington Post*, 19 August 2021. https://www.washingtonpost.com/politics/2021/08/19/trailer-an -american-dream-afghans-us-confront-post-withdrawal-politics/.

West, Keon, and Joda Lloyd. 2017. "The Role of Labeling and Bias in the Portrayals of Acts of 'Terrorism': Media Representations of Muslims vs. Non-Muslims." *Journal of Muslim Minority Affairs* 37, no. 2: 211–22. https:// doi.org/10.1080/13602004.2017.1345103.

Yaraghi, Niam. 2019. "How Should Social Media Platforms Combat Misinformation and Hate Speech." Brookings. 9 April 2019. https://www .brookings.edu/blog/techtank/2019/04/09/how-should-social-media -platforms-combat-misinformation-and-hate-speech/.

Yurkadul, Gökçe, and Anna C. Korteweg. 2021. "Boundary Regimes and the Gendered Racialized Production of Muslim Masculinities: Cases from Canada and Germany." *Journal of Immigrant and Refugee Studies* 19, no. 1: 39–54. https://doi.org/10.1080/15562948.2020.1833271.

Zine, Jasmin. 2009. "Unsettling the Nation: Gender, Race and Muslim Cultural Politics in Canada." *Studies in Ethnicity and Nationalism* 9, no. 1: 146–93. https://doi.org/10.1111/j.1754-9469.2009.01036.x.

Education, Memory, and Belonging

7 Islamophobia and Imperial Amnesia

SYED ADNAN HUSSAIN

Forgetting, and I would even say historical error, are an essential factor in the formation of a nation, and it is in this way that the progress of historical studies is often a danger for nationality. Historical investigation, in fact, sheds light on the acts of violence that took place at the origin of all political formations, even those whose consequences have been the most beneficial. Unity is always done brutally. – Ernest Renan (1882, 7–8)

The above translated quote is from Ernest Renan, one of the most famous and decorated French imperial intellectuals of the nineteenth century. Renan here speaks of the importance of forgetting in the construction of a nation. It is essential, Renan declares, that we do not dwell too deeply on the violence that makes a nation possible, and to that end, a national forgetting is necessary. He was speaking of the legacy of bloodshed that made French unity possible, and we also see this dynamic at play in settler colonial states. A shifting politics, however, demands a reassessment of these forgotten legacies, especially of the costs that made states like Canada possible. What should we remember and how do we respond to historic injustice? An ethical relationship to the past demands that we not forget legacies of violence and disruption that were justified through logics of possession and civilizing.[1]

Renan remains famous in French but is best known to English speakers as one of the targets of Edward Said's *Orientalism*, in which he interrogates Renan's racism and civilizational bias (Said 2003).[2] For Renan, civilization eclipses race (a linguistic category in his work) and

---

1 Special thanks are owed to Anver Emon and Daphna Levit who teased many threads into better cloth.
2 Anderson's famous thesis on the Nation draws deeply on Renan's thought (Anderson 2006).

even outlives the nation as an eternal inheritance from the Greek and Roman past. Renan believed that a European "religion" of "law, liberty and respect for man" would chart the future (Renan 1862, 28). The greatest enemy of this future was Islam and Muslims, who represented for Renan the "complete negation of Europe" (Renan 1862, 27). This idea, that Islam was a vestige of the past and remains uncivilizable, dominates conversations about the presence of Muslims in the West. This seems particularly odd as a majority of the Muslim world was colonized and "civilized" by Europe in the nineteenth and twentieth centuries.

Civilizational superiority undergirded the Anglicization of the British Empire under which the common law absorbed aspects of Buddhist, Parsi, Hindu, and Islamic law. Or, as the Privy Council Papers, the records of the highest court of appeal in the empire, attest: "Contrary to popular conception, Islamic law formed a formal and significant part of British Law."[3] These entanglements are often forgotten, through an imperial amnesia, when Muslims assert faith-based claims in different former colonies and Commonwealth states, such as Canada. Instead, a narrow, stagnant form of the sharia dominates the conversation and Muslims are treated as strangers (Emon 2006).

This essay explores how imperial amnesia perpetuates the othering at the heart of Islamophobic rejectionism, with specific focus on Canada. Imperial amnesia is a forgetting of the costs that make a nation or an empire possible. It includes forgetting that the imperial encounter transforms both sides. This essay begins by detailing how imperial amnesia or forgetting is connected to Islamophobia and explores the mechanisms that made Islam familiar to the British Empire, particularly in property and personal law. I provide examples of this forgetting in action in Canada and in the sharia debates in Ontario. This forgetting undermines Muslim attempts to participate fully in Canadian public life, exposing them to civilizational assassins and destroying any serious hope for a reparative future. Muslims are treated as a civilizational Other despite having already paid the price of "being civilized."

Islamophobia and Forgetting

The Ontario government describes Islamophobia as: "stereotypes, bias or acts of hostility towards individual Muslims or followers of Islam in general. In addition to individual acts of intolerance and racial

---

3   See, for example, the Privy Council Papers website (2022).

profiling, Islamophobia leads to viewing Muslims as a greater security threat on an institutional, systemic and societal level" (Ontario Human Rights Commission 2006, 10). This definition reflects a shift in understanding of Islamophobia as a form of racial discrimination, but it is ultimately limited to seeing Islamophobia as a series of individual actions and consequences. Absent from the government's analysis are the consequences of the systemic nature of this problem. To that end, Jasmine Zine offers the following: "a fear and hatred of Islam and Muslim (and those perceived as Muslims) that translate[s] into individual actions and ideological and systemic forms of oppression that support the logic and rationale of specific power relations" (Zine 2022, 14). The difference in language is significant because the second definition is conscious that Islamophobia enables certain power relations and politics. Among these politics is the idea, asserted by Renan above, that Muslims are the negation of Europe. This spectre rears its head frequently in debates in Canada and Europe, and it obscures the reality of long intertwined histories.

When we forget this history, rejectionist fears can too-easily shape the narrative. In *Casting Out: The Evictions of Muslims from Western Law & Politics*, Sherene H. Razack shows how the discourse around Muslims is often shaped by certain framing allegories. Three figures emerge in the "clash of civilizations" rhetoric: the first, the "dangerous Muslim man," his victim the "imperilled Muslim woman," and their saviour the "civilized European." These narratives take on a life of their own and impact the ways that Muslims see themselves and are seen by others. Muslims are effectively evicted from Western society, as too "other" to integrate *as* Muslims. Muslim women, the logic goes, need protection from the dead Muslim men that made Islamic law and the living ones who enforce it.

This simple civilizational talk proves a powerful unifying force for white supremacists, feminists, secular Muslims, xenophobes, Hindu Nationalists, and Liberal and Conservative presses that suddenly find themselves strange bedfellows in the assault against any forms of Muslim public self-expression. This groundswell helped prepare the ideological landscape for the Zero Tolerance for Barbaric Cultural Practices Act of 2014 which *en face* frames the law as a sword in the struggle against barbarism for the sake of civility. Québec Law 21 and other restrictions against so-called "sharia creep" are similarly rooted in rhetoric of civilizational self-defence. These laws are not neutral acts whereby the full citizenship of immigrant women or Muslim children is being protected, but rather acts of civilizational othering which perpetuate the subordination of Muslims.

But it wasn't always this way.

How Muslim Personal Law Became Familiar

Imperial Possessive Logics – Property

It was by means of the common law that lawyers became the translators of empire and its logics. William Blackstone (d. 1780), an imperial judge and legal scholar whose legacy still looms large in legal history, argued in his *Commentaries on the Laws of England* (1770) that the common law was the perfection of human reason (Blackstone and Archbold 1825). It's a Whiggish account, firmly rooted in narratives of emerging from darkness into light (becoming enlightened), portraying a march of history that would come to justify the white man's burden to civilize the world.

Key to the project of civilization, and in line with the philosophy of the time, was the notion that the greatest responsibility of the state was to enshrine and protect private property. For Blackstone, the central common good or public good was state protection of individual property rights (Harris 2004). It is in some ways a simple argument: people with property will care about its protection from those without and will invest in strong institutions that will protect those rights. Aileen Moreton-Robinson calls this a "possessive logic" that operates in the "white possessions" of Canada, the United States, Hawaii, New Zealand, and Australia. It is "a mode of rationalization ... that is underpinned by a desire to invest in reproducing and reaffirming the nation state's ownership, control, and domination" (Moreton-Robinson 2015, xii). This logic flowed from utilitarian philosophy which theorized that the maximization of utility should be the metric for determining all property decisions. Logically then, the Indigenous people had failed to adequately modify the land, or dominate it sufficiently, which meant that those that would do so, i.e., settlers, *should* take possession. Private property simultaneously was tied to enfranchisement and became a prerequisite of the full rights and participation as a citizen. We must remember that these settlers arrived only after the dismantling of the commons in England, whereby lands held in common, a messy sharing system that obliged an organic relational politics, had been enclosed into private property.

Law and legal philosophy re-evaluated land in terms of potential yield and not in terms of relationships to the land, and this logic would allow for the largest dispossessions in human history. Relationships to the land, for colonizers, were no longer seen as sources of knowledge or as critical to social reproduction (and survival) but as resources to be exploited.[4] In Canada, for example, instead of a commons we have Crown land, or privatized land administered on behalf of the public. Federal administrators see this land not through the nexus of relationships with the people who inhabit the land, but rather through an extractivist lens whereby it exists as something to be exploited to benefit the few. A related philosophy of privatization had devastating effects in British India.

Few Canadians know the significance of the name Dalhousie beyond that of a university in Nova Scotia. The school was founded by Nova Scotia's Lieutenant Governor George Ramsey the ninth Earl of Dalhousie (1770–1838) in 1818, who would go on to become governor general of Canada in 1820. A career soldier, Dalhousie served the empire against the Irish in the "Irish Rebellion" of 1798, against the French in Egypt and Europe, and finally as commander-in-chief in India.[5] His health suffered, and he returned to his native Scotland to pass four years later, but the Dalhousies were not done with India as his son's career in the East would eclipse his own. Andrew Broun-Ramsay, the first Marquess of Dalhousie, lived in Canada and worked his way up the ranks of British government to become the president of the board of trade in 1845 (the grand high capitalist). From there, he rose to become governor general of India in 1848. The oppressiveness of his policies is frequently cited as bringing about the revolt (or First War of Independence) of 1857 which culminated in the deposition of native rule and the installation of the British Raj. His aggressive Anglicization projects, utilitarian land policies, and cultural superiority are remembered in South Asia for mass Indigenous land dispossession through the doctrine of lapse where princely states without a British-recognized male heir would lapse to British control. Dalhousie would write, "I can not conceive it possible for any one to dispute the policy of taking advantage of every opportunity which presents itself for consolidating the territories which already belong to us, by taking possession of States that may lapse in the middle of them" (quoted in Metcalf and Metcalf 2012, 95). The doctrine of lapse was only in effect from 1848–56 but it massively expanded the empire through the absorption of seven princely states, making the conflict of '57 inevitable. Dispossession, annexation, and privatization are how the empire spread and came to rule over millions of Muslims.[6]

---

4 The most prominent scholarly voice on the commons is Silvia Federici. See, for example, Federici and Linebaugh (2019).

5 For an assessment of his legacy consider the 2019 report, *Report on Lord Dalhousie's History on Slavery and Race.*

6 The French similarly robustly engaged with Islamic legal traditions in their colonies; see Christelow (2014).

Muslim Personal Law

Under Warren Hastings, the first British governor general of India, cases of inheritance, marriage, or other religious causes would be based on the Qur'an for Muslims and would follow the laws of "Shaster with respect to the Gentoos [Hindus]." To make this possible, the British worked with local authorities and began a project of mass translation by Orientalist scholars. These intellectual enablers of empire searched for a Muslim Justinian or grand synthesizer. Failing in their search, they settled for legal codes developed by the Mughals and Ottomans and checked against a handful of well-regarded medieval texts (Hallaq 2009). After the uprising in 1857, codification efforts largely dispensed with native Muslim authorities, and Anglo-Muhammadan law – a hybrid legal system – emerged. This resulted in the translation of a deep cultural and historical relationship with the sharia into mere laws of personal status and property administered in British courts. Through these translated legal abstractions, communal identities were hardened and the relationship of the law to the community, which was often multireligious, was changed. Muslim practices were rendered into the possessive logic of the common law and designed to be implemented by English judges or native collaborators in the colony. Islamic law as a field of study appeared in Western universities without the lived experience of the law. Islamic legal textbooks in European languages reified the early tradition and created a core canon of literature, the knowledge of which would allow experts to dispense with traditional authority holders all together. This accompanied a massive expansion of the acquisition of Islamic manuscripts by imperial archives such as the British Library, and this inflow of data allowed a plethora of theories to emerge about how Muslims should be managed by scholars training for civil service jobs throughout the empire.

In this remapping, a lamentable casualty was a deeper concern for the promotion of the common good required of all good rulers. The legal system was constructed to support the economic circulation of wealth and not to support a pietistic polity. The only references to public good according to the model code contained in Wilson's *Digest* of Anglo-Muhammad Law of 1895 is to some general charitable endowments (sing. *waqf*). These had to be created to perpetuate the faith by, for example, establishing a mosque, or to care for vulnerable populations like orphans (Wilson 1895). Through narrowings like these, Muslim personal law became recognizable and actionable in imperial courts. Muslims themselves knew this was not the sharia as they knew it but, rather, a new thing framed by a daisy chain of contracts. These changes made it possible for Muslims to travel to London for education; gentry such as Syed Khilafat Hussain, my great-grandfather, travelled to England to study at Lincoln's Inn in the nineteenth century. He even took a wife (much to the chagrin of both families), his second, my great-grandmother Alice Maude Clarke.

The Anglo-Muhammadan law, as my *Par-dada* practised, was a legalistic iteration of Islam. Its mark of distinction was that it was recognizable to the colonial state and courts even if it was less familiar to its native subjects. His family were landowners and Syeds (Sayyid), which meant their opinions carried weight in their communities back home in Orain. If their advice was sought it would come through an intimacy with the tradition earned by way of a rigorous traditional education with tutors in numerous religious and cultural subjects. Decision-making at the level of traditional authority often avoids the imperial courts and seeks redress at the level of the community, but for those who benefited from the new authorities, the common law offered a multicultural alternative. The tension between cultures manifested on the biological level in both families of my great-grandfather, and his choices rippled throughout the lives of his children that experimented with these new identities. As a sampling of wonderfully complicated names indicates, these were a new breed: Syed Shamshuddin Ahmed, Delicia Hussain Jehan Clarke, Venetia Noorjehan Seth, and Syed Adolphus Enayat Hussain. His life oscillated between that of a traditional Muslim patriarch and a westernized lawyer. The sharia as he would have learned it was the means by which the Qur'an and the prophetic traditions of Muhammad (*sunna*) were refined into a guidance for living an upright life. He studied Persian, Arabic, and Urdu, which would enable his interactions with other Muslims, and lastly English which would make possible travel to England. His education in England would have taught him that the primary purpose of the law was to protect assets. In the case of the colonies, it was about protecting investments in the uninterrupted flow of capital.

Muslim imperial lawyers like my *Par-dada* worked with a version of Muslim family law that was poorly formulated but wore the trappings of a longer tradition. It was teachable to outsiders by outsiders, and it was also tolerable to those Muslims who recognized the authority of the new regime. Better yet, the new Muslim legal construct became an exportable commodity, and its codes appear in tweaked forms throughout the British Empire in Asia and Africa. The world was being made British, in part through the relationships and logics of the common law. This constituted a flattening of the world into "reasonable persons" who would be measured by a new scale: consider it as a civilization project in two acts, through the *juris* we achieve *civilis*.

This history of the expansion of the law is well known to comparative law scholars and legal historians. All law students in South
Asia still study criminal and civil codes often framed during the pre-
Independence codification (especially during the 1860s), and they do so
in English, the official language of the law. It seems so lamentable that
where Muslims have asserted basic claims in Western countries there is
nary a glance across the Commonwealth at a rich tradition that evolved
through these entanglements. Instead, what we see is an Islamophobic
hysteria that has undermined these claims at every turn. In Ontario,
many were swept up in the moral panic and the collapse of the faith-
based arbitration system was lauded as a triumph of liberal secularism.
But the reality is that it drove those negotiations back into the community and out of the scrutiny of the public.

Islamophobia, Forgetting, and the Ontario Arbitration Act

The Ontario Arbitration Act of 1991 allowed for religious arbitration
in private matters. Following its passage in 1992, Christian and Jewish
groups developed legally binding arbitration on a wide variety of issues as long as they did not violate Canadian law. Arbitration (or alternative dispute resolution, ADR) is frequently included as a remedy in
cases of contractual dispute, and this law merely extended arbitration
to the realm of religion. When Syed Mumtaz Ali, a retired lawyer, and
spokesperson for the Islamic Institute of Civil Justice announced his
intent to offer arbitration on issues of Muslim law in 2003, the backlash
was significant. Scholars have noted that the announcement became a
media frenzy, whereas Christian and Jewish arbitration had not raised
any concern (Korteweg and Selby 2012, 18). Muslims, as Renan noted
over a century ago, posed a unique threat in the eyes of the public and
a moral panic ensued.

Public debate, though bombastic, was ultimately meagre and re-
hashed Orientalist tropes, white nativist anxiety, and open racism as
detailed in the articles in Korteweg and Selby's *Debating Sharia* (2012).
Dominique Cardona's National Film Board documentary on the *Sharia
in Canada* is illustrative: the "Bad Muslims" came across as misguided
and misogynistic and the "Good Muslims" trumpeted secularism, political liberalism, and state protection of women (Cardona 2006). The
documentary contained no deep history of the matters at play and instead relied on interviews with embroiled parties that sensationalized
issues that were extremely simple at their core. Muslim marriages historically and at present are based primarily on contracts, which is why
they were relatively easy to adapt in the empire. Families in modern

day Pakistan will often debate the terms of the marriage contract in a manner similar to prenuptial agreements in Canada. A simple Google search reveals that the same holds true today in Canada, where a number of Toronto law firms offer "Sharia compliant" marriage contracts based on a system of carefully authored prenuptial agreements.

To add to the absurdity of the tale, and as a way of illustrating the amnesia at play, consider the following: A number of the public rallies on the sharia debate took place in Queen's Park between the statues of Queen Victoria, Empress of India, and King George VII, Emperor of India, a statue purchased from New Delhi. The Empire was alive and well in the Canadian imagination, but Muslims were not a part of that story. Less than one hundred years ago, a Christian Canadian and Muslim Indian could have attended the Inns of Court (law school-like clubs) in London and could even argue cases before the Privy Council. Their causes of action could even arise from matters germane to their individual faith traditions. The records of these cases would be housed in both colonies. The common thread was English and access to the common law. How can it be that Muslims adjusted their lives to the common law only to have the same law refuse to recognize their claims?

Unlearning Imperialism

In a 2019 book, Ariella A'sha Azoulay speaks of cultivating *potential history*, in which we begin by imagining what the healing of the ongoing violence of imperialism could look like. Nationalist and civilizational histories are a means of conveying rights by making the order of the present seem *right* (Azoulay 2019). Discarded are those that don't simply conform. Take, for example, Indigenous populations whose claims of injustice are seen as an *inconvenience* (to echo Thomas King), and any hope of repair becomes simply unthought. The alternative to this tallying of human relations is to develop a *potential history* that refuses to recognize these self-serving imperial logics and works actively to move us towards a liveable future. It is an attempt to tell better stories of our intimacies and entanglements and reject the amnesiac responses to historical injustice.

In Canada, the project of unlearning imperialism is accounting for the past, not merely forgetting. Take, for instance, the mandate of the recent Truth and Reconciliation Commission (TRC), which was created to conduct an autopsy of the residential school program, an assimilationist strategy that operated as a genocidal civilizational project. The TRC report eviscerates the civilizing program of the settler state. As settler logic dictated, "Indians" had to be integrated into the national project by any means necessary. Well, perhaps not by any means, as its agents realized that dead "Indian" children would shatter the civility of their project, and so they hid the bones that are only now being uncovered. Truth, we are realizing, requires that the gruesome arithmetic of counting children's remains not end with a mere tally and apology but rather forces us to interrogate the logics that made this monstrosity possible.

In Canada, the settler state's dismantling of Indigenous worlds was pursued through various assimilationist approaches. In the 1960s, following the revelations of the Hawthorne Report (Hawthorne 1966), Canada was faced with the grim reality that Indigenous communities were "citizens minus." The report showed how endemic poverty, healthcare discrepancies, and access to basic resources were lagging in Indigenous communities when compared to "White communities." The Hawthorne Report first rejected assimilation as an effective strategy and proposed a new "citizens plus" status that would help to correct for historic injustice. The government's response was to ignore the proposals of the report and their Indigenous consultants; it instead set about solving the "Indian problem" through the elimination of "Indian status." The White Paper of 1969 was an assimilationist ploy that would transform Indians into mere citizens by dismantling the treaty system and shifting land into Indigenous "ownership," thus rendering it taxable. This legal sleight of hand cloaked Indigenous dispossession in the language of full liberal citizenship. The furore came quickly.

Indigenous communities saw through the ploy and responses like the *Citizens Plus* (The Red Paper) document from Alberta refocused the claims on the issue of justice and the solutions proposed in the Hawthorne Report. Particular vitriol was reserved for the transformation of the current Crown lands into Indigenous title rather than shifting the lands held in trust to Indigenous control. The government intended to flatten the relationship of the land into private property, to which the authors of *Citizens Plus* responded: "The true owners of the land are not yet born" (Indian Chiefs of Alberta 1970, 198). Under the prevalent model of land use, such a situation was not deemed legally possible. The report argued for a reparative model that would make people who had been wronged whole and it reminded Canadians that the price for reparations was not a handout. "Indian people paid for them by surrendering their land" (8). How could we forget?

We Are Here Because You Were There

We began this chapter by reviewing Renan's notion that forgetting is a historical necessity for any nation given that all unity begins with brutality. His proposal was to repress past injustice as it gets in the way of progress. Renan saw the past as something to be instrumentalized in service to the present and not as the basis for a moral reckoning. It is a defensive analysis. Renan imagined European civilization was under threat from internal and external enemies. We see this same defensiveness today in the rhetoric of white nationalism and its anxiety over immigrants and multiculturalism, which undergirds Islamophobia.

We Are Here Because You Were There is a slogan that has begun to appear on signs in post-colonial immigrant protests through imperial metropoles like London and Paris. The phrase was coined by Ambalavaner Sivandan, a Sri Lankan-British writer, and is also the title of Ian Patel's study of a grand Imperial blunder whereby the British Nationality Act of 1948 granted a large number of non-white citizens of the colonies the ability to become British citizens (Patel 2021). Patel's book details some of the backflips by the British government to limit this non-white right of landing, from East Africa for example, or to divert its responsibilities to other colonies like Canada. The British feared that Britain's cultural identity would be threatened if too many brown bodies arrived too quickly. The possibility that immigration would operate as a form of reparation for the looting made possible by the British Empire receives little consideration.[7] Imperial amnesia persists because it protects the redistribution of wealth made possible by empire.

To counter Renan, what would a nation that remembers past injustice look like? For Canada, remembering includes understanding that the empire that made it possible entangled its history with a majority of Muslims on the planet. To forget this most basic fact forces Muslims to account for themselves as strangers when they have paid the cost of familiarity. To cultivate better histories that detail our entanglements also allows immigrants to accept that they will inherit some of the responsibility for the injustice that made Canada possible. If we are to push back against the possessive logic that atomized and strip-mined the world, we must become a people that remembers.

WORKS CITED

Anderson, Benedict. 2006. *Imagined Communities: Reflections on the Origin and Spread of Nationalism.* Rev. ed. London: Verso.

---

7   Carmen G. Gonzalez has suggested migration in the Americas as a form of reparation for the climate crisis (2020).

Azoulay, Ariella Aisha. 2019. *Potential History: Unlearning Imperialism*. London: Verso Books.

Blackstone, William, Edward Christian, and John Frederick Archbold. 1925. *Commentaries on the Laws of England: In Four Books*. 16th ed. London: A Strahan.

Cardona, Dominique. 2006. *Sharia in Canada – La Charia Au Canada*. Ottawa: National Film Board of Canada.

Christelow, A. 2014. *Muslim Law Courts and the French Colonial State in Algeria*. Princeton, NJ: Princeton University Press.

Emon, Anver M. 2006. "Conceiving Islamic Law in a Pluralist Society: History, Politics and Multicultural Jurisprudence." *Singapore Journal of Legal Studies* (December): 331–55. http://www.jstor.org/stable/24869084.

Federici, Silvia, and Peter Linebaugh. 2019. *Re-enchanting the World: Feminism and the Politics of the Commons*. Oakland, CA: PM Press.

Gonzalez, Carmen G. 2020. "Migration as Reparation: Climate Change and the Disruption of Borders." *Loyola Law Review* 66: 401–44. https://ssrn.com/abstract=3727725.

Hallaq, Wael B. 2009. *Shari'a: Theory, Practice, Transformations*. Cambridge: Cambridge University Press.

Harris, Cole. 2004. "How Did Colonialism Dispossess? Comments from an Edge of Empire." *Annals of the Association of American Geographers* 94, no. 1: 165–82. https://doi.org/10.1111/j.1467-8306.2004.09401009.x.

Hawthorne, H.B., ed. 1966. *A Survey of the Contemporary Indians of Canada*. Ottawa: Indian Affairs Branch.

Indian Chiefs of Alberta. 1970. *Citizens Plus*. Edmonton: Indian Association of Alberta.

Korteweg, Anna C., and Jennifer A. Selby, eds. 2012. *Debating Sharia: Islam, Gender Politics, and Family Law Arbitration*. Toronto: University of Toronto Press.

Lord Dalhousie Scholarly Panel on Slavery and Race. 2019. *Report on Lord Dalhousie's History on Slavery and Race*. Accessed 12 March 2022. https://cdn.dal.ca/content/dam/dalhousie/pdf/dept/ldp/Lord%20Dal%20Panel%20Final%20Report_web.pdf.

Metcalf, Barbara Daly, and Thomas R. Metcalf. 2012. *A Concise History of Modern India*. Cambridge Concise Histories. 3rd ed. Cambridge: Cambridge University Press.

Moreton-Robinson, Aileen. 2015. *The White Possessive: Property, Power, and Indigenous Sovereignty*. Minneapolis: University of Minnesota Press.

Ontario Human Rights Commission. 2006. *Policy and Guidelines on Racism and Racial Discrimination* Toronto: Ontario Human Rights Commission.

Privy Council Papers. 2022. "Islamic Law." Accessed 12 March 2022. https://privycouncilpapers.exeter.ac.uk/contexts/law-and-the-british-empire/the-laws/islamic-law/.

Patel, Ian Sanjay. 2021. *We're Here Because You Were There: Immigration and the End of Empire*. London: Verso.

Renan, Ernest. 1862. *De la part des peuples sémitiques dans l'histoire de la civilisation; Discours d'ouverture du cours de langues Hébraïque, Chaldäique et Syriaque au Collége de France*. 6th ed. Ed. M. Lévy Frères.

–. 1882. *Qu'est-Ce Qu'une Nation? Conférence Faite En Sorbonne, Le 11 Mars 1882*. Paris: Calmann Lévy.

Said, Edward W. 2003. *Orientalism*. New York: Penguin Books.

Wilson, R.K. 1895. *A Digest of Anglo-Muhammadan Law. Setting Forth in the Form of a Code... The Special Rules Now Applicable to Muhammadans... By the Civil Courts of British India*. London: W. Thacker & Co.

Zine, Jasmin. 2022. *Under Siege: Islamophobia and the 9/11 Generation*. Kingston: McGill-Queen's University Press.

8 Public to Private Schooling: A Research Agenda

MELANIE ADRIAN

Introduction

Islamophobia is on the rise in Canada and this increase has been shown to affect Muslim youth in public schools. Concomitantly, there has been an increase in the number of private Islamic schools across the country. This chapter broadly documents some of the main challenges for Muslim youth in public educational settings and outlines the rise of private Islamic schools in Canada. The chapter speaks to some of the reasons that parents are increasingly choosing private Islamic schooling over public education and highlights avenues for further research. The increase in private Islamic schools cannot be singularly attributed to the rise of Islamophobia. Other factors are at play including considerations of race, gender, and class, among others. We need studies that carefully delineate and understand these issues along intersectional lines and evaluate how Islamophobia affects Muslim youth within educational contexts.

This chapter raises some of the research areas that are in urgent need of analysis. I am not arguing in favour of public or private schooling, but instead I am aiming to raise several questions for both: for those students facing Islamophobic or anti-Muslim environments in public schools, how is this impacting their understanding of nationalism and feelings of belonging and inclusion? That is, are they firmly poised and supported to make positive contributions to the public sphere as citizens? For those students enrolled in private Islamic schools, how is civic belonging fostered, and how do the students understand their role as members of the public sphere and the democratic polity more generally?

Definition of Islamophobia

Before turning to the question of Islamophobia in public schools and the rise of private Islamic schools, I should note that the seminal definition of Islamophobia was formulated in 1997 in a landmark report entitled *Islamophobia: A Challenge for Us All. Report of the Runnymede Trust Commission on British Muslims and Islamophobia* ("the Runnymede Report"). The Runnymede Report was the first of its kind to examine discrimination and hate acts directed against Muslims and was the result of a commission called to study the subject (Runnymede Trust 1997). It was not the first instance of Islamophobia, but it was the first time a commission was specifically created to examine this particular phenomenon (Allen 2010).

The definition of Islamophobia developed in the Runnymede Report is based on "open" and "closed" views of Islam which are evaluated using eight distinctions in how Islam and Muslims are seen: monolithic/diverse, separate/interacting, inferior/different, enemy/partner, manipulative/sincere, criticism of West rejected/considered, discrimination defended/criticized, and Islamophobia seen as natural/problematic. Providing more than just a definition, the commission at the time outlined the primary ways in which Islamophobia presented itself. This way of understanding Islamophobia has been widely critiqued for its conceptual and theoretical weakness, self-perpetuating nature, and reductionistic tendencies (Allen 2010, 193).

Since 1997, distinctive schools of thought have developed, each using a different lens in framing Islamophobia. Farid Hafez, for example, charts three schools: one focuses on Islamophobia as prejudice, another understands Islamophobia as racism in a postcolonial frame, and the third sees Islamophobia as racism using both postcolonial and decolonial approaches (Hafez 2018). For the purposes of this chapter, Islamophobia is defined as "any unfounded or disproportionate fear and/or hatred of Islam or Muslims (or people perceived to be Muslim), leading to violence and systemic discrimination." I borrow this definition from the submission on Islamophobia in Canada to the United Nations Special Rapporteur on Freedom of Religion or Belief by the International Civil Liberties Monitoring Group (ICLMG), Islamic Social Services Association, and Noor Cultural Centre (2020).[1] I use this definition

---

1   The submission can be found online at https://www.ohchr.org/sites/default/files
/Documents/Issues/Religion/Islamophobia-AntiMuslim/Civil%20Society%20or%20
Individuals/Noor-ICLMG-ISSA.pdf.

recognizing that Islamophobia is gendered and intersects with race and class (Bakali 2016). This definition is useful as it shifts the conversation away from an impressionistic evaluation and towards what is seen, heard, and felt. These are all measurable and identifiable actions and reactions. Importantly, Islamophobia is not about hurt feelings or poor behaviour. Islamophobic acts are based on fear and groundless suppositions that lead to violence and discrimination.

Rise of Islamophobia and Public Schools

While the rise of Islamophobia in Canada is relatively easy to map, the rise of Islamophobia in public schools is more difficult to trace. No widespread studies exist that would allow thoughtful understanding or analysis. This is partially because education is regulated provincially, and thus any study would have to engage the ministries of education in all ten provinces and three territories. More importantly, however, Islamophobia or Islamophobic acts as such have not been tracked or recorded in a systematic way in the public education setting.

It is fair to relate a recorded rise of Islamophobia in Canada generally to the public school system more specifically. That is, as far as the public education system is a part of our public sphere, it is not unreasonable to suppose that these attitudes prevail in all parts of our public sphere, including the public schools. Helpfully, there are also a number of smaller studies that demonstrate this link. I will discuss these below after a brief introduction of the rise of Islamophobia.

The rise of Islamophobia in Canada has been documented, although more could be done to centralize this knowledge. One indicator of Islamophobia is the number of hate crimes[2] directed against Muslims. The number of anti-Muslim hate crimes more than tripled between 2012 and 2015. This is notable especially since overall hate crimes during this time decreased (Leber 2017, 3). Moreover, more Muslims have been killed in Canada in targeted hate crimes than in any other G7 country in the last five years (NCCM 2021). One need only mention the Quebec City Mosque attack in 2017 or the four members of one London (Ontario) family who were deliberately run over by a car in June 2021

---

2 According to Statistics Canada, police-reported hate crime is "defined as a criminal violation against a person or property motivated by hate, based on race, national or ethnic origin, language, colour, religion, sex, age, mental or physical disability, sexual orientation or gender identity or expression, or any other similar factor" (Wang 2022, 5). Available here: https://www150.statcan.gc.ca/n1/pub/85-002-x/2022001/article/00005-eng.htm.

because they were Muslims. Between 2019 and 2020, hate crimes rose sharply by a further 37 per cent (Wang and Moreau 2022, 3).

Media and social media platforms are also a good indicator of the rise of Islamophobia more generally. All in all, Islamophobia is increasing on social media platforms. Between 2015 and 2016, for example, there was a 600 per cent rise in the level of intolerance and hate speech in social media postings. One study focused on the use of certain hashtags such as #banmuslims and #siegheil (NCCM 2021, 4). Furthermore, in 2019, 60 per cent of Canadians reported having witnessed hate speech on social media (NCCM 2021, 4).

In their article analysing 345 academic studies on media representations of Muslims and Islam from 2000 to 2015, Saifuddin Ahmed and Jörg Matthes found that Muslims and Islam were portrayed poorly by the media. As Ahmed and Matthes write, "Post 9/11, media portrayals of Muslims and Islam worldwide were mostly negative, with Muslims and Islam being framed within the context of religious extremism and a clash of civilizations and cultures" (Ahmed and Matthes 2017, 231). The persistent and continuous framing of Muslims and Islam in the media has helped give rise to negative attitudes towards Muslims generally, including Muslim youth specifically (Karim 2003).

Given this context, it is no wonder that in the few studies conducted with Muslim youth in public schools in Canada one of the themes that emerges is that Muslim youth are consistently asked to *represent* and *educate* in regard to their religion. On one hand, they are asked to defend a non-violent vision of Islam or, alternatively, explain why violence happens in reference to Islam (Ahmed 2013). Acts of violence involving Islam and Muslims – abroad or in Canada – that make the headlines are something they know they will be asked to justify to their teachers and friends. Few other youth groups, if any, are expected to personally and consistently bear the weight of international events in these ways. Asma Ahmed, in her work with Muslim students in one urban public high school in Ontario, shows that these acts of representation and education are prevalent in the lives of Muslim youth as they are asked to respond to and explain negative myths and stereotypes about Islam (Ahmed 2016, 107).

The identity of Muslim youth as *Muslims*, as opposed to other aspects of who they are – children, young scholars, artists, athletes, etc. – is favoured and privileged (Ahmed 2021). This has been shown to isolate certain Muslim youth, particularly young women who choose to wear a headscarf (*hijab*) to school as they are the most obviously identified adherents of Islam. The twin charges of *representation* and *education* bear heavily on some Muslim youth, especially at a time of rapid physical and psychological growth that may parallel changing relationships with their families, religion, and community. This form of pressure, and its relationship to Islamophobia, remains understudied.

Being singled out for one aspect of their identities can lead to a sense of separation. A small study of seven *hijabi* (headscarf wearing) girls in a public school in Ottawa demonstrates this sense of isolation: "The essence of how a hijabi experiences social activities ... was described as 'Feeling Left Out.' This was the one statement that all participants made in each interview when speaking about their involvement or lack thereof, in school social activities" (Alvi 2008, 111). Thus, in addition to being singled out as Muslims and being asked to account for the actions of fellow Muslims both locally and globally, Muslim youth may also feel isolated due to their manifestation of religious belief. Additionally, the complex interrelationships between religion and race seem to amplify the context (Aziz 2015; Bakali 2016).

These initial findings seem to suggest that more research needs to be done to understand the implications for multicultural education specifically and multiculturalism and the understanding/recognition of diversity more generally. We must also understand in more detail how this affects visions of belonging – to school, to the public sphere, and principles of democracy more generally (Gutmann 1999).

Studies need to look at how the treatment of Muslim youth in public high schools is related to Islamophobia and how isolation affects visions of belonging to the public sphere. Elementary and high schools are central to influencing youth development and are critical spaces that teach civic and political engagement. These serve to frame an individual's vision and relationship to the state and the democratic polity. Multicultural states, given their focus on holding a space for diversity, must be concerned both with unity and social cohesion. As James Banks states, "every pluralistic nation-state must also be concerned about unity, social cohesion, and a set of shared values that will cement the commonwealth" (Banks 2017, 142–4). The way in which multicultural states like Canada balance diversity and a sense of shared nationhood has been scrutinized in a wide variety of scholarly and non-scholarly circles.

In addition to representing Islam, educating others about their religion, and being isolated for displaying their religiosity, Muslim youth have also faced difficulties in engaging in religious practice in public schools.[3] These difficulties have, at times, triggered public

---

3 The Government of Ontario's Human Rights Code (R.S.O. 1990, c. H.19) provides for reasonable accommodation of religious practice for students in public schools.

demonstrations of difference which have resulted in expressions of anti-Muslim hate. In 2017, for example, the Peel District School Board in Ontario was at the epicentre of one such conflict. The conflict arose when the board changed a long-held policy that allowed Muslim students to write sermons for their Friday prayers. These sermons had to be read and approved by the school beforehand, which placed an administrative burden on school leadership. The policy change was eventually reversed, but not before a nasty and ill-willed public meeting that was infused with deliberate misinformation. As representatives of the Peel Public Board later said, they were "appalled by the anti-Muslim rhetoric and prejudice ... seen on social media, read in emails, and heard first-hand at our board meetings" (Murphy 2017). This included a public desecration of the Qur'an and anti-Muslim hate speech.

These examples of limits to religious freedom and public controversies can lead to the further isolation of Muslim youth and have been shown to raise a wide variety of concerns among the youth and their parents. In my own ongoing research with Muslim youth over the last six years, these themes arose again and again in our discussions. Based in two private Islamic Schools since 2016, I have had the opportunity to speak with about seventy-five individuals – parents, students, and administrators – about their experiences in both private and public school settings. The data from these sessions has not been adequately analysed, but I use some of the voices here to highlight preliminary remarks vis-à-vis the need for further research on these subjects and their relationship to Islamophobia.

In addition to representing and educating about Islam as well as the possibility of isolation, some parents who were raised in the public system worried about their children's exposure to discrimination and Islamophobia and the stress this added to the everyday. They worried about the effect this would have on their children's sense of self.

For some, there is a fundamental disconnect between home and school. As one parent said: "a lot of them [their children and friends of their children] shared with me that they lived a schizophrenic life – [they are] one person in school with their friends, and they were a completely different person when they come home." The distinct worlds a student inhabits is often felt as separate, in part: "because their parents wanted them to act a certain way. They wanted them to speak in a different language. Even the value system was different."[4] This parent had

---

4   Parent Interview, 3 November 2016.

registered their child for private Islamic schooling after some time in the public system, suggesting that "one of the big reasons I like Islamic school, and to me that is the biggest advantage of an Islamic school versus a public school, is that the child grows up with a consistent identity."[5] The values in the school are seen as more aligned to the home and thus the child is not obligated to navigate two realities with distinct expectations.

This schism between home life and school life as described by this parent is not unknown to researchers and parents alike; as teenage youth find themselves in the larger society, new ideas and ways of being are tried and tested. Researchers working at the intersection of integration, minority communities, and belonging in the context of Islam and Islamophobia studies could ask how, if at all, this differs from non-minority or other minority communities. That is, is this aspect of what is described as a split identity part of the growth of the teenager? Or is this particular context shaping this differently? How might these answers reflect on the question of belonging and participation in the public sphere?

In terms of further research, careful consideration needs to be given to the different facets that may cause isolation among some Muslim youth. From the studies that have been done on Muslim youth in Canadian schools, we know that the task of representation and education is pushing a certain percentage of these youth onto the fringes of belonging. We also know that the wider context fuelling anti-Muslim hate and the presence of hate speech in schools has deleterious effects on Muslim youth (Ahmed 2016, 637–77). How these actions and effects intersect, if at all, with Islamophobia, needs careful attention.

Rise of Private Islamic Schools

There are many reasons cited by parents and youth alike about their choice to attend a private Islamic school. It is not the purpose of this chapter to outline these reasons in their entirety as this is done elsewhere (Zine 2008). I have charted a few of the main tensions above to bring out some ideas for further study vis-à-vis Islamophobia. I turn now to briefly examine the upswing in private Islamic schools in Ontario and consider why this may be happening.

Private Islamic schools are flourishing in Ontario, both in terms of their pedagogical approaches and their numbers. There are largely two

---

5   Parent Interview, 3 November 2016.

types of Islamic schools operating in Ontario. One is a night-or-weekend school that largely focuses on teaching the Qur'an, Arabic, and/or Islamic history. Students would attend this school outside of their public school hours.

The second type of school is the Islamic day school. This school teaches the Ontario curriculum and supplements these subjects with Arabic, Islamic history, and the Qur'an. These full-time day schools are registered with the Ministry of Education, meet the ministry requirements, and are inspected as any other private and public school in the province. Islamic day schools break for Islamic holidays and organize their days around prayer times at least once daily. They mandate school uniforms, which includes loose flowing gowns and headscarves (as of grade 4 or 6) for girls and pants and shirts for boys. There is an emphasis in many of the schools to apply a postcolonial lens to subjects, which for some schools and teachers includes an emphasis on Islamic inventions and ideas. What a postcolonial lens is and how it is taught is something that has been and continues to be actively discussed by school leadership and pedagogy experts.[6]

The rise of both types of private Islamic schools is captured statistically. In 2007–8, there were 36 registered Islamic Schools in Ontario. By 2018–19, there were 128 registered schools (Figure 8.1). Thirty-six of these schools have no registered pupils in that school year and 19 have not had registered students since 2007–8. If we limit our count to the number of schools which have had or have registered students in 2018–19, we are left with 92 schools. Thus, within an eleven-year timespan, the number of schools increased from 36 to 92.

Most of the schools are small, with forty-four having a registration of under 100 students. Thirty-six schools have between 100 and 299 students, nine schools have 300–499 students, one school has 500–699, and two schools have between 700 and 900 students (Figure 8. 2).

Given this increase in the numbers of schools and pupils, I wondered what percentage of Muslim school-aged children this represented in Ontario. That is, I wondered what percentage of Muslim households chose private Islamic education for their children. The number was a bit tricky to come up with and was complicated by the fact that the last household survey was conducted in 2011 in Canada and the results of

---

6   The Muslim Association of Canada, for example, runs the largest network of private schools across Canada. They organize and hold annual pedagogy conferences and employ instructional designers to support their school staff. I attended several of their conferences throughout the years from 2016 onwards. See https://www .macnet.ca/our-schools.

Figure 8.1. Number of private Islamic schools with student enrolment, 2007–8 to 2018–19.

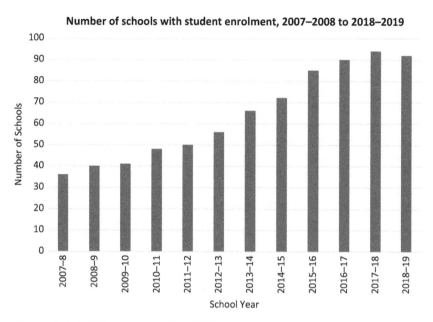

Source: Ontario Ministry of Education, 2021.

Figure 8.2. Number of private Islamic schools by enrolment, 2018–19.

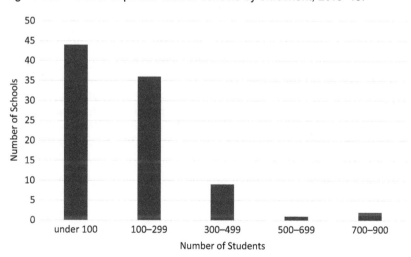

Source: Ontario Ministry of Education

the most recent census were not available prior to the publication of this chapter. Given these restrictions, I nevertheless estimate that about 9 per cent of Muslim households choose private Islamic education (Statistics Canada 2013).[7]

This new tide of Islamic schools is providing a rigorous educational alternative for parents who seek an Islamic environment for their child. As already mentioned, some parents are concerned about the effects of the public education context on their children, the exposure to values that they see as different from their own, and the expectation that their children speak for Muslim communities around the world.

Some parents in my study who enrolled their children in an Islamic school after a few years in public school described the relief they felt because they no longer carried the entire responsibility for the religious education of their children at home. Attending a private Islamic school meant that their children were learning to include prayer in their daily lives, that the school calendar followed religious holidays, and that certain norms were followed in the hallways of the school community.[8] Many parents were relieved that their girls in particular no longer faced the pressure of dressing in certain ways.[9]

There are two themes that emerged in my preliminary analysis of the data. The first theme that emerged highlighted the importance parents placed on passing along their religious and cultural heritage to their children. According to some of the parents I spoke with, this can mean that they wish for a more comprehensive religious education compared to the one they had. They wanted their children to learn to pray, read, and understand the Qur'an, and understand Islamic history. As one father told me, he is happy with private Islamic education as his children are not just memorizing the Qur'an, they are gaining an understanding the ideas and concepts that animate it. In his words: "I also learned [the] Qur'an when I was a child [but] I don't understand the language, just bits and pieces ... When I am reading the Qur'an, I cannot understand it. Here they are actually teaching you the meanings with it. Which I think is way more useful."[10] For this father, the meanings behind words and their histories function as an important piece of his children's education.

---

7   The National Household Survey Profile (NHS) is the most recent reliable source on religion in Canada.

8   These norms varied from school to school. The discussion on how they are shaped lies outside the confines of this chapter.

9   Parent Interviews, 26 September 2016, 3 November 2016.

10 Parent Interview, 1 December 2016.

The second theme that emerged is that parents appreciated that their children were learning the language of the Qur'an – Arabic – and thereby deepening their understanding of the complexity of the sacred text. This same father highlighted how important it was to him that his children learn concepts around religious practice and consciously participate. He states: "I also had Islamic study class when I was growing up. I think the Islamic study class here is better than the ones I had as a kid. The ones I had … they just tell you things in a certain way, perhaps a bit polarized. Here it is a little bit more conceptual."[11] The idea that his children will be exposed to a complex way of thinking around religious practice and history motivated him to keep his children in a private educational setting.

Conclusion and Future Research

Islamophobia is on the rise in Canada and this trend may be affecting how some Muslim youth experience their daily realities in public schools. More studies, particularly comparative studies with non-Muslim youth, need to be done to understand how the rise in Islamophobia as well as anti-Muslim hate acts are affecting Muslim youth. We know from the few studies conducted thus far that Muslim youth in public school settings express a feeling of isolation. This may be complicated by the fact that they are asked, time and again, to represent all Muslims and explain the actions of Muslims in other parts of the world.

In a context of rising Islamophobia, I chart the growth of two different types of private Islamic schools. One is an after-school program teaching a range of subjects from Arabic and Qu'ran studies to Islamic history. The other type of school is a full-time day school that offers all of the subjects required by the Ontario Ministry of Education in addition to Islamic history, Arabic, and Qu'ran studies. The number of schools that offer Islamic instruction, both part-time and full-time, are increasing, and more thought needs to be given to this trend as well as its relationship to Islamophobia. Many questions arise given the upswing in private Islamic schools, and we need more research in all of these areas to understand the complex interrelationships at play.

Some of the questions we might study include the following: How are private Islamic schools teaching civic and democratic values and norms? What level of interaction do students have with non-Muslim students in private and public settings? What is the lived reality and

---

11   Parent Interview, 1 December 2016.

effect of social isolation for Muslim youth in public schools and private schools? What does the rise in Islamic schools signal, if anything, for multicultural norms and values? Moreover, how do Muslim youth envision nationalism and social cohesion and their role in shaping Canadian society?

WORKS CITED

Ahmed, Asma. 2013. "London Islamic School: Millstone or Milestone?" *Discipline, Devotion and Dissent: Jewish, Catholic and Islamic Schooling in Canada*, edited by Graham P. McDonough, Nadeem A. Memon, and Avi I. Mintz, 145–68. Waterloo, ON: Wilfrid Laurier University Press.

–. 2016. "Exploring the Experiences of Muslim Students in an Urban Ontario Public School." PhD diss., Western University.

–. 2021. "Muslim Youth Yearning for Normal Lives." *Annals of Social Studies Education Research for Teachers* 2, no. 1 (May): 31–9. https://doi.org/10.29173/assert16.

Ahmed, Saifuddin, and Jörg Matthes. 2017. "Media Representation of Muslims and Islam from 2000 to 2015: A Meta-analysis." *International Communication Gazette* 79, no. 3: 219–44. https://doi.org/10.1177/1748048516656305.

Allen, Chris. 2010. *Islamophobia*. Farnham: Ashgate.

Alvi, Saba. 2008. "An Analysis of How Hijabi Youth Experience Social Activities in Ottawa Secondary Schools." Master's thesis, University of Ottawa.

Aziz, Nurjehan. 2015. *The Relevance of Islamic Identity in Canada: Culture, Politics and Self*. Toronto: Mawenzi House.

Bakali, Naved. 2016. *Islamophobia: Understanding Anti-Muslim Racism through the Lived Experiences of Muslim Youth*. Rotterdam: Sense.

Banks, James A., ed. 2017. *Citizen Education and Global Migration: Implications for Theory, Research, and Teaching*. Washington, DC: American Educational Research Association.

Gutmann, Amy. 1999. *Democratic Education*. Princeton: Princeton University Press.

Hafez, Farid. 2018. "Schools of Thought in Islamophobia Studies: Prejudice, Racism and Decoloniality." *Islamophobia Studies Journal* 4, no. 2: 210–25. https://doi.org/10.13169/islastudj.4.2.0210.

International Civil Liberties Monitoring Group (ICLMG), Islamic Social Services Association, and Noor Cultural Centre. 2020. *Islamophobia in Canada: Submission to the UN Special Rapporteur on Freedom of Religion or Belief*. 30 November 2020 https://www.ohchr.org/sites/default/files

/Documents/Issues/Religion/Islamophobia-AntiMuslim/Civil%20
Society%20or%20Individuals/Noor-ICLMG-ISSA.pdf.

Karim, Karim H. 2003. *Islamic Peril: Media and Global Violence.* Montreal: Black
Rose Books.

Leber, Ben. 2017. *Police-Reported Hate Crime in Canada, 2015.* https://www150
.statcan.gc.ca/n1/pub/85-002-x/2017001/article/14832-eng.htm.

Murphy, Jessica. 2017. "Toronto-Area Peel District School Board in Muslim
Prayer Row." BBC News. 12 April 2017. https://www.bbc.com/news
/world-us-canada-39508319.

National Council of Canadian Muslims (NCCM). 2021. *NCCM Policy
Recommendations for National Summit on Islamophobia.* 19 July 2021. https://
www.nccm.ca/islamophobiasummit/.

Runnymede Trust. 1997. *Islamophobia: A Challenge For Us All.* London:
Runnymede Trust.

Statistics Canada. 2013. *National Household Survey Profile, 2011.* Statistics
Canada Catalogue no. 99-004-XWE. https://www12.statcan.gc.ca/nhs
-enm/2011/dp-pd/prof/index.cfm?Lang=E.

Wang, Jing Hui, and Greg Moreau. 2022. *Police Reported Hate Crime in Canada,
2020.* https://www150.statcan.gc.ca/n1/pub/85-002-x/2022001/article
/00005-eng.htm.

Zine, Jasmin. 2008. *Canadian Islamic Schools: Unraveling the Politics of Faith,
Gender, Knowledge, and Identity.* Toronto: University of Toronto Press.

9 Countering Islamophobia in Higher Education: A Critical Pedagogy Perspective

SHELIZA IBRAHIM

Introduction

Islamophobia refers to "the specificities of contemporary forms of racism directed against Muslims" (Rizvi 2005, 171). As a scholar of education, I question how experiences of schooling systematically furthers white supremacy ideologies and the dehumanization of Muslim people. Consider the London, Ontario attacker who killed a Muslim family by running them over with his vehicle. The killer attended Strathroy District Collegiate Institute and then Fanshawe College in London, Ontario (Dubinski and Gollom 2021). Both schools and Canadian schools in general could be examined to question how experiences in these educational institutions failed to challenge the attacker's racist beliefs through unconscious bias and microaggressions. Institutionalized schooling has the potential to transform thinking or to reaffirm harmful ideologies. Many factors are at play, but education can serve as a space for unlearning many colonial norms rooted in white supremacy. My own experience as an educator in London, Ontario at Western University further contributes to this discussion.

For example, in 2016 I had a student exhibit a mindset of indifference and apathy for historically marginalized communities. Specifically, in the pedagogy and methods course I was teaching in science education, I included some instruction and content that raised issues of under-representation of minority groups (i.e., gendered, racial) in STEM fields (Moss-Racusin et al. 2014), and ways of incorporating Indigenous ways of knowing such as traditional ecological knowledge for understanding science phenomena (Adams, Ibrahim, and Lim 2010). Upon completion of the course, an anonymous comment from one of my students stated that social justice issues are not required in science and that science subjects should strictly focus on science phenomena and conceptual understanding. On one hand, it is plausible that this student had a more rationalist-realist frame of reference, assuming that scientists' topics, methods, and ways of using knowledge are strictly logical and systematic (Bencze 2017). Their comment was also aligned with what they equate the nature of science to be (Lederman et al. 2002). However, deeper issues are at play when students believe that knowledge generation processes in the sciences do not involve factors like gender, religion, race, culture, emotions, politics, economics, and personal and social biases (Bencze 2017).

These incidences occurring in London, Ontario (i.e., the attack on a Muslim family and the example of my student at Western University) further substantiate how a region like London seems to involve multiple overt incidences where ideologies of white supremacy surface (some with catastrophic/fatal outcomes and some with seemingly unconscious biases/microaggressions). I have merely added my experience to the ongoing racism that exists in this locale because incidences in London, Ontario and Western University have already been documented by Martis's (2020) recollection of race and campus life (Boon et al. 2021). In this light, the ways in which systemic racism impacts post-secondary education, students, and the larger community is in need of comprehensive study. In this chapter, I set out to explore current scholarship. Before that though, it should be noted that the complex systems that manifest Islamophobia around the world continue to rise. When examining white supremacy on a global scale, literature, popular media, social media, news, and current events all document incidences of Islamophobia (Hasan 2021) – with the most current incident coming from France (reported across news sites, Instagram, and Twitter) that the French Senate passed the ban of Hijabs in athletic competitions (Petrequin 2022).

Reports tend to capture the effect of racism but never the root – or cause – white supremacy. Racism happens to the racialized, the "visible" minority, and those who get to be "invisible" are those to whom the nation belongs and for whom it was built (Yu 2022). Given this reality, higher education can be a powerful tool to dismantle white supremacy. Historically, education has been a powerful tool in upholding it – residential schooling being a case in point. Here, however, I consider the potential for higher education to serve as a significant catalyst for change. I aim to reimagine what my practice might look like for myself and other faculty who actively teach and research within academia. Incidents of hate against people who identify as Muslim are grounded in colonialist ideologies. Racism "manifests differently in different contexts" (Rollock et al. 2015, 14). Thus, in our time, Islamophobia materializes into forms aligned with the historical moment. Amidst the world's response to the colonial oppression of anti-Black policing, the suppression of Indigenous ways of knowing in the residential school system and subsequent genocide of thousands of Indigenous children, and land dispossession and ethnic cleansing of Palestinians, we are witnessing forms of dehumanization further compounded by the COVID-19 pandemic.

Student Life and Academia

Focusing on post-secondary institutions, this chapter considers Islamophobia in higher education, specifically exploring two capacities. First, framed in student achievement, the chapter asks how post-secondary institutions prepare Muslim students for the world. Second, framed in institutional work, this chapter explores how Islamophobia is being addressed, if at all.

With respect to undergrad and graduate Muslim students, I draw on Freire's banking concept, which is the notion that schooling prepares students to be "adapted to the world." In an excerpt from *Pedagogy of the Oppressed*, Freire (2000) states:

> It follows logically from the banking notion of consciousness that the educator's role is to regulate the way the world "enters into" the students. The teacher's task is to organize a process which already occurs spontaneously, to "fill" the students by making deposits of information which he or she considers to constitute true knowledge. And since people "receive" the world as passive entities, education should make them more passive still, and adapt them to the world. The educated individual is the adapted person, because she or he is better "fit" for the world. Translated into practice, this concept is well suited for the purposes of the oppressors, whose tranquility rests on how well people fit the world the oppressors have created and how little they question it.

I unpack this truth in order to identify how higher education might challenge the banking concept and prepare students to change the networks/systems of the world rather than adapt to systems that were not designed for them. Students often enter higher education with a narrow focus. That is, they expect to adapt in order to suit the job market rather than to influence societal structures through transformative civic action. Students often enter into academic spaces as the institutions *are*, whereby students conform inauthentically.

With regards to the examination of current work on Islamophobia in post-secondary institutions, this chapter examines selected literature that references the kinds of work underway towards awareness of racism/Islamophobia or pedagogical change in post-secondary teaching and learning that is working towards dismantling systemic racism towards Muslims. As a critical pedagogy educator, I do question my representation, interpretation, voice, and capacity to write and research on Islamophobia. My critical lens as a science and mathematics scholar prompts me to ask whether I have the expertise to voice and speak on behalf of the work and research for Muslim advocacy. Yet, as a scholar and a researcher in university pedagogy, and as one who has journeyed through academia as a Muslim, I reflect on the ways in which I have numbed myself to the realities of this space, navigating with complacency and shying away from activism for my faith. In my courses, I share my story and teaching as a form of activism for me, but this is not reflected in my writing and research. Through this personal reflection, I examine post-secondary education and the possibilities for bettering it.

I conclude this chapter by applying critical pedagogy as a theoretical framework to review the literature and identify post-secondary spaces that honour critically engaged educational experiences. Drawing on theories of critical pedagogy to explore transformative pedagogical practices might situate students in democratic knowledge-making spaces. Contextualized through discourses of anti-racism and Islamophobia, I draw on Jean Anyon's (2009) perspective on critical engagement with social justice issues, suggesting three areas of pedagogical practice that require further research and conceptualization. These are (1) teaching mechanisms that encourage students to participate in public contention; (2) exploring identity as an evolving social construction of self, where politicizing self serves just cause; and (3) embodying knowledge as a means towards critical consciousness and advocacy. Further examination of these areas may offer opportunities to create intellectual hubs for undergraduate experience that invite both historically marginalized and privileged communities to create a discourse of unity that challenges the hate at its root.

Higher Education and Islamophobia, a Discourse Analysis

Research examining racial inequality in higher education reports varying foci. Some scholarship addresses the readiness of universities to support marginalized students such as supports and access to advanced coursework, counselling, and financial aid resources that prepare racialized students to transition to university life. They also report the disproportionate impact of systemic barriers that cause dropout and debt burden (Erwin and Thomsen 2021). Other research reports racial inequality affecting all levels of stratified higher education from admissions to graduation (Bensimon 2020). These examples highlight where research interest currently rests when it comes to understanding racial inequity in university contexts more broadly. Zeroing in on scholarship that examines Islamophobia and/or anti-Muslim racism in higher education, we find literature that speaks to how conceptualizing Islamophobia's impact by using one theoretical framework is not sufficient. For example, Gholami argues that racial and religious disadvantage must be understood separately, through intersectionality and critical race theory for Muslim students (2021). When focusing on female Muslim students only, research reports Orientalist representations (Said 2003) of veiled female students confronting microaggressions during schooling (Zine 2006), Orientalism being a concept by which the West perceives the East as backward, lacking democracy, and abrogating women's rights (Said 2003). Studies that address the multiple burdens faced by Muslim women pursuing university degrees are limited, but there are theoretical frameworks that draw on feminism and critical race theory, for example, in the context of a case study surveying Muslims in France on banning the headscarf (Wing and Smith 2005 – banning the hijab is an ongoing issue in France spanning decades). Still, explicit references to higher education contexts are limited. Digging into critical race theory (Crenshaw et al. 1995; Delgado 1995) or critical race feminism is beyond the scope of this review, but it is fair to say that institutional approaches to race and religion have been reported to inculcate structuration and perpetuation of academic disadvantage for Muslim students in post-secondary school (Gholami 2021) instead of easing it. It is evident that studies that reflect the intersectional experiences of Muslim students (i.e., multiple marginalized identities, such as race, ethnicity, and LGBTQ status) are few, and our understanding of the multiple burdens of oppression and discrimination has not been robustly identified or analysed (Ahmadi and Cole 2020). A review of the literature further substantiates emergent themes that do not fully tackle the systemic dismantling of Islamophobia in higher education, but instead identify its existence and constructions within institutionalized spaces of post-secondary schooling and report on the supports the institutions offer to students to *adapt* to university life. These themes emerged through a keyword search in peer-reviewed databases of scholarly and empirical studies, and in Google Scholar. Keywords were "Islamophobia," "Anti-Muslim Racism," "Race," "Higher Education,"

"University," "Equity, Diversity, and Inclusion," and "EDI/DEI." Employing a qualitative methodology to analyse the discourse (Gee 2011) in these articles where relationships between the articles collected suggest grounded interpretations (Charmaz 2014), I could identify a series of emergent themes.

1 Normalized hegemony conditioning institutions of schooling to operate on central authority (Ahmadi and Cole 2020; Gholami 2021)
2 Proposing EDI workshops and professional development for faculty/staff where anti-bias skills training is expected to combat all forms of racism and prejudice (Carter, Onyeador, and Lewis 2020; Janmohamed 2005; Lin, Lake, and Rice 2008), including Islamophobia (Siddiq 2021)
3 The advent of social emotional learning for mental well-being and wellness (Beard et al. 2021; Jagers, Rivas-Drake, and Williams 2019; Sekerka and Yacobian 2018; Zembylas 2012) as a learning strategy that is expected to teach how to live in a pluralistic and democratic society (Zine 2002; Ramarajan and Runell 2007) and cope with institutionalized Islamophobia

These emergent themes highlight the ways in which higher education studies reference Islamophobia, often in cursory attempts at enacting EDI. Such work is commendable and represents an important step; as scholarship in this area grows, more possibilities for incorporating Islamophobia teachings/awareness in higher education are likely to emerge. Regardless, this search did not yield many results, suggesting that greater evidence from empirical studies on Islamophobia in higher education is needed. In the meantime, this review is telling, as it indicates how Islamophobia and anti-Muslim racism are being addressed on the fringe of broader studies of anti-bias racism, EDI, and critical race theory. It also shows how Islamophobia is operationalized as an issue addressed within the bandwidth of all education training and learning in diversity. Indeed, the emergent themes from this narrow survey of the literature highlight the ways in which higher education fails to support the specific and complex needs of explicitly marginalized communities of Muslim students and their intersectionality (Gholami 2021). In anti-bias skills training, which as of late is seen as a crucial part of public education, the dialogue is broad and aimed at developing cultural competence for all equity-seeking groups. This might render the training shallow with respect to the depth and degree of understanding needed for the complex history and impact of Islamophobia.

Colonial Gaps and Decolonization in Higher Education

Historically, Islamophobia has been understood through the racialization of Muslims (contextually, such as post-9/11, and in media, through topics such as gender equities etc.) and through histories of colonialism such as Orientalism (Razack 2021). The extent of colonialism within higher education professional development sessions has not been adequately explored, and we lack a full appreciation of how critical it is that faculty apply the kinds of teaching philosophies that will dismantle white supremacy and create meaningful change for Muslim students. The wave of equity, diversity, and inclusion (EDI or DEI if referred to as diversity, equity, and inclusion) workshops for lecturers, professors, researchers, and university staff is an effort to answer the call for anti-bias education, but there is little to no empirical data on whether these workshops are effective. Anti-Islamophobia guides/resources/handbooks for educators are meant to address one of the world's most vulnerable and misunderstood minority groups (Siddiq 2021), but they usually only circulate when hate crimes are reported in the mainstream media. This is similar to the way in which the Black Lives Matter movement attracted public attention when incidents of police brutality were widely reported or how wider awareness of truth and reconciliation is only triggered by the discovery of the graves of missing Indigenous children. When there is a lull in this cycle, it means educational institutions are prioritizing something else, but EDI should be a mainstay of university life and training. Justice and equity for marginalized people is simply not embodied in the teaching philosophies of educators in their daily teaching or research. As a university educator, the burden of focusing on content delivery and conceptual understanding within our respective fields necessitates the teaching philosophies that guide our pedagogical instruction. Unfortunately, systemic bias and microaggressions that perpetuate Islamophobia continue unchecked, primarily because theoretical philosophies such as culturally responsive pedagogy are not prioritized, especially in undergraduate courses like mathematics (Leonard 2019). Decolonizing the elite spaces of higher education founded on ideologies of white supremacy requires disrupting the construct of higher education at its historical and perpetual core. The hegemonic normalization of *it is what it is* in higher education problematizes the difficulty in making systemic change. Muslim students must simply live with their identity and varying intersectionality without challenging why they might experience difference or biased treatment. Indeed, anyone who identifies with any racialized, religious, or gendered minority group understands that they may be susceptible to harm from bigotry. This is the accepted norm as one navigates campus life (Wong et al. 2021). For Muslims, it is referred to as institutionalized Islamophobia (Ahmadi and Cole 2020).

The literature shows that connections between Islamophobia and colonialism are not central to professional development or teaching philosophies. Colonialism and white supremacy as ideologies assume domination over others. The ideologies that are grounded in colonialism and white supremacy create the "othering" whereby white supremacy can maintain social, political, historical, and institutional dominion over "othered" groups (Saad 2020). Social systems where white people have structural advantages over other ethnic groups exist in seemingly democratic spaces like universities and colleges. The hegemony encompasses the way in which "People's responses to their discontents ... are culturally conditioned by being made to accept uncritically, the values, norms, perceptions, and beliefs that support and define the structures of central authority" (Owusu 2003, 59). Thus, hegemonic ideology is dominant, seldomly questioned, and normalized as "common sense" (Kumashiro 2015). In higher education, school is a space for whiteness to enact authorization and legitimatization of what and who are acceptable and what and who are not – the included and excluded. The interaction between whiteness and schooling ratifies social, economic, and cultural benefits by endorsing and cultivating whiteness as a dominant identity and cultural practice (Ladson-Billings 1998; Leonardo 2002; Ladson-Billings and Tate 1995).

The cultural and hegemonic matrix of whiteness, as a construction of privilege and power, functions as a material and tangible instrument of authorization and legitimacy of personhood. This is particularly pronounced in a time in which we see record levels of environmental crises, wars, and large numbers of political refugees and asylum seekers (see Gerrard 2017). To further substantiate this issue, even if there is an influx of initiatives towards anti-(Muslim) racism in the aftermath of a hate crime, it still also marks the heightened supremacy of whiteness by those feeling threatened (Thobani 2007). If a group in power or a person belonging to a race of authority feels threatened or afraid that the advantages they have been systemically awarded are being jeopardized, that person/group may/can act defensively and oppressively (DiAngelo 2018), and this sometimes leads to heinous acts. These persons/groups include the mass shooter in the Quebec mosque shooting of 2017 (Mahrouse 2018) or the twenty-year-old who killed four Muslim family members in 2021. They can also be a collective of women and men as teachers, administrators, and governing officials in residential schools who suppressed Indigenous ways of knowing to the point of murdering thousands of children. In addition, media representations of Muslims further propagate false identities to stoke fear and suspicion (Housee 2012) in order to "reinstate white racial equilibrium and maintain control" (DiAngelo 2011). Dismantling whiteness feels futile (Housee 2012), but education offers hope. Schooling itself is structured by colonialism and, thus by design, institutionalizes Islamophobia in a way that is experienced by Muslim students (Ahmadi and Cole 2020). A normalization in the way Muslim students experience Islamophobia is perpetuated and maintained through the colonial structures embedded systematically in education. Higher education must answer the call, not only to shed light on Islamophobia and anti-Muslim racism, but to serve our students, both Muslim and non-Muslim. Post-secondary institutions must also go inward to examine their own ordering of knowledge systems that uphold structural racism in its spaces.

In this light, proposing systemic adjustments to the practices of teaching faculty and conduct in higher education is usually done through tools to address EDI. Decolonizing education is one such framing for dismantling the systemic privileging of whiteness. There is literature that uses this framing to support truth and reconciliation within Indigenous education (Binda and Lall 2013), whereby the process of decolonization rejuvenates and renews the genuine cultural truth through an inclusive system. The redemptive quality of decolonizing academia (Kumar 2009) posits education, as Chief Atleo stated, as a "tool of freedom and liberty" instead of a "tool of oppression" (Binda and Lall 2013, 19) as enacted upon Indigenous societies. However, I do not adopt this particular framing in this chapter because decolonization might imply a reversal of what was done (and continues to be done); colonization cannot be *undone*. Acknowledgment of colonial existence is paramount. In doing so, one knows that colonialism cannot be reversed. It is simply impossible to decolonize entire ordering systems of knowledge. Thus, acknowledgment invokes truth; it makes known colonialist presence in the historical document and the colonial impact upon the present and future. This includes intergenerational trauma, unconscious bias, systemic privileging, and discriminatory practices across all levels of governance and life.

Methodological Approaches/Challenges: Where to Begin?

Critical pedagogy offers a possible frame to begin this analysis. This theoretical framework furthers acceptance and truth regarding colonial actions and does not historicize it as a thing of the past. Applied to this review, critical pedagogy stimulates criticality and unlearning in order to humanize the lives of those who identify as Muslim and those whose identities are mistaken as Muslim (and thus, experience forms of Islamophobia and anti-Muslim hate) (Jhutti-Johal and Singh 2021). Educating in post-secondary contexts requires consideration of pedagogical frameworks that not only teach conceptual understanding but critical reflection of the nature of being human. Aligned with three ambitious reimaginings of critical pedagogy (Anyon 2009), I look beyond the discourse of critical pedagogy to propose three ways that Islamophobia can be addressed in higher education:

1 teaching mechanisms that encourage students to participate in public contention,
2 exploring identity as an evolving social construction of self, where politicizing self serves just cause, and
3 embodying knowledge as a means towards critical consciousness and advocacy.

Future Research

Acknowledging the gaps explored above, I will briefly lay out how this approach might be taken up in higher education spaces.

1. Faculty Supporting Students' Participation in Public Contention

Post-secondary schooling exists as a dynamic and physical space but also as a relational space which interacts with notions of belonging, identity-building, and identity legitimation within a wider socio-cultural discourse. If we attempt to reconstruct instead of decolonize academia, we allow stories of truth to disrupt spaces. This might suggest that we can reframe decolonization as a way of asserting our Islamic/Muslim subjectivity and breaking the hegemony of the Western episteme. As Anyon has written: "Influencing whether people become involved in political contention has to do with how they interpret their political and economic surroundings" (390). That interpretation is limited when post-secondary schooling erases/supresses incidents of Islamophobia. Students do not organize around issues because of their political stances. In fact, research has reported that it is people's participation in activism that modifies their political identity or *change in consciousness.* A change in their view (i.e., political identity) is a consequence of their agency. This is at the individual level, but individuals then develop collective identity as social change agents and organize to improve their communities (Anyon 2009). Mechanisms that either teach students to participate in public action or offer opportunities to participate in activism in higher education are crucial. Research is needed to examine if these opportunities are offered in post-secondary institutions and, if so, whether the student body is being made aware of them. Further research can also examine whether Muslim and Non-Muslim students would feel supported if they were to engage in public work defending human rights for Muslims, or if they fear consequences would render them unmarketable, unemployable, and problem students. In my view, faculty and educators have a role to play in bringing students into social networks, especially as it has been shown that students are more likely to participate in activism when they have a sense that prior engagement has been effective (Passy and Giugni 2001). Faculty have an opportunity to teach students meaningful civic participation as these students may go on to undertake important civic work in their communities. A vital undertaking in current times, since "more Muslims have been killed in targeted hate-attacks in Canada than any other G-7 country in the past 5 years because of Islamophobia" (NCCM 2021). It is hopeful that advocacy work with students and faculty will lead to foundational understanding about hatred and Orientalism, but this kind of civic engagement can also give undergraduates and graduates other critical life skills. Indeed, studies report that lower socioeconomic students of colour who had engaged in civic activism displayed an increase in positive personal development, improvement in their academic engagement, and enhanced student achievement (Benson et al. 2012; Zeldin and Price 1995). These indicators suggest that participation in civic action can be an important tool in (1) dismantling institutionalized Islamophobia and (2) fostering a culture of belonging for Muslim students, both of which may be fundamental catalysts for post-secondary success. Further research in this area is needed.

2. Students' Recognition of Self in University Epistemologies

Exploring identity as an evolving social construction allows students to discern how conditions related to systemic barriers such as poverty are not connected to personal failings. The evolution of this identity might be connected to social and emotional learning experiences that are currently embedded in curriculum pedagogy in higher education. I suggest that this framing is problematic and draw on a study reporting that social and emotional learning cannot repair the "hegemonic miseducation" impacting the health and wellness of communities of colour and their colonial relationship with inequitable social systems (Camangian and Cariaga 2021). Muslim students must also contend with the ways in which the ordering of knowledge systems at the university level discounts Islamic epistemologies. University can serve as a place for unlearning and learning, especially since Muslim students' early education experiences (kindergarten to grade twelve) have not applied curricula that address Islamophobia. Only recently the National Council of Canadian Muslims (NCCM), published recommendations (2021) as a result of the motion passed in the House of Commons on 11 June 2021 to convene an Emergency National Action Summit on Islamophobia. One recommendation is that the ministries of education consult with boards and Muslim communities to develop curriculum, resources, and programs that affirm Muslim identities (NCCM 2021). Curriculum and resources are forthcoming and needed at the university level as well. Legitimization of colonial knowledge makes it difficult to teach other knowledge systems (recall the science student perturbed by learning Indigenous traditional ecological knowledge in a science course referenced in introduction). As Boaventura de Sousa Santos (2014) has shown, colonialism entails "epistemicide" – the erasure of entire ordering systems of knowledge. Historically, challenges to the canon of knowledge were met with oppression and racism, and when other systems of knowing could not be destroyed outright, as was the case with Islam (and those of First Nations), they were often profoundly reorganized. Texts remain unchanged, but the consciousness of the reader and the nature of knowing itself were fundamentally altered. I propose that faculty and staff open up spaces of dialogue for knowledge systems to be discussed within and beside the systems of knowledge they teach. Empirical research exploring how pedagogical practices include Islamic knowledge systems and other knowledge systems would offer important findings on how pedagogy is developed and how students are impacted. Some existing work examines the pedagogy and psychology of *humanization* as opposed to social and emotional learning (Camangian and Cariaga 2021), so that educators support the emergence of racialized students' self-determination and recognition of self. The details of such studies and methodology need further conceptualization. Nevertheless, this is a critical area for future study.

3. Acceptance of Cognitive Justice and the Pedagogies That Counteract Colonialism

The application of critical pedagogy uncovers complex decisions concerning justice, democracy, and competing ethical claims (Kincheloe 2004) so that faculty and staff move beyond the canon of knowledge, single storied texts, and colonial curricula, which in turn potentially emphasize an emancipatory and transformational educational practice. Of course, higher education might not be capable of teaching solutions for inequities, but instead it can help "learners facilitate critical thinking and engagement to address the fundamental issues of power, privilege, and oppression" (Sampson 2018). Notions of racism, prejudice, and discrimination have been examined in Canadian history textbooks and report how racism is largely conceptualized as an individualized problem/behaviour, imagined as existing within temporal and spatial locations/events (Montgomery 2005). This is problematic and means that supremacy ideologies of power, privilege, and oppression are not taught as impacting systems or generations since time immemorial. Critical pedagogy can be a gateway to reimagining instruction and teaching that guides learners towards deeper reflection and action. The potential for social agency is what Freire (2014) refers to as *conscientization*, and in that shift students become aware that knowledge is not fixed, that individuals and collectivity have the power to transform it and to transform their reality. For Muslim students, this can show up in the form of cognitive justice (Santos 2014) which recognizes how diverse people across the globe interpret the world and provide meaning to their existence – offering varied knowledge systems. The widespread acceptance of cognitive justice could raise consciousness surrounding bias and microaggressions that public spaces perpetuate about Islam and other systems of knowing. This would require important pedagogical changes in courses that include teachings on Orientalism. Students would come to know how depictions of the Orient are a result of discursive formations (Foucault 2006); that is, what we know about Muslims is socially constructed with bias and power contributing to the representation of Muslim identity. I argue that understanding Orientalism allows scholars, students, and faculty "to interrogate more deeply the marginalisation of certain Canadian communities" (Richardson 2014). Said states, "without examining Orientalism as a discourse one cannot possibly understand the enormously systematic discipline by which European culture was able to manage – and even produce – the Orient" (2003, 3). The Orient discourse continues to be perpetuated through the containment and representation of dominating frameworks, like education (or the media). Learning about the Orient might suggest accepting that the Orient exists - the Orient exists as a manifestation of the colonizer. But, if we steer away from that tension and instead recognize that it's in the learning of what Orientalism is, that one begins to learn how representations of *anything* is embedded in discourses of power, culture, institutions, and so on. Introducing frameworks such as critical pedagogy (Freire 2000), power and knowledge (Foucault 2006), or Orientalism (Said 2003) offer a possibility for learners to deconstruct the Western gaze on Muslim identities (and other colonial representations), and for Muslims to reflect on their own identities, which allows them to loosen the embrace of words and things (Foucault 2006) that narrate their representation in a negative light. Continued research needs to examine pedagogical instruction/vision that might help us counteract colonial incursions in our consciousnesses and work against the hegemony and imperialism of education. Radical knowledge practices that might disrupt academia need further examination in current research.

Hope

Institutions for learning are hopeful places. Yet, students have reported that guidance counsellors in high schools did not take their educational goals seriously because they held the misconception that education is not valued for Muslim women (Zine 2001). Similar incidents likely occur in higher education, but student experiences of Islamophobia/anti-Muslim racism in higher education settings lack robust empirical documentation. I also add that I write this piece just after Statistics Canada's annual report on police-reported hate crimes, revealing a significant increase from 84 hate crimes against Muslims in 2020 to 144 incidences in 2021 (Moreau 2022). This 71 per cent increase in reported hate crimes against Muslims is a strong indication of the urgency of research in this field and knowledge mobilization. These hate crimes consist of threats and attacks on mosques and hijabi women, some of which resulted in lethal outcomes. The death of innocent victims weighs heavily, and the scholarly exploration for justice and change for Muslims are forms of activism that I adopt as an academic. This chapter highlights the gaps in the efforts to counter Islamophobia and suggests specific theoretical framings for examining socio-justice issues and systematically reconstructing Islamic knowledge with truth, humanization, and conscientization. Faculty and staff can foster epistemological reflection and critical engagement that can advance social justice, while we as Muslims in these spaces (student, staff, or faculty) seek systemic change in the institutions that change us. Such is the act of embodied learning and unlearning. In a way, these institutions are fluid, and our work seeks to reimagine higher education via well-meaning foundations that are ethical for all. We hope that these interventions (even if they are EDI workshops) are not wasted, nor that our labour creating these interventions and learning within them serve to be purposeless. Instead, let them guide the work towards critical pedagogy in post-secondary schooling that enhances the lives of all our students – Muslim and non-Muslim – and removes Islamophobia and racism in the deep roots of its making. Higher education can be a powerful space for hope in this endeavour.

WORKS CITED

Adams, Jennifer D., Sheliza Ibrahim, and Miyoun Lim. 2010. "Invoking the Ontological Realm of Place: A Dialogic Response." In *Cultural Studies and Environmentalism: The Confluence of Ecojustice, Place-Based (Science) Education, and Indigenous Knowledge Systems*, edited by Deborah J. Tippins, Michael P. Mueller, Michiel van Eijick, and Jennifer D. Adams, 215–28. New York: Springer.

Ahmadi, Shafiqa, and Darnell Cole. 2020. *Islamophobia in Higher Education: Combating Discrimination and Creating Understanding*. Sterling, VA: Stylus Publishing.

Anyon, Jean. 2009. "Critical Pedagogy Is Not Enough: Social Justice Education, Political Participation, and the Politicization of Students." In *The Routledge International Handbook of Critical Education*, edited by Michael W. Apple, Wayne Au, and Luis Armando Gandin, 389–95. New York: Routledge.

Beard, Karen Stansberry, Joanne Baltazar Vakil, Theodore Chao, and Cory D. Hilty. 2021. "Time for Change: Understanding Teacher Social-Emotional Learning Supports for Anti-Racism and Student Well-Being during COVID-19, and Beyond." *Education and Urban Society*. https://doi.org/10.1177/00131245211062527.

Bensimon, Estela M. 2020. "The Case for an Anti-Racist Stance toward Paying Off Higher Education's Racial Debt." *Change: The Magazine of Higher Learning* 52, no. 2: 7–11. https://doi.org/10.1080/00091383.2020.1732752.

Benson, Peter L., Nancy Leffert, Peter C. Scales, and Dale A. Blyth. 2012. "Beyond the 'Village' Rhetoric: Creating Healthy Communities for Children and Adolescents." *Applied Developmental Science* 16, no. 1: 3–23. https://doi.org/10.1080/10888691.2012.642771.

Bencze, J.L., ed. 2017. *Science & Technology Education Promoting Wellbeing for Individuals, Societies & Environments*. Cham, Switzerland: Springer.

Binda, K.P., and Mel Lall. 2013. "Decolonizing Indigenous Education in Canada." *Education, Dominance and Identity*, vol. 1, edited by Diane B. Napier and Suzanne Majhanovich, 11–27. Rotterdam: Sense Publishers. https://doi.org/10.1007/978-94-6209-125-2_2.

Boon, Sonja, Laurie McNeill, Julie Rak, and Candida Rifkind. 2021. "Reading and Teaching Canadian Auto/biography in 2021: On Eternity Martis'

They Said This Would Be Fun: Race, Campus Life, and Growing Up and Samra Habib's *We Have Always Been Here: A Queer Muslim Memoir." Canadian Literature*, no. 244: 144–59.

Camangian, Patrick, and Stephanie Cariaga. 2021. "Social and Emotional Learning Is Hegemonic Miseducation: Students Deserve Humanization Instead." *Race, Ethnicity and Education*: 1–21. https://doi.org/10.1080/13613324.2020.1798374.

Carter, Evelyn R., Ivuoma N. Onyeador, Neil A. Lewis Jr. 2020. "Developing & Discovering Effective Anti-bias Training: Challenges & Recommendations." *Behavioral Science & Policy Association* 6, no. 1 (August): 57–70. https://doi.org/10.1353/bsp.2020.0005.

Charmaz, Kathy. 2014. *Constructing Grounded Theory*. 2nd ed. Los Angeles: Sage.

Crenshaw, Kimberlé, Neil Gotanda, Gary Peller, and Kendall Thomas, eds. 1995. *Critical Race Theory: The Key Writings That Formed the Movement*. New York: The New Press.

Delgado, Richard. 1995. *Critical Race Theory: The Cutting Edge*. Philadelphia, PA: Temple University Press.

DiAngelo, Robin. 2011. "White Fragility." *The International Journal of Critical Pedagogy* 3, no. 3: 54–70.

–. 2018. *White Fragility: Why It's So Hard for White People to Talk about Racism*. Boston: Beacon Press.

Dubinski, Kate, and Mark Gollom. 2021. "What We Know about the Accused in the Fatal Attack on a Muslim Family in London, Ont." CBC News. 9 June 2021. https://www.cbc.ca/news/canada/london/london-murder-suspect-muslim-family-1.6057164.

Erwin, B., and J. Thomsen. 2021. *Addressing Inequities in Higher Education. Policy Guide*. Denver: Education Commission of the States.

Foucault, Michel. 2006. *The Archaeology of Knowledge*, translated by A.M. Sheridan Smith. London: Routledge.

Freire, Paulo. 2000. *Pedagogy of the Oppressed*. 30th anniversary ed. New York: Continuum.

–. 2014. *Pedagogy of Hope: Reliving Pedagogy of the Oppressed*. London: Bloomsbury Academic.

Gee, James Paul. 2011. *An Introduction to Discourse Analysis: Theory and Method*. London: Routledge.

Gerrard, Jessica. 2017. "The Refugee Crisis, Non-citizens, Border Politics and Education." *Discourse: Studies in the Cultural Politics of Education* 38, no. 6: 880–91. https://doi.org/10.1080/01596306.2016.1227959.

Gholami, Reza. 2021. "Critical Race Theory and Islamophobia: Challenging Inequity in Higher Education." *Race, Ethnicity and Education* 24, no. 3: 319–37. https://doi.org/10.1080/13613324.2021.1879770.

Hasan, Wafaa. 2021. "'How Did We Get Here?' Facing the Political Histories of Islamophobia and Anti-Arab Racism in Canada." Politics Today. 29 June 2021. https://politicstoday.org/facing-the-political-histories-of -islamophobia-and-anti-arab-racism-in-canada/.

Housee, Shirin. 2012. "What's the Point? Anti-racism and Students' Voices Against Islamophobia." *Race, Ethnicity and Education* 15, no. 1: 101–20. https://doi.org/10.1080/13613324.2012.638867.

Kumashiro, Kevin K. 2015. *Against Common Sense: Teaching and Learning toward Social Justice.* 3rd ed. Routledge. https://doi.org/10.4324 /9781315765525

Jagers, Robert J., Deborah Rivas-Drake, and Brittney Williams. 2019. "Transformative Social and Emotional Learning (SEL): Toward SEL in Service of Educational Equity and Excellence." *Educational Psychologist* 54, no. 3: 162–84. https://doi.org/10.1080/00461520.2019.1623032.

Janmohamed, Zeenat. 2005. "Chapter Eight: Rethinking Anti-bias Approaches in Early Childhood Education: A Shift toward Anti-racism Education." *Counterpoints* 252: 163–82. https://www.jstor.org/stable/42978749.

Jhutti-Johal, Jagbir, and Hardeep Singh. 2021. *Racialization, Islamophobia and Mistaken Identity: The Sikh Experience.* London: Routledge.

Kincheloe, Joe L. 2004. *Critical Pedagogy Primer.* New York: Peter Lang.

Kumar, Malreddy P. 2009. "Aboriginal Education in Canada: A Postcolonial Analysis." *AlterNative: An International Journal of Indigenous Peoples* 5, no. 1: 42–57. https://doi.org/10.1177/117718010900500104.

Ladson-Billings, Gloria. 1998. "Just What Is Critical Race Theory and What's It Doing in a Nice Field Like Education?" *International Journal of Qualitative Studies in Education* 11, no. 1: 7–24. https://doi.org/10.1080 /095183998236863.

Ladson-Billings, Gloria, and William F. Tate. 1995. "Toward a Critical Race Theory of Education." *Teachers College Record* 97, no. 1: 47. https://doi.org /10.1177/016146819509700104.

Lederman, Norm G., Fouad Abd-El-Khalick, Randy L. Bell, Renée S. Schwartz. 2002. "Views of Nature of Science Questionnaire: Toward Valid and Meaningful Assessment of Learners' Conceptions of Nature of Science." *Journal of Research in Science Teaching* 39, no. 6: 497–521. https:// doi.org/10.1002/tea.10034.

Leonard, Jacqueline. 2019. *Culturally Specific Pedagogy in the Mathematics Classroom: Strategies for Teachers and Students.* 2nd ed. New York: Routledge.

Leonardo, Zeus. 2002. "The Souls of White Folk: Critical Pedagogy, Whiteness Studies, and Globalization Discourse." *Race, Ethnicity and Education* 5, no. 1: 29–50. https://doi.org/10.1080/13613320120117180.

Lin, Miranda, Vickie E. Lake, and Diana Rice. 2008. "Teaching Anti-bias Curriculum in Teacher Education Programs: What and How." *Teacher*

Education Quarterly 35, no. 2: 187–200. https://www.jstor.org/stable /23479231.

Martis, Eternity. 2020. *They Said This Would Be Fun: Race, Campus Life, and Growing Up*. Toronto: McClelland & Stewart.

Mahrouse, Gada. 2018. "Minimizing and Denying Racial Violence: Insights from the Québec Mosque Shooting." *Canadian Journal of Women and the Law* 30, no. 3: 471–93. https://doi.org/10.3138/cjwl.30.3.006.

Montgomery, K. 2005. "Imagining the Antiracist State: Representations of Racism in Canadian History Textbooks." *Discourse* 26 no. 4: 427–42. https:// doi.org/10.1080/01596300500319712.

Moreau, Greg. 2022. Police-Reported Crime Statistics in Canada, 2021. Statistics Canada. 3 August 2022. https://www150.statcan.gc.ca/n1 /pub/85-002-x/2022001/article/00013-eng.htm.

Moss-Racusin, Corinne A., Jojanneke van der Toorn, John F. Dovidio, Victoria L. Brescoll, Mark J. Graham, and Jo Handelsman. 2014. "Scientific Diversity Interventions." *Science* 343, no. 6171: 615–16. https://doi.org/10.1126 /science.1245936.

National Council of Canadian Muslims (NCCM). 2021. *NCCM Policy Recommendations for National Summit on Islamophobia*. 19 July 2021. https:// www.nccm.ca/islamophobiasummit/.

Owusu, Robert Y. 2003. *Toward a Recovery of Kwame Nkrumah's Liberation Philosophy and the Role of Religious Advocacy in Contemporary Ghana*. Trenton, NJ: Africa World Press.

Passy, Florence, and Marco Giugni. 2001. "Social Networks and Individual Perceptions: Explaining Differential Participation in Social Movements." *Sociological Forum* 16, no. 1: 123–53. https://doi.org/10.1023 /A:1007613403970.

Petrequin, Samuel. 2022. "French Senators Vote to Ban Veils in Sports Competitions." CTV News. 19 January 2022. https://www.ctvnews.ca/ sports/french-senators-vote-to-ban-veils-in-sports-competitions-1.5745692.

Ramarajan, Dhaya, and Marcella Runell. 2007. "Confronting Islamophobia in Education." *Intercultural Education* 18, no. 2: 87–97. https://doi.org/10.1080 /14675980701327197.

Razack, Sherene H. 2021. "Alternatives: What Anti-Muslim Racism Can Tell Us about Christianity, White Supremacy, and the US Insurrection 2021." *Studies in Political Economy* 102, no. 2: 223–31. https://doi.org/10.1080 /07078552.2021.1949788.

Richardson, Chris. 2014. "Orientalism at Home: The Case of 'Canada's Toughest Neighbourhood.'" *British Journal of Canadian Studies* 27 no. 1: 75–95. https://doi.org/10.3828/bjcs.2014.5.

Rizvi, Fazal. 2005. "Representations of Islam and Education for Justice." In *Race Identity, and Representation in Education*, edited by Cameron McCarthy,

Warren Crichlow, Greg Dimitriadis, and Nadine Dolby, 2nd ed., 167–78. New York: Routledge.

Rollock, Nicola, David Gillborn, Carol Vincent, and Stephen J. Ball. 2015. *The Colour of Class: The Educational Strategies of the Black Middle Classes*. London: Routledge.

Saad, Layla. 2020. *Me and White Supremacy: How to Recognise Your Privilege, Combat Racism and Change the World*. London: Quercus.

Said, Edward. 2003. "Orientalism." Counterpunch. 5 August 2003. https:// www.counterpunch.org/2003/08/05/orientalism/.

Sampson, Lynette. 2018. "8 Critical Pedagogy through Participatory Video." In *Democracy 2.0: Media Political Literacy and Critical Engagement*, edited by Paul R. Carr, Michael Hoechsmann, and Gina Thésée, 127–46. Leiden: Brill.

Santos, Boaventura de Sousa. 2014. *Epistemologies of the South. Justice against Epistemicide*. New York: Paradigm.

Sekerka, Leslie E., and Marianne M. Yacobian. 2018. "Fostering Workplace Respect in an Era of Anti-Muslimism and Islamophobia: A Proactive Approach for Management." *Equality, Diversity and Inclusion an International Journal* 37, no. 8: 813–31. https://doi.org/10.1108/EDI-11-2017-0265.

Siddiq, Raniya N. 2021. "Anti-bias Education for Islamophobia." Master's thesis: California State Polytechnic University.

Thobani, Sunera. 2007. "White Wars: Western Feminisms and the 'War on Terror.'" *Feminist Theory* 8, no. 2: 169–85. https://doi.org/10.1177 /1464700107078140.

Wing, Adrien K., and Monica N. Smith. 2005. "Critical Race Feminism Lifts the Veil? Muslim Women, France, and the Headscarf Ban." *UC Davis Law Review* 39, no. 3: 743–90. https://ssrn.com/abstract=1130247.

Wong, Billy, Reham Elmorally, Meggie Copsey-Blake, Ellie Highwood, and Joy Singarayer. 2021. "Is Race Still Relevant? Student Perceptions and Experiences of Racism in Higher Education." *Cambridge Journal of Education* 51, no. 3: 359–75. https://doi.org/10.1080/0305764X.2020.1831441.

Yu, Henry. 2022. "The White Elephant in the Room: Anti-Asian Racism in Canada." Beyond: People, Ideas, and Actions for a Better World. Accessed 14 January 2022. https://beyond.ubc.ca/henry-yu-white-elephant/.

Zeldin, Shepherd, and Lauren A. Price. 1995. "Creating Supportive Communities for Adolescent Development: Challenges to Scholars: An Introduction." *Journal of Adolescent Research* 10, no. 1: 6–14. https://doi.org /10.1177/0743554895101002.

Zembylas, Michalinos. 2012. "Pedagogies of Strategic Empathy: Navigating through the Emotional Complexities of Anti-racism in Higher Education." *Teaching in Higher Education* 17, no. 2: 113–25. https://doi.org/10.1080 /13562517.2011.611869.

Zine, Jasmin. 2001. "Muslim Youth in Canadian Schools: Education and the Politics of Religious Identity." *Anthropology and Education Quarterly* 32, no. 4: 413. https://doi.org/10.1525/aeq.2001.32.4.399.

–. 2002. "Inclusive Schooling in a Plural Society: Removing the Margins." *Education Canada* 42, no. 3. https://www.edcan.ca/wp-content/uploads/EdCan-2002-v42-n3-Zine.pdf.

–. 2006. "Unveiled Sentiments: Gendered Islamophobia and Experiences of Veiling among Muslim Girls in a Canadian Islamic School." *Equity & Excellence in Education* 39, no. 3: 239–52. https://doi.org/10.1080/10665680600788503.

10 Archives as Tools to Combat Islamophobia

MOSKA ROKAY

Introduction

This chapter introduces a method to combat Islamophobia through the archival field. Islamophobia may not be clearly evident within archival studies, yet there are ways in which archives can prevent and mitigate it. I argue that traditional Canadian archival institutions have the ability to assist in countering Islamophobic narratives, and I show how and why these institutions have previously not been in positions to address social justice issues. I first consider how archives in Western Europe and North America were formed, and the traditional principles that underpin them. Archives, as repositories of primary source documents, have long been treated as neutral and passive when it comes to a nation's collective memory and historical record. I then briefly discuss community archives and the Muslims in Canada Archives (MiCA), which may offer solutions to many of the gaps seen in Canada's archival record. Finally, I conclude with suggestions on how mainstream archival institutions can combat Islamophobia today in part by raising awareness of and for Canadian Muslim histories.

To be clear, when I refer to any "mainstream archival institution" or "major archival institution" I mean the archives of large, entrenched institutions such as federal, provincial, or municipal bodies, universities and colleges, and major companies. These archives typically have mandates to prioritize the documentation of their parent organizations and are usually about as old as these organizations.

A Brief Consideration of Western Archival Approaches

To understand how Canadian archives can become tools to combat Islamophobia, it is critical to understand the history of Western archival theory and practice – approaches which have traditionally not been positioned to account for or advance social justice. Current Western archival theory and practice finds its foundations, principles, and procedures in Europe. Influential archival theorist, Terry Cook, identifies four critical paradigm shifts in archival theory, which began with political upheavals in Europe around the French Revolution: evidence, memory, identity, and community (Cook 2013). As the new nations at the time began to develop their unique identities and governance structures, it became increasingly important for fledgling governments to legitimize themselves through control and evidence of their history and documentary heritage (Cook 2013). If these governments could manage and regulate the archives of a nation's previous history up until the republic's inception, they could control how the citizens of new nations would understand their own past and present. Thus, began an era of institutional recordkeeping based on concepts of provenance, original order, and *respect des fonds* that would sweep most of Europe and, eventually, make its way to North America. These principles were meant to keep the archive objective and neutral while the archivist remained supposedly unbiased in the history-making process (Cook 2013).

Archival practices that emerged were largely established by archival theorists from major institutions, including government bodies at various levels of authority (municipal to federal). These practices largely served to provide evidence of the activities of their parent institutions at the time (Cook 2013). Of course, once they placed importance on the evidentiary value of records, archivists realized that they needed to also determine theories and practices of proving the authenticity of the documents. One way to determine authenticity was by understanding the origin of a record or, in other words, its provenance. If you could be certain of the creator of a record, you could prove the authenticity of that record (Eastwood 2017). Another similar and equally vital principle is respect des fonds, which acknowledges the importance of keeping like records from the same creator together in one unit (Duchein 1983). When they work together, understanding the provenance and respect des fonds highlights the importance of determining the original creator of a grouping of records and, from there, ensuring that those records with the same origin stay together in order to retain the contexts of their creation.

The concept of original order is also quite straightforward. This principle highlights the importance of maintaining the original order in which an aggregate of records comes into the archives as much as possible. The understanding is that the placement and format of the donated records in relationship to each other gives critical context to the creation of the records as well as the mind of the creator of the records (Schellenberg 1961). Order also contributes to authenticity in that the researcher learns how the records may have been used in day-to-day activities of the parent institution.

These concepts, principles, and ideas of archival theory and practice were meant to ensure the neutrality and objectivity of the archive and the archivist, often then known as the custodian of the archive. It was believed that by adhering to these ideas, the average historian, researcher, or government official would enter a supposedly impartial, unbiased repository of records. These principles and practices laid out the roadmap for the pillars of archives within large, long-standing institutions in North America.

Archival Institutions in North America

As these European practices made their way to North America in the nineteenth and twentieth centuries, archivists in Canada and the United States found that they did not face some of the issues endured by their European counterparts. To take one example, North American archivists did not need to place as much importance on verifying the authenticity of three-hundred-year-old records because the nations were young in comparison to those in Europe. Their government institutions continued, however, to produce countless records since their respective inceptions.

While the European archival theories and practices were retained and became entrenched in North American archival institutions, the twentieth century saw the establishment of several practices unique to the recordkeeping circumstances in the United States and Canada.

Documentation Strategy

In the United States, many theories and ideas emerged to reflect the growing recordkeeping needs of major institutions within the country. German archival theorist Hans Booms's concepts of archival acquisition and appraisal began to inspire American archivists to create innovative documentation strategies. Booms was an advocate for archival acquisition of records with consultation of experts, determining what organizational records were most valued, and if the records adequately documented the functions of those organizations (Booms 1987). Applying these basic principles, Helen L. Samuels, an American archivist, came up with a way in which her institution could fill in the major gaps in its archival record. Her documentation strategy included a process in which the institution consulted a council of experts including records creators, scholars, historians, researchers, and administrators to assist with identifying major gaps in the record and to understand the kinds of records being created to document the respective gaps. She also argued for building ongoing relationships with this council of experts to continue consultations (Samuels 1986). Though Samuels applied this to a large postsecondary institution, this strategy worked well in identifying gaps and documenting the activities within any institution.

"Total Archives"

Meanwhile, in Canada, archivists launched the "total archives" documentation strategy and rapidly began to implement it nationwide. The "total archives" strategy refers to a commitment by government archival institutions to document all aspects and activities of Canada through both institutional and individual records (Consultive Group on Canadian Archives 1980). This meant that the governmental archives at the federal, provincial, and municipal levels sought out in-kind acquisition of the records of all Canadians in order to have a more representative picture of Canadian life. This shift deviated significantly from European and American archival traditions (Haworth 1993), which at the time focused only on the records of government bodies. It was an enormous endeavour that even today impacts how public archival institutions function. One way archivists could identify gaps in records was through unmistakable conditions brought upon by external pressures. For example, after the Second World War and the subsequent Cold War, new waves of Northern and Western European immigrants began arriving in Canada. In response to this influx, Canadian archivists began documenting these groups, knowing they were not previously represented in the Canadian archival record (Daniel 2014). Although it was reactionary and not an active, concerted effort, archivists in the twentieth century were able to document the arrival and presence of some of these Western European groups.

As major archival institutions practised a strategy of total archives, it eventually became clear how difficult it would be to ensure every aspect of Canadian life was represented in the archives. The Canadian archival community rejected English archival theorist Hilary Jenkinson's insistence, in 1922, that the creators of records (i.e., the institution) should ultimately get to choose what enters the archives over an archivist's judgment and appraisal (Jenkinson 1922, 41, 128–9). However, Canadian archives faced challenges in upholding this strategy as the primary repositories of the records of their parent organizations (i.e., government body, university institution, etc.). Despite the application of a total archives strategy, gaps emerged within the archival record, and minority groups fell through the cracks, leaving many voices out of Canada's documentary heritage.

Archives Are Not Neutral

Archives are not neutral. While the adoption of a documentation strategy from Canada's neighbour to the south may have rectified and filled some of the gaps in the late twentieth century, an archivist's relationships, subjective knowledge, and perspectives often drove active documentation strategies in practice. Throughout its history, the archival profession in North America has largely been Caucasian/white and even in the twenty-first century, diversity within the profession has been lacking. In 2004, the Society of American Archivists conducted a study to understand the demographics of its membership and discovered that an overwhelming 84 per cent of its members were white/Caucasian (Irons Walch et al. 2006). More recently, the 2016 Canadian census determined that about 135 Canadians identified themselves as visible minority archivists out of a total 1,950 archivists in Canada (Statistics Canada 2018). Only about 7 per cent self-identified as a visible minority. If the active, concerted efforts of a documentation strategy to acquire materials into an archive is based on the knowledge and relationships of archivists, and a majority of professional archivists are white, it is safe to assume that outreach and spread into Canadian society is biased. A Caucasian/white archivist may not have insider access to communities of visible, marginalized minorities; this bias may not be the fault of any or all white archivists. The point, however, is that this lack of diversity within the profession means outreach capacities are limited to perspectives and connections of and for a certain group.

By this logic, the lack of archival representation in major institutions of many marginalized groups can be attributed to these groups having little to no relationship with any Canadian archives or archivists. Many identity-based communities (i.e., Indigenous Peoples, ethnic minorities, queer communities, groups established from activities or past events, and so on) thus began to recognize the need for archives of their own communities because they did not see themselves adequately represented in official records (Caswell 2014). Cook's aforementioned fourth paradigm, community, refers to the emergence of community-based grassroots archiving initiatives starting in the late twentieth century (Cook 2013). In the late twentieth century and twenty-first century, many identity-based communities utilized emerging digital technologies as well as the Internet as accessible, innovative alternatives to document their communities' collective memories (Caswell 2014; Caswell, Cifor, and Ramirez 2016). While major archival institutions contend with the lack of diversity in the profession and subsequent outreach activities, identity-based communities gather and collect their own memories in order to fill in piercing silences in Canada's official archival record.

Community Archives as Social Justice: MiCA

The creation of these community archives are acts of social justice. For most communities that do not feel that they adequately exist in the archival record, the community archive becomes a tool for the amplification of a silenced voice, the community's voice. It is a chance for a marginalized community to tell its own stories in its own words. In a similar vein, some communities are not just absent in the archival record but also bear the burden of having skewed, generalized, and often harmful representations painted by media and society. The Canadian Muslim community is an instructive example of such a group: mainstream media, overwhelmingly non-Muslim, have filled the stories, identities, and representations of this community with narratives of terrorism, war, violence, and extremism. Community archives can become platforms to speak back to and against these representations because they can choose not to be entrenched in traditional, Western European principles and practices; they can be grassroots and consult the community in order to shape their foundations.

MiCA emerged out of the Institute of Islamic Studies at the University of Toronto after consultations with Canadian Muslim-led organizations, researchers, and Canadian Muslim community members in 2018. MiCA showcases Canadian Muslim stories that reflect lived realities by becoming a repository for primary source documents by or about Canadian Muslim individuals, families, and organizations. When these records live in one place, it becomes easier and much more accessible for anyone to learn more about Canadian Muslim history. If there are more records and sources, as a community archive, MiCA can be a space to combat Islamophobia through its platform of alternative storytelling.

Locating Primary Sources on Muslims

In order to understand the significance of a community archive for Canadian Muslim communities, we must first explore the current ways a researcher or member of the general public can access primary sources about Canadian Muslims. While Muslims are reflected in major archival institutions in Canada such as Library and Archives Canada and provincial archives across the country, these institutions are not positioned to carry out active social justice campaigns such as combating Islamophobia. Their mandates often do not leave room for such initiatives. Nevertheless, while some Canadian Muslims and Muslim organizations are reflected in some archives across Canada, their records and stories remain dormant in these institutions and, therefore, they are under-utilized as tools for social justice and alternative Canadian Muslim representation.

A multitude of archives at many different levels of government and across universities are scattered across the country. It can thus be difficult for those hoping to dive into analogue archival material, such as records of Canadian Muslims, to physically go to each archive across the country. As a result, researchers often must turn to more accessible primary source documents to uncover Canadian Muslim histories, such as newspaper archives. Many mainstream newspapers have digitized their issues and made them easily accessible online. Through keyword searches like "Muslims" or "Islam" one can pour over hundreds of newspapers to discover events and activities of Canadian Muslim communities over time. This is certainly a viable albeit time-consuming option. But one might run into trouble given that some of the earliest Canadian Muslims, including those that arrived in the late 1800s and early 1900s, either voluntarily anglicized their names, or immigration officials did it for them in order to facilitate assimilation into Canadian society (Hogben 2021). Many of these earlier Muslims and their records have likely been lost to history. If a researcher were to attempt to find them by searching for surnames common in Muslim-majority cultures, they may not be successful.[1]

MiCA aims to bring together the records of Canadian Muslims in one dedicated archive whose main priority will always be the documentary heritage and histories of Canadian Muslims. By focusing on self-identifying Muslims, MiCA is an active, concerted effort to

---

1 Another important consideration is the variations in the spelling of "Muslim" as well as the different terms that non-Muslims have labelled Muslims throughout history. Previous, incorrect terms have been "Mohammedan" and "Islamic Canadian." These varied spellings and terms make it even more difficult to search for actual Muslims in vast databases, especially considering Muslims themselves would never label themselves in such ways. I provide examples of how erroneous search terms created by non-Muslims deter discoverability of Canadian Muslims in archives in the following policy report: Rokay, Moska. 2019. "Archives of Muslims in Canada: Environmental Scan." *Institute of Islamic Studies Occasional Paper Series* 1, no. 2.

document Canadian Muslim lived experiences and is, inherently, countering mainstream, skewed narratives of Muslims. It has the potential to combat Islamophobia by its sheer existence but also through deliberate, organized programming. MiCA is not a passive, neutral archive and will never be: it is meant to disrupt and combat prevailing and prejudiced narratives.

Mainstream Archival Interventions

While a community archive for Canadian Muslims will allow the community to tell its own stories in its own words, MiCA cannot combat Islamophobia on its own. Canadian archives of major institutions such as governments, universities/colleges, and libraries may not have the capacity, human resources, or mandates to actively seek Canadian Muslim collections. But there are a number of ways these institutions can still support the fight against Islamophobia. Mainstream archival institutions should use their power, knowledge, resources, and authority in the Canadian archival field to support community archives.

Islamic History/Heritage Month

In 2007, the Canadian Parliament officially proclaimed October as Canadian Islamic Heritage Month and, in 2016, the province of Ontario proclaimed October as Islamic Heritage Month through the Islamic Heritage Month Act. This month is a special time to recognize the contributions and achievements of Canadian Muslims and to acknowledge and condemn the rampant Islamophobia across the country. Archives can do their part by creating social media campaigns, as well as physical or digital exhibits for the month showcasing Canadian Muslims in their holdings. If there are no Canadian Muslims in the archival holdings or no records that document Canadian Muslim activities, archives can also invite MiCA and its contributors to speak about the project in order to raise awareness of MiCA's existence to a broader membership. Similarly, it would also be a good opportunity to invite scholars of Canadian Muslim history to either give talks on the contributions of Muslims in Canada or consult them to identify gaps in the archive's holdings.

Building Relationships

Archives should conduct careful outreach strategies to build relationships with Canadian Muslims or Canadian Muslim organizations.

While a mainstream repository may not have space for any more records, they can still teach Canadian Muslim communities about the importance of archives. To do this, mainstream archival institutions should endeavour to build lasting relationships with Muslim-led organizations and local mosques in their regions in order to enter their spaces and create more awareness of the existence of archives. By informing more Canadian Muslims about the power and process of archives, archival institutions support the battle against Islamophobia by inspiring Canadian Muslims to potentially engage with an archive to ensure informed, consensual donations of records.[2] Moreover, one way to reach these Muslim communities can be through the hiring of Muslim archivists. Some Canadian Muslim organizations and masjids may be more comfortable with a member of their own community entering their spaces. Canadian Muslim archivists are more likely to have the cultural or religious competencies to engage with these communities and perhaps even identify subcommunities hitherto unknown to archival institutions.

Records Management

As identified in Anver Emon and Nadia Hasan's 2021 report, *Under Layered Suspicion*, many Muslim-led charities in Canada have faced disproportionate discrimination by the Canada Revenue Agency and even had their charity statuses revoked. One of the important recommendations they make for Canadian Muslim-led charities is to establish a records management and archival system to organize their records. A challenge for researchers to access and learn about specific Muslim-led organizations has been their lack of structured archives and records management systems. Major archival institutions can intervene here in order to provide records management training to Muslim-led charities. This effort can help ensure that Canadian Muslim-led organizations are no longer targets of Islamophobic practices, and in turn facilitate

---

2   On the other hand, it is clear that one of the risks of public access to Canadian Muslim records could be increased surveillance of Canadian Muslims as well. A discussion of these risks is out of scope for this paper but certainly an issue that MiCA faces with Muslim donors of records every day. We do not yet have a clear-cut, perfect solution for this but are actively attempting to mitigate this risk in several ways. One way archivists can mitigate this risk is by allowing for flexible restrictions: Muslims must be able to restrict their records however they please in order to feel safe. I encourage archives and archivists to be as flexible with their policies as possible.

archives becoming an instrument for building strong relationships with Canadian Muslim organizations.

Conclusions

Major Canadian archival institutions have practices and procedures entrenched in Western European – and later North American – record-keeping traditions that have focused on the documentation of mainstream institutions. Although some practices have changed and shifted, the foundations of mainstream archival institutions have remained stable for decades. It will take more time and consistent effort to chip away at the Western practices that helped establish these archival institutions. As noted above, many of these principles centre authenticity and the evidentiary value of records as opposed to community archival practices that focus on the communities they represent.

Mainstream archival institutions still maintain great influence and are consistently consulted for historical research. But they can actually leverage this public trust by participating in activities to support the active fight against Islamophobia. These institutions may not have the capacity to engage in active anti-Islamophobia campaigns or conduct extensive outreach programs to Canadian Muslim communities. However, participation in Islamic History Month, building ongoing relationships with Muslim organizations and mosques, and helping to provide records management consulting for Muslim organizations are just some ways mainstream archival institutions can participate in and advance anti-Islamophobic programming.

A community archive for Canadian Muslim groups brings together the scattered archival records of Canadian Muslims that currently exist in various different archival institutions across the country. It helps build reciprocal relationships of trust with the community and physically acquires records of Canadian Muslims that have not yet been donated to archives. MiCA aims to be this platform for the absent Muslim voices in Canada's archival record. By creating one platform that can both point to records that exist within its own repository and those that exist in other archives, MiCA allows for more accessible research on and about Canadian Muslims. At the same time, MiCA will have the capacity to dedicate efforts to active anti-Islamophobia programs and campaigns. In its essence, MiCA counters negative, prevailing narratives about Canadian Muslim communities and combats Islamophobia through active archival acquisition of records donations. By preserving, sharing, and exhibiting the records of Canadian Muslims, MiCA is a critical platform for telling the stories of their everyday, lived experiences and, thus, countering the skewed, one-dimensional narratives of war, terrorism, and extremism that prevail among Western media outlets. With more Muslims telling their own stories in their own words through their records, they simultaneously talk back to Islamophobic narratives.

WORKS CITED

Booms, Hans. 1987. "Society and the Formation of a Documentary Heritage: Issues in the Appraisal of Archival Sources." Translated and edited by Hermina Joldersma and Richard Klumpenhouwer. *Archivaria* 24 (January): 69–107.

Caswell, Michelle. 2014. "Seeing Yourself in History: Community Archives and the Fight Against Symbolic Annihilation." *The Public Historian* 36, no. 4: 26–37. https://doi.org/10.1525/tph.2014.36.4.26.

Caswell, Michelle, Marika Cifor, and Mario H. Ramirez. 2016. "'To Suddenly Discover Yourself Existing': Uncovering the Impact of Community Archives." *American Archivist* 79, no. 1: 56–81. https://doi.org/10.17723 /0360-9081.79.1.56.

Consultive Group on Canadian Archives. 1980. *Canadian Archives: Report to the Social Sciences and Humanities Research Council of Canada*. Social Sciences and Humanities Ottawa: Research Council of Canada.

Cook, Terry. 2013. "Evidence, Memory, Identity, and Community: Four Shifting Archival Paradigms." *Archival Science* 13, no. 2/3: 95–120. https:// doi.org/10.1007/s10502-012-9180-7.

Daniel, Dominique. 2014. "Archival Representations of Immigration and Ethnicity in North American History: From the Ethnicization of Archives to the Archivization of Ethnicity." *Archival Science* 14, no. 2 (May): 169–203. https://doi.org/10.1007/s10502-013-9209-6.

Duchein, Michel. 1983. "Theoretical Principles and Practical Problems of Respect *des fonds* in Archival Science." *Archivaria* 16 (Summer): 64–82.

Eastwood, Terry. 2017. "A Contested Realm: The Nature of Archives and the Orientation of Archival Science." *Currents of Archival Thinking*, edited by Heather MacNeil and Terry Eastwood, 3–21. Santa Barbara, CA: Libraries Unlimited.

Emon, Anver M., and Nadia Z. Hasan. 2021. *Under Layered Suspicion: A Review of CRA Audits of Muslim-Led Charities*. Toronto: Institute of Islamic Studies. www.layeredsuspicion.ca.

Haworth, Kent M. 1993. "The Voyage of RAD: From the Old World to the New." *Archivaria* 35 (Spring): 55–63.

Hogben, Murray. 2021 *Minarets on the Horizon: Muslim Pioneers in Canada.* Toronto: Mawenzi House.

Jenkinson, Hilary. 1922. *A Manual of Archive Administration Including the Problems of War Archives and Archive Making.* Vol. 4. Oxford: Clarendon Press.

Samuels, Helen W. 1986. "Who Controls the Past." *American Archivist* 49, no. 2 (Spring): 109–24. https://doi.org/10.17723/aarc.49.2.t76m2130txw40746.

Schellenberg, T.R. 1961. "Archival Principles of Arrangement." *American Archivist* 24, no. 1 (January): 11–24. https://doi.org/10.17723/aarc.24.1 .l330351406231083.

Irons Walch, Victoria, Nancy Beaumont, Elizabeth Yakel, Jeannette Bastian, Nancy Zimmelman, Susan Davis, and Anne Diffendal. 2006. "A*CENSUS: (Archival Census and Education Needs Survey in the United States)." *The American Archivist* 69, no. 2: 291–419. https://doi.org/10.17723/aarc.69 .2.d474374017506522.

Statistics Canada. 2018. "Occupation - National Occupational Classification (NOC) 2016 (691), Employment Income Statistics (3), Highest Certificate, Diploma or Degree (7), Visible Minority (15), Work Activity During the Reference Year (4), Age (4D) and Sex (3) for the Population Aged 15 Years and Over Who Worked in 2015 and Reported Employment Income in 2015, in Private Households of Canada, Provinces and Territories and Census Metropolitan Areas, 2016 Census - 25% Sample Data. 2016 Census of Population, Statistics Canada Catalogue number 98-400-X2016356, Ottawa, Ont.: Statistics Canada 2016." 28 March 2018. https://www150.statcan .gc.ca/n1/en/catalogue/98-400-X2016356.

Democracy, (In)Equality, and Exclusion

11 How Low Can We Go? Combating Systemic Islamophobia with the Unwritten Constitutional Principle of Respect for Minorities

NATASHA BAKHT

Canada's constitution has a Charter of Rights and Freedoms (1982)[1] that protects a series of rights, both individual and collective, from government intrusion. The Charter is for many Canadians "a justice-seeking document" (Berger 2005) that promises a better, more inclusive society for everyone, irrespective of immutable differences. For members of non-dominant minority communities, the Charter has often provided protection from laws and policies that directly or inadvertently promote majoritarian interests or perspectives. While the rights in the Charter are not absolute, they require government justification if they are to be infringed. At the time of the Charter's creation, section 33 or "the notwithstanding clause" was negotiated. It permits governments to override fundamental freedoms including religious freedom and freedom of expression (s. 2), legal rights (ss. 7–14), and equality rights (s. 15) for a five-year renewable period. The inclusion of section 33 in the Charter was a political compromise, decried by many as diluting critical protections to appease certain provinces at the time of constitutional negotiation. Until recently, there has been a culture of restraint around the use of section 33 (Albert 2008, 1041–3). Political commentators predicted that governments would rarely use it, and if they did, it would be to their political peril.

Recent events have raised doubt as to the efficacy of this implicit political constraint on the use of section 33. The world has seen a rise in populist governments that promote an anti-Muslim agenda (Kundnani

I am very grateful for the invaluable conversations I have had with my co-parent and fellow proponent of justice, Prof. Lynda Collins.

1 *Canadian Charter of Rights and Freedoms*, Part I of the Constitution Act, 1982, being Schedule B to the Canada Act 1982, (UK), 1982, c 11.

2015). One instantiation of this systemic Islamophobia is a transnational suppression of visible Muslimness, primarily targeted at women, through law (Bakht 2022, 20). Legal bans of the hijab and niqab in a variety of contexts have spread from country to country, sharing justifications and tactics irrespective of local context or logic (Bakht 2020, 116–24). In 2019, the Quebec government enacted An Act Respecting the Laicity of the State[2] (Law 21), a law that prohibits all people who wear religious symbols from working in key sectors of the public service and prevents those who cover their faces for religious reasons from receiving public services in certain circumstances. Law 21 undoubtedly violates a whole range of constitutionally protected rights of several religious minorities, in particular Muslim women. Yet the government of Quebec's pre-emptive invocation of section 33 has immunized the law from typical avenues of Charter challenge.

Globally, provisions like section 33 coupled with the rise of right-wing populist governments undermine the very purpose of a bill of rights – to protect minorities from the threat of the "tyranny of the majority" (*R. v. Big M Drug Mart Ltd.* (1985) 1 SCR 295, para. 96). For constitutional rights to mean anything, particularly the most basic and crucial rights to which section 33 applies, the notwithstanding clause must be used rarely. And yet this "exceptional" status is challenged by governments that insist on promoting majoritarian values – in the case of Quebec, a fierce anti-religious secularism – that undermine the practices of vulnerable minorities. Section 33 has essentially permitted systemic Islamophobia to persist and grow. Before considering avenues for countering this situation, let me unpack the devastating consequences of Quebec's Law 21.

Law 21

As the court of first instance noted in *Hak c. Procureur général du Québec*,[3] Muslim women who wear religious clothing are disproportionately affected by Law 21 (*Hak*, para. 807). First, the law significantly and disproportionately curtails hijab- and niqab-wearing women's economic autonomy by prohibiting their ability to work in the public service and potentially barring them from certain private sector jobs (Law 21 s. 6). Thus, people who have spent years training or getting an education in specific fields are prohibited from seeking employment as public school

---

2 An Act Respecting the Laicity of the State, SQ 2019, c12 [Law 21].
3 *Hak c. Procureur général du Québec*, 2021 QCCS 1466 [*Hak*].

teachers, principals, government lawyers, or police officers. Those who wear religious clothing and already work in the public service are denied transfers or promotions. Some have made the difficult and onerous decision to move from Quebec to other provinces to work in their areas of expertise (Somos 2019).

Second, the denial of state services, whether an outright denial for those who cover their faces (Law 21, s. 10) or where the receipt of services is likely to be applied in a discriminatory manner (Law 21, s. 8; *Eldridge v. British Columbia (Attorney General)*, [1997] 3 SCR 624), will unduly affect many aspects of niqab-wearing women's lives. Women experience higher rates of poverty (Mossaman et al. 2015, 367–9; CEDAW 2017, para. 78) and are thus more likely to require government services such as public transportation and social assistance. Because women continue to be the primary caregivers for children, the elderly, and those who are ill or disabled (para. 47), they will also be acutely impacted by the requirement that an individual must show their face to access day care, public retirement homes, public therapeutic services, and hospitals. The denial of multiple levels of educational services, including French language training for immigrant women, will affect the long-term prospects of niqab-wearing women, compromising their personal development and prospects for a healthy life (Ansell 2017, 116). Having an education plays a pivotal and transformative role in the empowerment of women and in their ability to earn an income whether inside or outside of government.

Finally, and perhaps most gravely, by enacting legislation that promotes distrust and animosity towards specific groups, governments, through such bans of religious clothing, implicitly condone the segregation, marginalization, and exclusion of minorities and create an atmosphere where women in particular, who often wear visible symbols of their faith, are subject to harassment and violence as they occupy and travel through public spaces (Mason-Bish and Zempi 2018, 540–1). Governmental and judicial backing of discriminatory ideas legitimizes and emboldens certain public views. These ideas seep into mainstream consciousness and lower the bar in terms of what can appropriately and publicly be said about Muslims, and indeed what can be done to them (Pertiz 2014; Leber 2017; Steuter-Martin 2017; Kestler-D'Amours 2021). The increase in hate crimes targeting Muslims is undoubtedly related to the perpetuation of state-sanctioned anti-Muslim racism (Bakht 2020, 135).

While the court of first instance found that Law 21 had a cruel and dehumanizing impact on Muslim women (*Hak*, para. 69), it nonetheless upheld much of the law because the Quebec government invoked section 33 of the Charter. In other words, although Muslim women's religious freedom, freedom of expression, equality, and security of the person, among other rights, are being violated, this state of affairs is permitted to continue. Many have argued that the time has come to dispense with section 33 (Mailey 2019, 9–18; McLean and Froc 2021). While its repeal requires constitutional amendment that can be difficult to achieve, it is a course worth pursuing. Otherwise, we risk normalizing the use of section 33 as an everyday tool used by governments to bypass the Charter with extremely harmful repercussions for marginalized minorities. Until section 33 is made constitutional history, scholars and advocates will need to explore other approaches to combating an institutionalized mechanism that permits systemic Islamophobia.

The immunization of Law 21 from the usual routes of Charter challenge such as sections 2(a) and 15 has forced innovative advocacy drawing on multiple constitutional resources for Charter review (*Hak*).[4] Although dismissed by the Quebec Superior Court (*Hak*, para. 873–6), I am particularly swayed by the constitutional argument that an intersectional approach to sections 27 and 28, to which section 33 does not apply, offers a viable way to counter the legislation (Froc 2019, 20; Strauss 2021, 92; Bakht, forthcoming; *Secession Reference*, para. 53).[5]

Unwritten Principles

In this chapter, however, I explore another approach, that of unwritten constitutional principles to counter state-sanctioned systemic oppression. The Supreme Court of Canada characterized "unwritten constitutional principles [as] unwritten norms that are essential to a nation's history, identity, values and legal system" (McLachlin 2006, 163). The Court held that

> they are the vital unstated assumptions upon which the text is based ... [I]t would be impossible to conceive of our constitutional structure without them. The principles dictate major elements of the architecture of the Constitution itself and are as such its lifeblood. The principles assist in the

---

4   For example, in *Hak*, 2021 QCCS 1466, lawyers argued that Law 21 was contrary to the constitutional division of powers and unwritten constitutional principles.

5   This approach is particularly promising where in the hierarchy of constitutional sources, the written text of the Constitution should have primacy over unwritten portions. Reference Re Secession of Quebec, [1998] 2 SCR 217, para. 53 [*Secession Reference*].

interpretation of the text and the delineation of spheres of jurisdiction, the scope of rights and obligations, and the role of our political institutions. Equally important, observance of and respect for these principles is essential to the ongoing process of constitutional development and evolution of our Constitution as a "living tree." (*Secession Reference*, paras. 49, 51–2)

In *Reference Re Secession of Quebec*, the court identified four fundamental and organizing principles of the Constitution, respect for and protection of minorities being one such principle (*Secession Reference*, paras. 32, 68, 70, 74, 76).[6] The protection of minority rights was central in the negotiations leading to Confederation and a key consideration motivating the enactment of the Charter. The protection of minority rights is thus essential to the design of Canada's constitutional structure and ensures that minorities are not assimilated. The principle of respect for minorities was characterized as not merely descriptive, but "invested with powerful normative force, and ... binding on courts and governments" (*Secession Reference*, para. 54). The legitimacy of a modern democratic state depends on its adherence to a "bottom line" (Collins 2017, 2) of fundamental norms below which law and executive action cannot go (McLachlin 2006, 151). The Canadian Constitution contains an irreducible minimum core of human rights that transcends the political compromise embodied in section 33. If this were not the case, historic injustices that we are only beginning to come to terms with could easily be repeated for the sake of political convenience.

Indeed, the invocation of section 33 could hypothetically permit Canadian governments to replicate human rights abuses that are now universally decried. For example, the Indian residential school system, established in the nineteenth century, funded by the Canadian government, and administered by Christian churches, was a network of

---

6   The other three unwritten constitutional principles identified in the case were federalism, democracy and constitutionalism, and the rule of law. While the protection of minorities is the most obvious principle that is relevant to challenging Law 21, democracy and constitutionalism/rule of law are arguably also highly pertinent. The principle of democracy is richer than a system of simple majority rule. "A democratic system of government is committed to considering dissenting voices, and seeking to acknowledge and address those voices in the laws by which all in the community must live" (*Succession Reference*, paras. 68 and 76). The rule of law vouchsafes to citizens and residents a stable, predictable, and ordered society (*Succession Reference*, para. 70). The principle of constitutionalism provides an added safeguard for fundamental human rights and individual freedoms. "There are occasions when the majority will be tempted to ignore fundamental rights in order to accomplish collective goals more easily or effectively" (*Succession Reference*, para. 74).

boarding schools for Indigenous children where attendance was mandatory. It was created to separate Indigenous children from their parents, to destroy their language, culture, and religion, and to assimilate them into the dominant Canadian culture (Truth and Reconciliation Commission of Canada 2015). Thousands of children were exposed to physical and sexual abuse and died in these schools from malnutrition and disease (Truth and Reconciliation Commission of Canada 2015, 487, 560, 598). The children's unmarked mass graves are only now being uncovered (BBC News 2021). Had the Charter been in existence at that time, we would argue that the forced assimilative "education" of Indigenous children was a clear violation of their right to life, liberty, and security of the person under section 7, and to the equal protection and equal benefit of the law without discrimination under section 15. While most of us have barely come to terms with this horrendous past (let alone contemplating its repetition), a broad interpretation of section 33 would permit governments to do this again.

To take a second example, between 1885 and 1923, Chinese immigrants were required to pay a head tax of $50–$500 to enter Canada. During the thirty-eight years the tax was in effect, approximately 82,000 Chinese immigrants paid nearly $23 million towards this tax (Chan 2016). Although the labour of Chinese men was critical to building the Canadian Pacific Railway, discriminatory legislation – in fact, the first to exclude immigration based on ethnicity – was enacted once the railway neared completion. The head tax made it nearly financially impossible to bring families from China, creating a major gender imbalance within this community. The head tax was removed with the Chinese Immigration Act in 1923, which banned virtually all Chinese immigrants from Canada until its repeal in 1947. The systemic racism perpetuated by the Chinese Immigration Act denied people of Chinese descent the right to vote, to practice law or medicine, to hold public office, or even to seek employment on public works (Chan 2016). Legislation of this sort would be contrary to section 15 of the Charter which guarantees that every individual is equal before and under the law without discrimination based on race, nationality, or ethnic origin (*Tai Sing v. Maguire*, 101; *Wing Chong*, 150; *Mee Wah*, 403; *Gold Commissioner of Victoria District*, 260; *Corporation of Victoria*, 331).[7] However, if there is no constitutional backstop controlling the scope of section 33, then

---

7 The Supreme Court of British Columbia used the division of powers in the constitution but also the principles of English law that underlay that text to strike down a series of anti-Chinese provincial and local laws. See *Tai Sing v. Maguire* (1878) 1 BCR (Pt 1) 101 (SC); *R. v. Wing Chong* (1885) 1 BCR (Pt 2) 150 (SC); *R. v. Mee Wah* (1886) 3

politicians could override this critical protection by turning to the notwithstanding clause.

Similarly, if section 33 is truly an untrammelled discretion to abrogate crucial rights and freedoms, then Canada could conceivably engage in racist internment of minority communities. During World War II, the Canadian government forcibly relocated and interned Japanese Canadians in the name of national security. Japanese Canadians, many of whom were citizens by birth, were stripped of their homes and businesses and sent to internment camps and farms in British Columbia and other parts of Canada. This forced relocation subjected them to government-enforced curfews and interrogations, job and property losses, and forced repatriation to Japan. The camp conditions were dire; families were separated; people lived without privacy, in unsanitary environments, in the intense cold and in poverty (Marsh 2012). The effects of this chapter in Canadian history led to the fracturing of a community, intergenerational shame, and loss of language and culture. This episode would today be described as a violation of Japanese Canadians' liberty and security of the person under section 7 and their equal protection and equal benefit of the law without discrimination under section 15. And yet, because section 33 permits governments to ignore these rights when enacting laws, theoretically, this situation could arise again.

While technically the constitutionalized mechanism of section 33 gives governments the power to strip people of basic rights for at least five years, the unwritten constitutional principles that infuse and breathe life into the Constitution (*Secession Reference*, para. 50) cannot permit this to occur. Since the Second World War, it has been widely accepted in modern democracies that legal systems must adhere to certain basic norms. Non-discrimination on the basis of gender, race, or religion, for example, is included in this minimum moral content (McLachlin 2006, 150).[8] Essentially, the protection of minorities is a fundamental norm of justice so basic that it forms part of the legal structure of governance and must be upheld by the courts.

Some may suggest that the use of unwritten constitutional principles is acceptable only when the written text is unclear or incomplete.[9] The

---

BCR 403 (Cty Ct); *R. v. Gold Commissioner of Victoria District* (1886) 1 BCR (Pt 2) 260 (Div Ct); and *R. v. Corporation of Victoria* (1888) 1 BCR (Pt 2) 331 (SC).

8 International legal instruments that Canada has ratified and signalled its intention to be bound by are also sources that set out the norms of unwritten constitutional principles that can prevail over laws and executive action.

9 Unwritten constitutionalism is potentially dangerous, but this circumstance in which I propose that it be used is extraordinary.

Supreme Court identified the use of unwritten constitutional principles in *Secession Reference* as filling a gap when the text of Canada's Constitution was silent on whether a province could unilaterally secede from the federation (Constitution Act s.43(a)).[10] The written text of a constitution is certainly crucial. However, unwritten constitutional principles must also be relied on in a situation that is manifestly unconscionable or impossible to accept, one that would permit an ordinary law like Law 21 to undermine written and unwritten constitutional principles of the highest order. Such a contradiction that goes to the very heart of a constitutional democracy undermines not only the core values of our constitution, but also thwarts the legal certainty and predictability that is essential to its workings.

Blank Cheque?

Another way to examine this situation is to ask whether section 33 gives governments a constitutional "blank cheque." The answer to this question may be the gap or uncertainty that needs to be filled in the written text of the Constitution, which requires us to resort to unwritten constitutional principles (*Toronto*, paras. 65–6).[11] Does section 33 permit the commission of atrocities? For example, can governments commit torture or genocide by simply ousting key sections of the Charter for a five-year period? If these examples seem extreme or even absurd, I would argue that this reaction reflects an intuitive understanding that such atrocities are not only politically unacceptable, they are legally impermissible. In other words, the Constitution contains an irreducible core of human rights. Section 33 must have limits, though this may not seem obvious from the text of the Constitution. The federal government has officially apologized for each of the three aforementioned historic episodes of violence and racism in Canada's past (CBC Archives 2018a, 2018b; Government of Canada News Release 2006), promising to do better in the future. Ideally, the day-to-day work of governments are themselves influenced by unwritten constitutional principles that shape political decision-making (MacDonnell 2019, 175). However, if section 33 is a blank cheque for governments, these promises and indeed the Constitution itself may become self-defeating.

---

10 Arguably, the Constitution was not silent on the changing of Canadian boundaries. The amending formulas contained in Part V of the Constitution Act, 1982 address this issue. Constitution Act, 1982, *supra* note 2, s 43(a).

11 *Toronto (City) v. Ontario (Attorney General)*, 2021 SCC 34, paras. 65–6.

Because unwritten constitutional principles give rise to substantive legal obligations, their legal force will limit government action. As former Chief Justice McLachlin noted: "the task of judges is to do justice. Judges who enforce unjust laws – laws that run counter to fundamental assumptions about ... [a] just society – lose their legitimacy." She was referring to the lesson of the Nuremberg Trials, but she went on to state that it is "also a lesson that should embolden judges when faced with seemingly more mundane manifestations of injustice" (McLachlin 2006, 159). While the situation of Muslim women and other religious minorities in Quebec is not identical to the historic racism noted above, it is nonetheless a clear and extreme case of injustice with damaging implications for minorities that must be corrected. If this situation is tolerated or even normalized, it could also lead to further departures from the human rights norms that Canadians have come to expect and rely upon. Courts must not be afraid to assume their role in protecting certain fundamental principles as essential even in the face of section 33.

This is particularly important given the rise of global populism in the very particular form of anti-Muslim racism. Canada has not been immune to this trend. It is dangerous to retain a provision that essentially permits governments to promote and sustain systemic Islamophobia. Until section 33 is repealed, courts must rely on unwritten constitutional principles to ensure that minimum guarantees of core human rights are protected. If our Constitution is the justice-seeking document that Canadians believe it to be, if we have learned anything from the abuses of the past, and if our Constitution is truly a "living tree" that grows and evolves, we cannot allow section 33 to move us backward.

WORKS CITED

Albert, Richard. 2008. "Advisory Review: The Reincarnation of the Notwithstanding Clause." *Alberta Law Review* 45, no. 4: 1037–69. https://doi.org/10.29173/alr314.

Ansell, Nicola. 2017. "Achieving Gender Parity in Education: Achievements and Limitations of Millennium Development Goal 3." In *Laboring and Learning*, edited by Tracey Skelton, Tatek Abebe, and Johanna Waters, 111. Singapore: Springer.

Bakht, Natasha. 2020. *In Your Face: Law, Justice and Niqab-Wearing Women in Canada*. Toronto: Irwin Law.

–. 2022. "Transnational Anti-Muslim Racism: Routes in Law." *Meridians: Feminism, Race, Transnationalism* 20, no. 2: 291–7. https://muse.jhu.edu /article/856875 .

–. Forthcoming. "The Surprisingly Positive Impact of Section 27 of the Charter." In *The Surprising Constitution*, edited by Howard Kislowicz, Kerri Froc, and Richard Moon. Vancouver: UBC Press.

Berger, Benjamin L. 2005. "Judicial Appointments and Our Changing Constitution," *The Lawyers' Weekly*. LexisNexis. 16 September 2005.

BBC News. 2021. "Canada: 751 Unmarked Graves Found at Residential School." 24 June 2021. https://www.bbc.com/news/world-us -canada-57592243.

CBC Archives. 2018a. "Government Apologizes for Residential Schools in 2008." CBC News. 25 June 2018. https://www.cbc.ca/archives /government-apologizes-for-residential-schools-in-2008-1.4666041.

–. 2018b. "Government of Canada Apologizes to Japanese Canadians in 1988." CBC News. 22 September 2018. https://www.cbc.ca/archives /government-apologizes-to-japanese-canadians-in-1988-1.4680546.

Chan, Arlene. 2016. "Chinese Head Tax in Canada." *The Canadian Encyclopedia*. 8 September 2016. https://www.thecanadianencyclopedia.ca/en/article /chinese-head-tax-in-canada.

Collins, Lynda Margaret. 2017. "Ecological Sustainability as an Unwritten Constitutional Principle: Why Canada Courts Should Recognize an Environmental UCP." University of Ottawa Centre for Environmental Law & Global Sustainability. https://papers.ssrn.com/sol3/papers .cfm?abstract_id=3061938.

Committee on the Elimination of Discrimination against Women (CEDAW). 2017. *General Recommendation No. 36 (2017) on the Rights of Girls and Women to Education*. CEDAW/C/GC/26, 2017.

Froc, Kerri A. 2019. "Shouting into the Constitutional Void: Section 28 and Bill 21." *Constitutional Forum* 28, no. 4. https://doi.org/10.21991/cf29391.

Government of Canada News Release. 2006. "Prime Minister Harper Offers Full Apology for the Chinese Head Tax." 22 June 2006. https://www .canada.ca/en/news/archive/2006/06/prime-minister-harper-offers -full-apology-chinese-head-tax.html.

Kestler-D'Amours, Jillian. 2021. "Four Years after Quebec Mosque Attack, a Promise 'Not to Forget.'" Al Jazeera. 29 January 2021. https://www .aljazeera.com/news/2021/1/29/wounds-remain-fresh-four-years -after-quebec-mosque-attack.

Kundnani, Arun. 2015. *The Muslims Are Coming! Islamophobia, Extremism, and the Domestic War on Terror*. London: Verso.

Leber, Ben. 2017. *Police-Reported Hate Crime in Canada, 2015*. Statistics Canada. 14 June 2017. https://www150.statcan.gc.ca/n1/pub/85-002-x/2017001 /article/14832-eng.htm.

MacDonnell, Vanessa A. 2019. "Rethinking the Invisible Constitution: How Unwritten Constitutional Principles Shape Political Decision-Making," *McGill Law Journal* 65, no. 2. https://doi.org/10.7202/1075515ar.

Mailey, Richard. 2019. "The Notwithstanding Clause and the New Populism." *Constitutional Forum* 28, no. 4: 9–18. https://doi.org/10.21991/cf29390.

Marsh, James H. 2012. "Japanese Canadian Internment: Prisoners in Their Own Country." *Canadian Encyclopedia*. 23 February 2012. https://www.thecanadianencyclopedia.ca/en/article/japanese-internment-banished-and-beyond-tears-feature.

Mason-Bish, Hannah, and Irene Zempi. 2018. "Misogyny, Racism and Islamophobia: Street Harassment at the Intersections." *Feminist Criminology* 14, no. 5: 540–59. https://doi.org/10.1177/1557085118772088.

McLachlin, Beverley. 2006. "Unwritten Constitutional Principles: What Is Going On?" *New Zealand Journal of Public and International Law* 4 no. 2. https://www.wgtn.ac.nz/public-law/publications/nz-journal-of-public-and-international-law/previous-issues/volume-4-issue-2-december-2006/mclachlin.pdf.

McLean, Jason, and Kerri Anne Froc. 2021. "Notwithstanding the Notwithstanding Clause, the Charter Is Everyone's Business." *The Conversation*. 26 July 2021. https://theconversation.com/ mnotwithstanding-the-notwithstanding-clause-the-charter-is-everyones-business-163143.

Mossaman, Mary Jane, Natasha Bakht, Vanessa Gruben, and Karen Pearlston. 2015. *Families and the Law: Cases and Commentary*. 2nd ed. Concord, ON: Captus Press.

Pertiz, Ingrid. 2014. "Anti-Islam Vandalism Stokes Concerns." *Globe and Mail*, 22 February 2014.

Somos, Christy. 2019. "Sikh Teacher Moves from Quebec to B.C. after Bill 21 Implemented." CTV News. 10 October 2019. https://www.ctvnews.ca/canada/sikh-teacher-moves-from-quebec-to-b-c-after-bill-21-implemented-1.4633830.

Steuter-Martin, Marilla. 2017. "Hate Crimes Targeting Muslims Doubled in 2017, Says Quebec City Police Chief." CBC News. 5 December 2017. www.cbc.ca/news/canada/montreal/quebec-city-hate-crimes-1.4434028.

Strauss, Cee. 2021. "Section 28's Potential to Guarantee Substantive Gender Equality in *Hak c Procureur général du Québec*." *Canadian Journal of Women and the Law* 33, no. 1: 84–115. https://doi.org/10.3138/cjwl.33.1.04.

Truth and Reconciliation Commission of Canada. 2015. *Final Report of the Truth and Reconciliation Commission of Canada*. Vol 1. Kingston: McGill-Queen's University Press.

12 Moving Muslim Money

ANVER M. EMON

Whether domestically or internationally, commercial banks such as the Bank of Montreal, Canadian Imperial Bank of Canada, and the Hong Kong and Shanghai Banking Corporation, as well as online payment systems such as PayPal, offer customers the opportunity to instantaneously move money across borders. This apparently frictionless movement of money stands in stark contrast to the friction that people experience in crossing borders. Canada has a whole federal agency – the Canada Border Security Agency (CBSA) – that enforces "more than 90 acts and regulations that keep our country and Canadians safe" from those who might enter Canada to cause harm (Government of Canada, n.d.a.). Visa requirements, passport controls, and customs declarations are just a few sources of friction to border crossing. Moreover, certain categories of people encounter more friction than others. In the United States, the Trump administration's so-called "Muslim Ban" applied to Muslims by reference to certain Muslim-majority states that purportedly presented security concerns. In Canada, refugees seeking safe haven from conflicts in Syria, Afghanistan, and Egypt encounter friction worldwide as border patrol agencies and policies subject them to a regime of suspicion.

When we juxtapose the movement of money and people across borders, our first impression is that, unlike people, money crosses without friction. But moving money across borders is not frictionless for everyone. Much depends on who is moving it, its destination, and how the private financial sector, conscripted into the War on Terror, flags funds using privately developed software algorithms that report "suspicious transactions" to federal agencies charged with combating money laundering and terrorism financing.

This essay is not interested in the best practices for monitoring the financial activities of criminal organizations. Instead, it explores the extent to which Canadian law and policy has conscripted the financial sector in the War on Terror, and thereby enabled – through private sector technology and innovation – inordinate, untransparent, and unaccountable surveillance on and economic friction for racialized peoples, in particular Muslim Canadians (Iafolla 2015). My interest in this issue stems in part from research I have conducted with Nadia Hasan that examines Canada Revenue Agency audits of Muslim-led charities (Emon and Hasan 2021). In our report, *Under Layered Suspicion* (2021), we show how the Government of Canada's policies on terrorism financing link 100 per cent of terrorism financing risk to groups that map onto Canada's racial and religious minorities. Within that risk portfolio, though, the Government of Canada associates 80 per cent of all terrorism financing risk in Canada specifically with groups that map onto Canada's Muslim communities. In other words, to the extent risk assessment for terrorism financing is speculative, predictive, and future-oriented, there is a disproportionate adverse focus on Muslims in Canada.

Canada's anti-terrorism financing regime, when examined alongside the Proceeds of Crime (Money Laundering) and Terrorist Financing Act (PCMLTFA, S.C. 2000, c. 17) and its regulations (e.g., SOR/2001-307), prompts questions about the ways private financial institutions are conscripted into Canada's War on Terror, with limited requirements of public disclosure and accountability. Under the PCMLTFA, Canada's financial institutions are required to report "suspicious transactions" to federal bodies. They are asked to use risk-based assessment models to identify such suspicious transactions. Given the anti-terrorism financing regime in Canada that is facially discriminatory against Muslim Canadians, this essay asks how private banks identify "suspicious transactions," what their risk-based assessment models look like, and the impact these models have on Muslim Canadians. More directly, how might these models engender the "debanking" of Muslims?

"In most countries ... banking is the most important part of the financial system," asserts one guide on preventing terrorist financing, written for bank supervisors. "It is key to facilitating domestic and international payments, it serves as the intermediary for depositors and borrowers, and it provides other financially related products and services" (Chatain et al. 2009, 7). It thus follows that exclusion from basic financial services like deposit accounts and electronic payment systems on risk-based metrics has the capacity to create an underclass of citizens who cannot effectively participate in and contribute to the marketplace. If someone is "debanked," they are not simply inconvenienced, they are blocked from making basic, everyday purchases at venues that increasingly no longer accept payment in hard currency.

Much of the existing literature on "unbanked" people focuses on lower-class citizens and the poor who cannot access banks in the first place (Johnston and Morduch 2008; Brown et al. 2013).[1] This essay suggests that another important avenue for research is considering the extent to which anti-terrorism financing policies contribute to private sector "debanking" of Muslim clients on potentially biased risk assessment models, many of which are hidden from democratic scrutiny behind privacy laws and intellectual property protections. There are various intersections between the "unbanked" and the "debanked" when we consider income levels, race, even geographic location. Both raise general concerns about fair and equal access to financial services. But in the case of moving Muslim money, it is worth distinguishing between the two in order to highlight and conceptually clarify the effect of the various epistemologies of anti-terrorism financing regimes on Muslims and their money. For the purpose of this essay, being debanked anticipates the private financial sector itself, which is subject to domestic banking regulations that in turn mark out and police otherwise capable, willing, and existing clients.

Media outlets report cases of conventional banks "debanking" Muslim clients on suspicious grounds. Citibank, for example, was sued for religiously discriminating against a Muslim woman seeking to open a bank account that named her husband as beneficiary (Budryk 2019). Online payment system Venmo was sued when a Muslim Bangladeshi woman tried to use the financial payment service to reimburse her friend for a meal they ate at Al-Aqsa Restaurant in New York. Venmo halted the transaction because the reference to "Al-Aqsa" flagged its security filter system. Al-Aqsa, an Arabic term (literally translating as "the farthest"), is the name of a revered mosque in Jerusalem; the incident suggests that Venmo's algorithms filter and flag transactions related to Islam and/or Arabic terms, in turn discriminating against Muslims (Pereira 2019). On 22 April 2020, US Representative Rashida Tlaib and three of her congressional colleagues sent a letter to three major US banks to denounce the biased practices of the financial services industry adverse to those "banking while Muslim." They wrote, "[w]e have noticed these *de-risking* practices disproportionately impact Muslim Americans and Muslim organizations and charities, despite the

---

1   To the extent banking institutions preclude the poor from accessing basic financial services on risk-assessment bases – and thus become described as the "unbanked" – scholarly analyses about inclusiveness and access reflect concerns about the exclusionary effect of private sector banks' risk-based metrics.

emphasis by U.S. regulators that such organizations should not be categorically treated as high risk" (Tlaib et al. 2020). These US examples are hardly exceptional (Menendez and Masto 2018).[2] Similar "debanking" practices have also been reported in the UK (Laurie 2014) and Canada. In 2007, the Royal Bank of Canada faced accusations of discrimination when it closed the US-dollar accounts of its customers with dual-citizenship to a handful of countries, many of which are Muslim majority (e.g., Iraq, Iran, and Sudan) (Grant and Dobrota 2007).

Yet to date, the empirical data and analysis on "debanking" in Canada is limited (Iafolla 2015). More robust research in this area is needed in the interest of maximizing both transparent democracy and market participation among willing and able consumers. Government and private sector surveillance of Muslim money within and beyond Canada's borders is hidden from view by private sector protections of privacy, confidentiality, and intellectual property. These mechanisms are structured through legislation and banking regulations, and centrally overseen by Canada's financial investigation unit, FINTRAC. Analysis should thus begin with FINTRAC and its viral effects on Canada's financial sector.

Financial Intelligence Units and Canada's FINTRAC

During the Regan era, the US War on Drugs led governments around the world to develop new mechanisms to undermine the production, distribution, and consumption of illicit drugs. One mechanism was to target the proceeds of drugs sales. By 1989, it was estimated that over $300 billion in drug proceeds were laundered through the conventional banking systems in Hong Kong, Europe, and the United States (Emon and Hasan 2021, 15). This use of the conventional banking system prompted the creation of the Financial Action Task Force (FATF) during the 1989 G7 meeting in Paris. It was thought that a multilateral organization would be well placed to create unified global standards to coordinate state action against the proliferation of the drug trade. The standards were designed to help states develop the best practices for domestic financial regulation to prevent the financial sector from laundering the proceeds of the illicit drug trade. Implicit in some of these

---

2   In fact, in 2018 US Senators Robert Menendez (NJ) and Catherine Cortez Masto (NV) sent a letter to Bank of America CEO Brian T. Moynihan over concerns that their risk assessment policies operated adversely against immigrants, which took shape concurrent with then President Trump's actions against the Deferred Action for Childhood Arrivals Program (DACA or Dreamers).

best-practice standards was a recognition that financial institutions were privy to data on financial transactions that could in turn be interpreted to identify risk-factors corresponding to money-management techniques used by drug cartels.

As a multilateral organization, FATF could only offer best practices and standards because states exercise exclusive jurisdiction over domestic law, including the regulation of their financial sectors and institutions (e.g., banks). If data running through financial institutions were to be interpreted, it would need to be done so either by the banks themselves, by domestic governmental agencies, or some combination of the two. States ultimately created domestic agencies tasked with financial investigation. The first Financial Investigation Units (FIUs) took shape in the 1990s and proliferated thereafter, coinciding with the War on Terror launched by the US after 11 September 2001 (Gleason and Gottselig 2004, ix).

According to the World Bank and International Monetary Fund (IMF), an FIU "is a central national agency responsible for receiving, analysing, and transmitting disclosures on suspicious transactions to the competent authorities" (Gleason and Gottselig 2004). These governmental agencies operate on the presumption that financial services corporations have vital data relevant to combating money laundering and terrorism financing. These public institutions assess relevant data from private financial institutions and coordinate data sharing with relevant domestic police agencies (ix). Central to the function of FIUs is close cooperation with private sector financial institutions. Most of the relevant data on "suspicious transactions" is held by these private financial institutions; there is thus a symbiotic relationship between banks and anti-terrorism law enforcement agencies of the state. The regulatory framework is a crucial link between the public and private sectors; it is the mechanism by which the government conscripts private financial institutions as foot soldiers in the War on Terror.

Canada's FIU is called Financial Transactions and Reports Analysis Centre, or more simply FINTRAC. FINTRAC reports to the minister of finance, who oversees the country's whole-of-government anti-terrorism financing regime. As the Government of Canada explains:

> FINTRAC was created in 2000 pursuant to the Proceeds of Crime (Money Laundering) Act (PCMLA). At the time of its creation, FINTRAC's mandate was to assist in the detection, prevention and deterrence of money laundering by analyzing and assessing financial transactions and other information and making disclosures to police related to money laundering (Government of Canada, n.d.b.).

But in December 2001, after the 11 September attacks, the Canadian Parliament amended the PCMLA, passing the Proceeds of Crime, Money Laundering, and Terrorist Financing Act (PCMLTFA). Under this new legislative regime, still currently in place, FINTRAC's expanded mandate includes terrorism financing – and thereby the regulation and oversight of financial sector compliance with anti-terrorism financing protocols. The PCMLTFA requires financial service providers to disclose "suspicious financial transactions and … cross-border movements of currency and monetary instruments" (PCMLTFA, s. 3). Financial service providers that fall under the ambit of FINTRAC's mandate include banks and payment service providers (e.g., PayPal), among others. Under section 7 of the PCMLTFA, these service providers are required to report to FINTRAC:

> every financial transaction that occurs or that is attempted in the course of their activities and respect of which there are reasonable grounds to suspect that
>
> (a)   the transaction is related to the commission or the attempted commission of a money laundering offence; or
> (b)   the transaction is related to the commission or the attempted commission of a terrorist activity financing offence. (PCMLTFA, s. 7)

Section 7 is the legislative equivalent of the World Bank's and IMF's "suspicious transaction" concerns. Each financial service institution is required to create "a program" to ensure its compliance under the PCMLTFA, which includes "policies and procedures" by which the financial service institution assesses in the ordinary course of business "the risk of a money laundering offence or a terrorist activity financing offense" (PCMLTFA, s. 9.6(1), 9.6(2)). Failure of any financial service organization to comply with these legislative requirements results in heavy fines. In the event a financial entity violates its section 7 reporting obligations, and is convicted of doing so, it is liable to a maximum fine of 2 million CAD and/or imprisonment for a maximum term of five years (PCMLTFA, s. 75(1)). If the committed violation came at the direction of an officer of a corporation, the PCMLTFA pierces the corporate veil and considers the individual officer a party to the offence (PCMLTFA, s. 78).

Since the PCMLTFA creates a series of obligations (and financial liabilities) on the private sector, FINTRAC offers financial institutions guidance on how to craft a compliance program, devise a risk-based assessment model, and assess its reporting needs. FINTRAC advises financial service organizations to know their clients, appreciate their geographic location and where they move their money relative to the presence of crime/terrorism, and consider the shifting risk patterns across different foreign jurisdictions. The agency also provides a standardized form – Suspicious Transaction Report – for institutions to complete as part of their reporting obligations on specific transactions (Government of Canada, n.d.b.). The form provides space for the reporting entity to explain why a transaction may have been suspicious. According to the Regulations to the PCMLTFA, a reporting financial entity is required to provide a "[d]etailed description of grounds to suspect that transaction or attempted transaction is related to commission or attempted commission of money laundering offence or terrorist activity financing offense" (PCMLTFA, Schedule 1 Part G). Moreover, where the financial institution believes the transaction relates to the interests of a terrorist group, it must also explain how it "came to know that property in question is owned or controlled by or on behalf of terrorist group of listed person" (PCMLTFA, Schedule 2 Part B).

The flip side of this guidance is that FINTRAC subjects financial institutions and their compliance mechanisms to periodic review (PCMLTFA, s. 62.1). These statutory and regulatory measures show that though the government does not prescribe a particular risk-based assessment model for financial institutions to follow, it nonetheless reviews, evaluates, and thereby knows the various metrics used by different financial institutions that report suspicious transactions related to terrorism financing.

In its formal guidance to financial entities, FINTRAC recognizes that while "[t]there is no standard risk assessment methodology," a financial entity will undertake, among other things, the following in designing its methodology of risk analysis:

- Consider and assess business risks, which includes – "products, services and delivery channels, geography, new developments and technologies, affiliates if applicable," and any other relevant matters.
- Consider and assess clients and business relationships "based on the products, services and delivery channels they use, on their geography, and on their characteristics and patterns of activity."
- For high-risk relationships, put in place "the prescribed special measures."
- High-risk measures are relevant in cases, for example, where the financial entity is connected to high-risk countries, such as those subject to

- The Special Economic Measures Act (SEMA)
- FATF's list of high-risk countries and non-cooperative jurisdictions
- UN Security Council Resolutions
- The Freezing Assets of Corrupt Foreign Officials Act sanctions (Government of Canada, n.d.b.)

The above regulatory demands are just a few features of Canada's basic training for its institutional draftees in the War on Terror.

Because of their access to data, private sector financial institutions help make possible and give full effect to Canada's anti-terrorism financing regime. But this public-private collaboration in the War on Terror presents serious challenges that future research must undertake in the service of Canadian commitments to democratic accountability, equality, and anti-racism, including efforts to combat systemic Islamophobia.

Research Challenges

Economically, the ordinary cost of doing business is now higher given statutory compliance requirements and the schedule of fines in the event of failure (Standing Committee on Finance 2018).[3] Financial institutions must assess these costs in light of their duties to shareholders and profit maximization metrics. As they design their risk-based assessment metrics, it is reasonable to assume that they will prioritize profit maximization and share-holder interests over the liberties and rights of ordinary Canadians. It is likely their compliance measures will be over-inclusive out of an abundance of caution, in light of the statutory scheme of criminal fines and penalties. Cost-based analyses may indicate that over-inclusive measures that result in "debanking" a limited number of clients is less expensive than the statutory fines outlined in the PCMLTFA. Moreover, we can reasonably foresee that their compliance programs will enable existing governmental (and other such metrics) of anti-terrorism financing, which currently facially discriminate against racial and religious minorities, in particular Muslim Canadians.

The number of transactions a financial institution processes on a daily basis is exceedingly large, especially when we include electronic

---

3 Indeed, various Canadian financial entities complained to Canada's House of Commons about these costs, especially when borne by financial institutions and services that posed little risk of money laundering or terrorism financing.

transfer payment services banks increasingly provide. To review these transactions for purposes of PCMLTFA compliance, financial institutions implement computerized algorithms to flag reportable transactions. Indeed, one of Canada's largest banks, CIBC, hosts an Enterprise Anti-Money Laundering group, which is made up of specialists who use "analytics" and "innovative technologies" to address money laundering and terrorist financing (CIBC, n.d.). Software such as FinScan and ComplyAdvantage promise banks and other financial institutional customers "AI [artificial intelligence] solutions [that] enable suspicious entities and activities to be identified in real time. You can onboard faster, cut your costs, and reduce your risk exposure" (Comply Advantage, n.d.). But while these software packages aim to reduce the cost of compliance to banks and other financial service providers, they raise the possibility of discrimination against groups of consumers who are already subject to over-determinative policing and surveillance logics.

There is abundant literature suggesting that algorithms designed to manage information employ discriminatory metrics on racial and religious grounds, employing what Safiya Umoja Noble terms "technological redlining" (Noble 2018; Eubanks 2018). As analysts of big data and policing suggest, data-driven modes of risk assessment and surveillance have the potential to reproduce and scale up already existing social inequalities (Brayne 2017). Canadian financial institutions are certainly subject to laws and regulations against racial or religious discrimination. However, that does not change the fact that the relevant financial intelligence software is the intellectual property of financial institutions or third-party vendors and thereby shielded from public disclosure requirements. The evidence that might be used to file a claim of discrimination against financial institutions is itself protected by the very legal system that aims to combat discrimination.

In light of the economic incentives that enable discriminatory compliance, and the embedded bias already documented in information management software, FINTRAC would have a complex obligation to Canada, were it to undertake an equity-based review of the underlying technology used to identify suspect transactions. On the one hand, it needs to protect the financial sector from being used to launder the proceeds of crime and to financially support terrorist activities. On the other hand, economic incentives and biases in technology enable overbroad compliance measures that are potentially discriminatory. If FINTRAC were to integrate equity-oriented consumer protection within its mandate, it would have to undertake compliance review processes that also protect ordinary Canadians from violations of their liberties and freedoms as enshrined in the Charter and relevant human rights legislation. But FINTRAC's openly accessible publications or reports do not indicate that it is cognizant of this discriminatory potential in its regulatory mandate. Its publications presume an audience that is comprised of those already committed to or obligated under the PCM-LTFA and its regulatory regimes. While FINTRAC ensures that it takes privacy seriously (Government of Canada, n.d.b.),[4] it does not address how it preserves the equality interests of ordinary Canadians as it oversees financial institutions and their compliance measures, many of which can lead institutions to "debank" individual clients on potentially discriminatory grounds.

Conclusion

Because the Government of Canada insists that there is no strict method for financial institutions to assess risk, it insures itself against accusations that its anti-money laundering and anti-terrorism financing regime enables systemic biases within the private sector. Moreover, financial institutions and third-party vendors can invoke intellectual property rights to protect their programs from scrutiny even as they are conscripted into the government's War on Terror by virtue of legislation with costly sanctions. In the end, we are left with a financial investigative regime that is effectively immune from accountability. Our financial institutions are both service providers and soldiers, leaving consumers vulnerable to market exclusion in the name of the Wars on Terror and Drugs. In the financial field of battle, Canada's financial institutions use compliance protocols like army field manuals that vary from institution to institution but are undisclosed to the very public at risk of being collateral damage.

This essay raises critical concerns about Canada's conscription of its financial sector into the Wars on Terror and Drugs in the service of core principles of equality, inclusion, and democratic accountability. In doing so, this essay runs against a dominant current of literature written in service of the state and the financial sector conscripted to fight the War on Terror. Canada's financial intelligence regime contributes to a business of privatized national security, which arguably disincentivizes critical enquiry into its discriminatory impact. To support financial institutions in fulfilling their statutory requirements, third-party businesses now offer compliance services for banks. Consulting firms like Protivity provide risk analysis and compliance for financial service providers

---

4   See its privacy policy: https://www.fintrac-canafe.gc.ca/atip-aiprp/2011-pp-eng.

working in an increasingly complex regulatory environment. Protivity's staff includes former financial institution regulators and compliance officers, and its services promise clients effective compliance programs (Houston, n.d.). Anti-terrorism financing regimes ultimately produce their own economies that make critique of such regimes, let alone critically informed policy reversals, costly to private economic actors and the national economy as a whole. Any future researcher needs to enter this field of study fully aware of this current and its momentum.

Future researchers eager to gain insight into the private sector operation of anti-terrorism financing will need to identify anti-money laundering units within Canada's banks, for instance, and interview willing senior analysts and managers charged with upholding the bank's compliance programs. Computer scientists might deploy a critical race enquiry into the software used to service a bank's anti-money laundering and anti-terrorism financing program. Scholars of law, business, and the financial sector could conduct a series of Access to Information Program requests of government agencies to secure necessary documentation and records to identify the role of private sector institutions in the War on Terror and the metrics they use to identify suspect transactions and customers. The fact that securing such information will be a challenge attests to the democratic *un*accountability of Canada's national security strategies.

WORKS CITED

Brayne, Sarah. 2017. "Big Data Surveillance: The Case of Policing." *American Sociological Review* 82, no. 5: 977–1008. https://doi.org/10.1177/0003122417725865.

Brown, Ed, Francisco Castañeda, Jonathon Cloke, and Peter Taylor. 2013. "Towards Financial Geographies of the Unbanked: International Financial Markets, 'Bancarizacion' and Access to Financial Services in Latin America." *Geographical Journal* 179, no. 3: 198–210. https://doi.org/10.1111/geoj.12000.

Budryck, Zack. 2019. "Muslim Group Alleges Religious Discrimination by Citibank." The Hill. 23 June 2019. https://thehill.com/blogs/blog-briefing-room/news/454374-muslim-group-alleges-religious-discrimination-by-citibank.

Chatain, Pierre-Laurent, John McDowell, Cédric Mousset, Paul Allan Schott, and Emile van der Does de Willebois. 2009. *Preventing Money Laundering and Terrorism Financing: A Practical Guide for Bank Supervisors.* Washington, DC: World Bank. http://hdl.handle.net/10986/2638.

CIBC. n.d. "CIBC's AML/ATF and Sanctions Regime." Legal. Accessed 2 January 2022. https://www.cibc.com/en/legal/anti-money-laundering .html.

Comply Advantage. n.d. "Accelerate Onboarding While Reducing Risks." AML Banks. Accessed 26 March 2022. https://complyadvantage.com/aml -banks/.

Emon, Anver M., and Nadia Z. Hasan. 2021. *Under Layered Suspicion: A Review of CRA Audits of Muslim-Led Charities*. Toronto: Institute of Islamic Studies. www.layeredsuspicion.ca

Eubanks, Virginia. 2018. *Automating Inequality: How High-Tech Tools Profile, Police, and Punish the Poor*. New York: St. Martin's Press.

Gleason, Paul, and Glenn Gottselig. 2004. "Financial Intelligence Units: An Overview." International Monetary Fund. 17 June 2004. https://www.imf .org/en/Publications/Manuals-Guides/Issues/2016/12/30/Financial -Intelligence-Units-An-Overview-17369.

Government of Canada. n.d.a. "Canada Border Services Agency." Accessed 26 March 2022. https://www.cbsa-asfc.gc.ca/menu-eng.html.

–. n.d.b. "FINTRAC." Accessed 26 March 2022. https://www.fintrac-canafe .gc.ca/atip-aiprp/infosource-eng.

Grant, Tavia, and Alex Dobrota. 2007. "RBC Closed U.S.-Dollar Accounts for Dual Citizens." *Globe and Mail*, 17 January 2007. https://www .theglobeandmail.com/news/national/rbc-closed-us-dollar-accounts-for -dual-citizens/article17989434/.

Houston, Roger Z. n.d. "Anti-Money Laundering (AML) Compliance." Proviti. Accessed 26 March 2022. https://www.protiviti.com/CA-en /risk-and-compliance/anti-money-laundering-compliance.

Iafolla, Vanessa. 2015. "Anti-Money Laundering and Counter-Terrorist Financing Policy in Canada: Origins, Implementation, and Enforcement." PhD diss., University of Toronto.

Johnston, Don, and Jonathan Morduch. 2008. "The Unbanked: Evidence from Indonesia." *World Bank Economic Review* 22, no. 3: 517–37. https://doi.org /10.1093/wber/lhn016.

Laurie, Dominic. 2014. "HSCBC Closes Some Muslim Groups' Accounts." BBC News. 30 July 2014. https://www.bbc.com/news/business-28553921.

Menendez, Bob, and Cortez Masto. 2018. "Menendez and Cortez Masto to Moynihan." Bob Menendez United States Senator for New Jersey. 1 October 2018. https://www.menendez.senate.gov/imo/media/doc/Letter%20 to%20Bank%20of%20America.pdf.

Noble, Safiya Umoja. 2018. *Algorithms of Oppression: How Search Engines Reinforce Racism*. New York: New York University Press.

Pereira, Sydney. 2019. "Brooklyn Woman Accuses Venmo of 'Singling out Muslims' When Blocking Transactions." Gothamist. 24 December 2019.

https://gothamist.com/food/brooklyn-woman-accuses-venmo-singling
-out-muslims-when-blocking-transactions.

Proceeds of Crime (Money Laundering) and Terrorist Financing, Suspicious
Transaction Regulations SOR/2001–317.

Standing Committee on Finance. 2018. *Confronting Money Laundering and
Terrorist Financing: Moving Canada Forward*. 42nd Parliament, 1st Session.
November 2018. https://www.ourcommons.ca/Content/Committee/421
/FINA/Reports/RP10170742/finarp24/finarp24-e.pdf.

Tlaib, Rashida, Joyce Beatty, Emanuel Cleaver II, and Ilhan Omar. 2020.
"Letter to Jamie Dimon, Brian Moynihan, and Charles Scharf." 22 April
2020. https://cleaver.house.gov/sites/evo-subsites/cleaver-evo.house
.gov/files/Final_BWM_Banks.pdf.

Policing and the Law

13 The Need to Better Understand the Over-Policing and Under-Protection of Muslims

KENT ROACH

1. Introduction

The simultaneous over-policing and under-protection of Indigenous people in Canada has been apparent since the early 1990s. Similar findings also apply to Black, LGBTQ2S, the unhoused, those with live with mental health issues and other marginalized communities. At first glance, the fact that disadvantaged groups are both over-policed and under-protected[1] may seem paradoxical. Nevertheless, they are united by stereotypes that see members of the groups as associated with crime and danger and ultimately as less worthy of protection from both state and private actors (Roach 2022, chap. 3). All marginalized groups are subject to domination and fear of domination from both state and private actors. They are ultimately less free and equal (Braithwaite 2022).

This chapter will first briefly explain how Indigenous people are both over-policed and under-protected. The next part will examine the evidence in the public domain that supports the hypothesis that Muslims in Canada are similarly over-policed and under-protected. Over-policing of Muslims has resulted in the targeting of the innocent by national security actors. This has resulted in the abuse of human rights, both in Canada and abroad. Under-protection has resulted in hate crime and terrorism targeting Muslims. This has produced 25 deaths in Canada

---

1 I use the word "under-protected" as opposed to the more familiar term of under-policing because of increased recognition that some of the tasks done by the police may be done with less violence, more expertise, and perhaps less discrimination by other public agencies or community groups. See Roach (2022, chap. 7).

since 2014 compared to at most five acts of terrorism motivated by al Qaeda and Daesh since 2001.[2]

The final part of this chapter will examine areas and strategies for additional research about the over-policing and under-protection of Muslims. Understanding over-policing and under-protection can contribute to better understanding of systemic discrimination in general and Islamophobia in particular which involves the interaction of discriminatory conduct by public and private actors (Beydoun 2016, 111; Bahdi and Kanji 2018). The relevant private actors here include those who commit hate crimes and terrorism targeting Muslims, most notably violent far-right extremists.

Additional research can help explain dilemmas facing Muslim communities in Canada who may have been pushed away from the state by post 9/11 human rights abuses and the stereotyped targeting of Muslims as potential terrorists, but who now may be pulled towards the state by the fear of hate crime and terrorism directed against them. Such research will help explore how Muslim communities, like Indigenous, Black, and other marginalized communities, are influenced by an unjust historical legacy of policing as personified by highly publicized cases such as those of Maher Arar and others who were wrongly detained as terrorists and tortured in part on the basis of inaccurate intelligence supplied by Canadian officials. Additional research should also employ an intersectional lens to examine particular concerns that may apply to Muslim women, sexual minorities, recent migrants, and others in Canada's diverse Muslim communities (Sinno 2009).

Further research can contribute to a better understanding of the experiences and treatment of Canada's diverse Muslim communities and make up for the fact that crime statistics in Canada have not recorded religious and ethnic identity. It can also enrich understandings of Canada's security responses over time which appear to have discounted the danger of far-right violence targeting Muslims, Jews, and racialized groups.

Research can also create an evidence base for reforms. It is not clear that the answer to the systemic inequalities and double standards

---

2 The far-right attacks include those in Moncton (3 deaths), Quebec City (6 deaths), the Toronto van (11 deaths) and massage parlour attacks (1 death) and the London, Ontario attacks compared to the two deaths in 2014 in Ottawa and Saint-Jean-sur-Richelieu, two deaths in the Toronto Danforth shooting and a 2020 deadly hammer attack in Toronto. It could be argued that more plots motivated by al Qaeda and Daesh have been disrupted, but this only supports a thesis that terrorism law has been used as a form of "enemy criminal law" that have primarily targeted Muslims. See Roach (2021) and Canadian Network for Research on Terrorism, Security and Society (n.d.).

revealed by the over-policing and under-protection of Muslims is simply to increase the use of hate speech and terrorism prosecutions to apply more equitably to those who target Muslims. This is especially so because increased state powers will be used by security actors in a broader context of systemic discrimination and Islamophobia. For example, recent attempts under the *Emergencies Act*[3] to extend terrorism financing laws to apply to the far-right leaders of the "Freedom Convoy" have the potential to result in expanded laws that will be administered in a system of institutional Islamophobia. (Emon and Hasan 2021; McSorley 2021). Thus, even measures designed to target far-right extremists could be applied and enforced in a manner that harms Muslims and other marginalized groups. This suggests that reforms designed to stop the over-policing of Muslims may also be necessary to address the under-protection of Muslims.

2. Over-Policing and Under-Protection of Indigenous People

The over-policing/under-protection thesis was first developed by researchers examining the treatment of Indigenous peoples by the Canadian state. In its 1991 report, the Aboriginal Justice Inquiry of Manitoba focused on the killing of an Indigenous man, J.J. Harper, by the Winnipeg police and the decade of delay by the RCMP in laying charges against two of four white men who participated in the abduction and sexual assault of an Indigenous woman, Helen Betty Osborne (Manitoba 1991). In the same year, researchers found a similar pattern of over-policing of the James Bay Cree for minor public disorder crimes combined with a frequent failure to lay domestic violence charges. These researchers also noted this was similar to research into the circumstances faced by the urban Black population in the United States (Brodeur, La Prairie, and McDonnell 1991, 17). Both 1991 reports recommended increased Indigenous control over policing and the justice system as the main remedy for the combination of over-policing and under-protection they documented.

An enquiry into the police investigation that eventually led to the arrest and conviction of serial murderer Robert Pickton found a failure of the police to take an Indigenous-specific approach to investigating the disappearances of many Indigenous victims. A recent national enquiry into missing and murdered Indigenous women and children

---

3   RSC 1985 c. 22 (4th supp) and PC Order in Council 2022 – 0106 (14 February 2022) at https://orders-in-council.canada.ca/attachment.php?attach=41560&lang=en.

found that poor relations between the police and Indigenous people and the police's lack of understanding and use of stereotypes contributed to high but unknown numbers of missing and murdered Indigenous women and children (Missing and Murdered Indigenous Women and Girls Inquiry 2019).

Law enforcement continues to police Indigenous people in a manner that produces prison populations that are about 30 per cent Indigenous. CBC News's "Deadly Force Database" shows that from 2000 to 2020, 89 of the 555 people who died in deadly encounters with the Canadian police were Indigenous.

This database does not record religious identity. It does identify twelve people who died as "South Asian – East Indian, Pakistani, Sri Lankan." They include Ejaz Choudhry, a sixty-two-year-old man who did not speak English and was shot in 2020 during a wellness check by Peel police when he would not drop a knife. It also identifies forty-eight deceased as Black (Singh 2020). They include Abdirahman Abdi, a Somalian Canadian, killed by an Ottawa police officer who was subsequently acquitted of manslaughter, aggravated assault and assault with a weapon in late 2020. The Ottawa police subsequently settled a lawsuit brought by the Abdi family for an undisclosed amount. They also arrested and charged with mischief twelve people who tried to block an intersection in protest of the 2021 acquittal of the police officer charged with manslaughter in relation to Abdi's death (Roach 2022, chap. 5).

3. The Public Record of the Over-Policing and Under-Protection of Muslims

Over-Policing and High Policing

Muslim organizations in Canada feared over-policing in the wake of the 9/11 terrorist attacks. They were part of a successful lobby that placed a 5-year sunset on new police powers of preventive arrests and investigative hearings (Roach 2003, 25–74). They failed to secure an anti-discrimination clause despite the fact that Liberal backbencher and human rights lawyer Irwin Cotler was among its champions. To its credit, the 2001 Anti-Terrorism Act (ATA) recognized connections between hate and terrorism and included innovative but under-used provisions to allow hate speech, including that which vilified Muslims, to be taken off the Internet under judicial order. These powers have not yet been used leaving the policing of hate speech on the Internet to the private sector (Roach 2021).

Although Muslim groups and civil liberties groups focused on the ATA, much of the post 9/11 over-policing was, as is typical of high policing, conducted in secret. Even before 9/11, the Canadian state had been playing catch up after Ahmed Ressam was apprehended by American officials in 1999 when he was entering the United States from Canada with plans to bomb Los Angeles International Airport as part of the al Qaeda Millennium attack plots.

Mohamedu Slahi, famous for the book and movie *The Mauritanian*, attempted without success to obtain the information that Canadian officials passed on to the United States after investigating his attendance at the same Montreal mosque as Ressam. The courts made a questionable ruling that Slahi could not obtain such information because he was not a Canadian citizen.[4] This followed concerns that Muslim non-citizens were targeted in Canada in a way that would not have been accepted with respect to Canadian citizens. There are concerns that, as in the cases of Maher Arar, Abdullah Almalki, Ahmad Abou-Elmaati, and Muayyed Nureddin, Canadian officials may have passed on inaccurate intelligence based on guilt by association and stereotypes that may have played a role in Slahi's fourteen years of detention at Guantanamo Bay before being released. The Arar, Slahi, Almaki, Abou-Elmaati, and Nureddin cases all brutally illustrate a direct connection between over-policing, based on unverified suspicions of Muslims as terrorists, and under-protection, as all were tortured by foreign state officials.

The day after 9/11, an Algerian refugee applicant to Canada, Benamar Benatta, was taken across the Rainbow Bridge by Canadian officials and given to American officials where he was held for 1,780 days despite being cleared of involvement in terrorism. He later sued Canadian officials and settled for an undisclosed sum. He explained "this is racial profiling at its worst. These Canadian officials ruined my life without a second thought" (Bronskill 2015).

The Canadian Security Intelligence Service (CSIS) detained and rendered a terrorist suspect, Mohammed Jabarah, into American custody. Another Canadian, Liban Hussein, was listed by the US, Canada, and the UN as a terrorist financier on the basis of inaccurate intelligence. It took a court injunction to grant a passport to allow Abousfian Abdelrazick to travel back to Canada from Sudan after he was listed by the US and UN as a terrorist financier, before such listings were withdrawn (Forcese and Roach 2010, 253–8). This also suggests that future research should critically examine intelligence practices including the

---

4 *Slahi v. Canada (Justice)*, 2009 FCA 259 leave to appeal denied 2010 CanLII 7376 (SCC).

dangers of guilt by association and the role of bias and stereotypes; it should also explore why such a preventive intelligence mindset has not been applied in Canada to white, far-right, and Christian extremists. Evidence before the Public Order Emergency Commission revealed that CSIS did not think that the Truckers Convoy was a threat to national security and that collection of intelligence on the occupation was offloaded onto the police, who are subject to less regulation than CSIS when they collect intelligence.

It is important to situate Islamophobia in a geopolitical context. A desire to please the American government contributed to most of the above abuses. Canada is a net importer of intelligence and relies on the United States with respect to security and trade. Future research could also examine how arguments based on Canada's security, foreign policy, and economic needs can also be influenced by bias and stereotypes.

Over-policing of Muslims has continued since the initial response to 9/11. The RCMP paid over $1 million in overtime to 150 Mounties in a five-month 2013 anti-terrorism sting of John Nuttall and Amanda Korody, who were recent converts to Islam and recovering heroin addicts (Merali 2018). The RCMP persisted despite warnings from lawyers about a "police generated crime" and that "you have a person who can do nothing without the assistance of the police."[5] The courts rejected the prosecution on much the same basis. Why did the police proceed as they did in the face of legal advice? How might stereotypes have enforced their tunnel vision in this case?

Under-Protection

Although the 1985 Air India bombings did not target Muslims, a 2010 commission of enquiry found that Canadian security officials did not devote sufficient resources to terrorism inspired by foreign events. Despite specific intelligence, Canada failed to prevent the planting of a bomb on the one Air India airplane that left Canada every week. Poor treatment of potential witnesses in the Indo-Canadian community contributed to failed prosecutions. The result was that only one person in a murderous

---

5   *R. v. Nuttall* 2016 BCSC 1404 at para 355 aff'd 2018 BCCA 479 at 440. This case found that while police had reasonable suspicions and that a reasonable person would not have committed a crime, that "the police went far beyond investigating a crime. They pushed and pushed and pushed the two defendants to come up with a workable plan. The police did everything necessary to facilitate the plan. I can find no fault with the trial judge's conclusion that the police manufactured the crime that was committed and were the primary actors in its commission."

conspiracy was convicted of manslaughter in relation to Canada's largest mass murder of 331 people. Research into Islamophobia must be alert to the intersection of religious and racial prejudice and implicit understandings of who is a citizen and who matters in Canadian society.

In 2002, the Canadian Islamic Congress reported 170 hate crimes against Muslims, a 1,500 per cent increase from the 11 hate crimes reported in 2000. In 2017, after the Quebec City mosque shooting and divisive debates over a parliamentary motion to denounce Islamophobia, hate crimes against Muslims reported to the police spiked at 349 incidents before decreasing to less than 100 in 2020 (Boynton 2021). This supports Braithwaite's concept that crime occurs in cascades (Braithwaite 2022, chap. 11). It also supports the idea that strong symbolic and practical state action may prevent such harmful cascades.

In 2015, then Justice Minister Peter Mackay explained a failure to lay terrorism charges against neo-Nazis who planned an armed attack on a Halifax mall as "not culturally motivated, therefore not linked to terrorism," a statement also echoed by the RCMP (Fitz-Morris 2015). Both Mackay and the RCMP's statements were legally incorrect because culture is not part of the Canadian definition of terrorism. Nevertheless, both statements echoed the infamous Zero Tolerance for Barbaric Cultural Practices Act (S.C. 2015 c. 29). The law made non-citizens inadmissible if they practised polygamy, criminalized various acts related to marriages of people under sixteen years of age, and restricted the defence of provocation to ensure that racial or religious slurs alone could not constitute provocation reducing murder to manslaughter. Some Muslim Canadians took Justice Minister Mackay's statement as coded language for "they weren't Muslims so thus not terrorism" (Forcese and Roach 2015, 281).

On 29 January 2017 a twenty-nine-year-old white man entered a Quebec City mosque with a semi-automatic rifle and a Glock pistol. A pig's head had been left at the mosque the year before during Ramadan. The man killed six men who were worshipping and critically injured another five within two minutes. He was an avid follower of white supremacists and was motivated by Canada's acceptance of migrants from Muslim majority countries that were the subject of the Trump ban. He was charged with first-degree murder but not under a provision added to the Criminal Code as part of the 2001 ATA, which allowed first-degree murder charges on the basis of a terrorist activity. He pled guilty to the six counts of first-degree murder and six counts of attempted murder. He told the court, "I am not a terrorist, I am not an Islamophobe" (BBC News 2020). Despite a Criminal Code provision that would have made him ineligible for parole for 150 years based on the six murder victims, he was made eligible for parole in 40 years, later lowered to 25 years by the Supreme Court of Canada (*R. v. Bissonnette*, 2022 SCC 23). Hate crimes against Muslims reported to the police tripled in 2017 (Statistics Canada 2018) again suggesting that the unspeakable massacre enabled a cascade of less serious but similarly Islamophobic crimes.

In late 2017, the Quebec legislature enacted a law prohibiting public servants from wearing religious symbols, with a stricter law being enacted notwithstanding Charter rights in 2019. A spokesperson for the Quebec City mosque where the massacre occurred commented: "Everything the public has given us: empathy, kindness, recognition, the government has taken back" (Scott 2021). This is in contrast to the enactment of a controversial and tough terrorism law enacted in 2015, in response to the killing of two members of the Canadian Armed Forces by terrorists motivated by Daesh (also known as ISIS). Unlike in New Zealand after the Christchurch massacre, increased gun control measures were not fast-tracked.

On 6 June 2021, a twenty-year-old white man motivated by anti-Muslim hatred and wearing swastikas used his pickup truck to attack a Muslim family, killing four and injuring a nine-year-old in London, Ontario. The RCMP's curt press release still characterized the killings as a "vehicle attack" and not a terrorist attack (RCMP 2021). This was in sharp contrast to the highly publicized press conferences held in June 2006 shortly after the arrest of the Toronto 18.[6] Unlike in the Quebec City case, federal prosecutors intervened a few days after initial charges to add terrorism charges. This was symbolic but symbols can be important.

In both the Quebec and London massacres, the perpetrators surrendered to the police and were apparently not on the radars of intelligence agencies. Studies also suggest that terrorism charges designed to prevent terrorism before it happens have never been laid in Canada since their post 9/11 enactment. In many cases in which terrorism charges punishable by ten years in prison or more were a possibility, less serious hate propaganda offences punishable by up to two years imprisonment have been laid instead (Nesbitt 2021).

As with the Quebec City attack, there was increased reporting of other hate attacks after the London attacks. For example, a Black Muslim woman was attacked in Edmonton after the London, Ontario attacks and had to be hospitalized overnight (Lachacz 2021). Two women wearing hijabs in St. Albert, Alberta were attacked by a masked man with a

---

6 For reflections on these prosecutions including their relation to Islamophobia see Nesbitt, Roach, and Hofmann (2021).

knife with one of them rendered unconscious (CBC News 2021). This follows what scholars have noted as the dialectic or interactive nature of Islamophobia in which some acts of public or private discrimination or attacks against Muslims may serve as a form of social licence or implicit approval for other such acts (Beydoun 2016, 111; Bahdi and Kanji 2018).

The cascade of crimes against Muslims was not also counteracted with state expressions of support or solidarity. For example, the Toronto police who were guarding a mosque arrested and charged two men threatening the mosque with breaking and entering, threatening death, and mischief to property. The police claimed there was no evidence of hate motivation, even though those at the mosque reported threats to blow up the building and shoot individuals (Woodward 2021). A similar approach appears to have been taken with first-degree murder charges against a man who reported neo-Nazi ties and who is alleged to have killed a caretaker at a Toronto mosque in 2020 (Canadian Press 2020).

Canada First, a far-right group formed after Canada listed the Proud Boys as a terrorist group, condemned "white" politicians as "traitors to their people" for calling the London attack terrorism or a hate crime. They stated on a page with images of Hitler:

The Muslims have been committing terrorist attacks on western nations for a long time now, including using vehicles such as rental trucks and vans. When they do it, our treasonous politicians call it a mental health problem, when even a blind man can see it's a terrorist attack … When one of these Muslim swine kills our people they instantly say "it's too soon to tell what the motive is," then two weeks to one month later they say, "it wasn't motivated by hate or terrorism, it's a mental health crisis." (Canadian Anti-Hate Network 2021, para. 18–20)

As seen in the above post, hateful attempts are made to justify crime against Muslims as a form of vigilante retaliation to acts of terrorism committed by some who may be inspired by al Qaeda or Daesh. This post also demonstrates the impact of social media disinformation as it falsely suggests that violent extremists are seen as having mental health problems whereas those motivated by far-right ideologies actually seem more likely to be so diagnosed. In any event, the links between over-policing and under-protection of Canadian Muslims seem to be rooted in stereotypes that associate Muslims with terrorism.[7]

---

7 One reaction to being under-protected by public officials is taking self-protective measures. This was a factor in the so-called "Freedom" occupation of Ottawa where private litigants obtained injunctions against honking, got freezing orders for assets,

In my view, the public evidence discussed above makes a strong prima facie case that Muslims in Canada suffer from both over-policing and under-protection as are other sometimes intersecting marginalized and disadvantaged groups.

4. Strategies for Additional Research

The connected phenomena of the over-policing and under-protection of Muslims provides a fertile context for research from a range of disciplines including criminology, law, politics, religion, sociology, and security studies.

Towards Better Understandings of Systemic Discrimination and Islamophobia

Additional research could enrich our understanding of Islamophobia as a complex form of systemic discrimination. It would provide an excellent context in which to examine how Islamophobia is "dialectic" in the sense that "state policies targeting Muslims endorse prevailing stereotypes and, in turn, embolden private animus toward Muslim subjects" (Beydoun 2016, 111; Bahdi and Kanji 2018). In the case of under-protection, the "private animus" goes beyond private acts of discrimination and includes hate crimes and terrorism or politically motivated violence. Such research should also integrate criminological research into crime cascades (Braithwaite 2022).

Research should explore the attitudes and preconceptions of security officials and study control groups of Muslims that work or have worked within these agencies. CSIS has settled lawsuits that have claimed that their Muslim employees have suffered discrimination, though typically with non-disclosure agreements.

Research should also be sensitive to the possibility of change over time. Given that at least twenty-five people have been killed in Canada by the far right and the February 2022 declaration of an emergency, researchers should examine whether Canadian police and security officials now have different attitudes and behaviour about far-right violent

---

and started a class action against the occupiers in part because of their perception that the police were slow to act. Somewhat similarly, there has been a series of defamation actions brought by Muslims to combat alleged falsehoods and hate speech (*Paramount Fine Foods v. Johnston*, 2021 ONSC 6558; *Soliman v. Bordman*, 2021 ONSC 7023). There is a need to examine the effectiveness and costs of private as opposed to public protection.

extremism than they have had in the past. Such research should also be attentive to differences in attitudes and approaches among leaders and the rank and file of security institutions.

Towards Better Understandings of the Interaction of Private and Public Discrimination

There should be comparative research on the extent to which Muslims in Canada suffer from over-policing and under-protection compared to Indigenous, Black, and other marginalized groups. Recent reports have referred to over-policing and under-protection as a connected "vicious circle" (Epstein 2021; Roach 2022) driven by the police's lack of under-standing of the group and distrust among the targeted communities. The accuracy of these conclusions and linkages should be examined by other researchers. Such research should be attentive to the intersecting nature of such disadvantaged groups and the prospect for strategic alliances to mobilize media and political attention.

Research comparing the systemic discrimination suffered by Muslims and other groups would also allow researchers to explore the extent to which socio-economic status as compared to discriminatory stereotypes and hate contribute to the problem, given that Muslims in Canada generally have high levels of income and education (Sinno 2009).

Towards Better Understanding of the Experiences of Canada's Diverse Muslim Communities

Focused interviews within Muslim communities should be under-taken to better understand how over-policing and under-protection is experienced. Care should be taken to respect the diversity of Canada's Muslim population and compare any differences that could emerge by age, gender, sect, and region. Such interviews should also include victimization studies and examine why Muslims as compared to other groups may not report hate crimes to the police. Without such research, police-reported hate crimes cannot be placed into their proper context, and barriers that could be reduced for reporting may not be examined.

There should also be research into the memory (or lack thereof) about past acts of over-policing and under-protection. To what extent do well-publicized acts such as the targeting of Maher Arar or the highly publicized press conference held after the initial arrest of the Toronto 18 in 2006 still influence attitudes (Nesbitt, Roach, and Hoffman 2021)? To what extent do public apologies and the settlement of lawsuits by Muslims such as Mr. Arar ease concerns about over-policing? How are memories of both over-policing and under-policing shaped over time?

Given the importance of public awareness, thought should also be given to how community groups and the media can gather and publicize data. There are dangers to relying exclusively on Statistics Canada or even the academy to collect the relevant data. For example, community activism and counting were necessary before missing and murdered Indigenous women was recognized as a public problem. We need to explore whether or not the same is true with respect to hate and other crimes against Muslims. The media's coverage of hate crime (Rodriguez 2020) should also be critically examined. This also suggests the need for research on barriers to the political mobilization of Muslim communities.

Towards Better Understandings of Policing Including "High" Policing

Additional research may also contribute to our understanding of systemic discrimination by security officials by extending this research from "low" or street policing that results in over-policing to "high" or intelligence-led policing with transnational elements.[8] The consequences of possible offloading of intelligence collection from CSIS to the police should be examined because the police have less expertise and are subject to less regulation when they collect intelligence.

Better Understanding of Plural Policing and the Role of the Private Sector

Attention should also be paid to plural policing that involves communities and the private sector. Elements of far-right violence directed towards Muslims, such as the availability of guns and the protections afforded to mosques, should be re-examined. One hypothesis that should be explored is that Muslim communities and mosques may have more expertise and perhaps more interest in protecting their members than security officials and the police. This then leads to the question of how the security officials and the police should work with and perhaps subsidize Muslim community groups as they take self-protective measures (Roach 2022, chap. 7).

The role of the private sector, especially social media companies, in contributing to over-policing and under-protection should be examined.

---

8   On the distinction between low and high policing see, Brodeur (2010).

Canada has Criminal Code provisions that allow hate and terrorist propaganda to be removed from the Internet by court order, but these provisions appear never to have been used. In any event, they are dwarfed by the daily decisions of social media companies on whether or not to take down such material. Another area that could be explored is why some Muslims have resorted to private civil litigation against hate speech as opposed to relying on criminal offences of hate speech and defamatory libel. The effectiveness of such approaches should be explored, as well as whether they are motivated by conclusions that the Canadian state cannot be relied upon to protect Muslims in Canada.

Providing an Evidence Base for Future Reforms to Combat Over-Policing and Under-Protection

If it is to be funded by government, additional research may require practical applications. A 2018 Heritage Committee of the House of Commons made recommendations for better data and research. At the same time, this seems to concede that the existing evidence base for the committee's other proposals, such as racial and cultural sensitivity training for the police, is weak (Standing Committee on Canadian Heritage 2018). Indeed, there are concerns that such training could possibly be counterproductive. More generally, there is a danger that remedies for over-policing and under-protection that are not supported by evidence may be counterproductive.

Another policy initiative that may lack a firm evidence base is the creation of the Canada Centre for Community Engagement and Prevention of Violence with its focus on Countering Violent Extremism programs. Concerns have been raised in the UK and elsewhere that such programs, when introduced in the context of Islamophobia, may securitize the response of non-security actors including schools and health care providers. Such an approach may not effectively respond to the under-protection of Muslim populations. At the same time, the idea that such programs can prevent violence and provide less coercive remedies should not be dismissed. The point is simply that research and continued evaluation are essential to ensure that even well-intended remedies to deal with the under-protection of Muslims do not backfire.

Should Security Efforts Be Ratcheted Up to Achieve Equality or Should They Be Reconceived?

Finally, research into policy responses and remedies for the over-policing and under-protection of Muslims must also assess the advantages and disadvantages of ratcheting up present policing and security efforts to include far-right extremists that target Muslims. The alternatives would be to reimagine security responses to place more emphasis on measures such as programs designed to counter violent extremism and plural policing that does not rely exclusively on state actions.

Ratcheting up present security efforts could help end discriminatory double standards that have contributed to both the over-policing and under-protection of Muslims. At the same time, however, researchers should also concern themselves with whether the existing measures are actually effective in providing protection to Muslims. Researchers should also consider that increased state security powers may be used to target innocent Muslims and violate their human rights.

Shirin Sinnar has stressed the need to ratchet up American counterterrorism to include domestic and often far-right terrorism (Sinnar 2019). My own research, however, has suggested that the challenge of far-right terrorism could give many states an opportunity to rethink coercive post 9/11 security strategies (Roach 2021). Examples of such security strategies would be the UN's listing of groups and individuals as terrorists associated with al Qaeda and Daesh. It is far from clear that attempting to add far-right extremists to lists of terrorists and financial outlaws is a strategy worth pursuing. Perhaps the whole listing process should be abandoned because it is unfair, discriminatory, and of dubious effectiveness.

The choice between ratcheting up or reconceiving security approaches to respond to under-protection does not have to be a binary or zero-sum choice. For example, concerns that programs to counter violent extremism have been influenced by Islamophobia and are discriminatory might be partially addressed by ensuring that proportionate attention is given to far right extremist.

Attempts should be made to disaggregate the symbolic and practical effects of reforms. For example, the charging of the man who killed four members of the family in London, Ontario with terrorism offences is a symbolic measure that may not make any difference to the man's future prospects of conviction or punishment. Hate speech prosecutions may have a role in combating the under-protection of Muslims, but so too may practical measures such as protecting mosques, increased gun control, or regulations to allow take downs or less amplification of hateful social media posts. Canada's decision to proscribe some far-right extremist groups such as the Proud Boys may have some symbolic value, but the actual effectiveness and fairness of proscription is dubious (Forcese and Roach 2018).

5. Conclusion

The existing public record reviewed in this chapter suggests that Muslims, like Indigenous Peoples and other often intersecting disadvantaged groups, experience systemic discrimination in the form of both over-policing and under-protection. This over-policing and under-protection is a promising site for future research into Islamophobia as a form of both public and private discrimination. Such research could also provide an evidence base to guide attempts to reduce both over-policing and under-protection as two sides of systemic discrimination and Islamophobia unfortunately faced by Muslims in Canada.

WORKS CITED

Bahdi, Reem, and Azeezah Kanji. 2018. "What Is Islamophobia?" *University of New Brunswick Law Journal* 69: 322–60. https://journals.lib.unb.ca/index.php/unblj/article/view/29035.

Beydoun, Khaled. 2016. "Islamophobia: Toward a Legal Definition and Framework." *Columbia Law Review* 116, no. 108: 108–25. https://ssrn.com/abstract=2933156.

Braithwaite, John. 2022. *Macrocriminology and Freedom.* Canberra: Australian National University Press.

Brodeur, Jean Paul. 2010. *The Policing Web.* New York: Oxford University Press.

Brodeur, Jean-Paul, Carol La Prairie, and Roger McDonnell. 1991. *Justice for the Cree: Final Report.* Nemaska: Grand Council of Crees (of Quebec) Cree Regional Authority.

Bronskill, Jim. 2015. "Refugee Sent to US after 9/11 Settles Lawsuit against Ottawa." *Globe and Mail,* 9 March 2015. https://www.theglobeandmail.com/news/national/refugee-sent-to-us-after-911-settles-lawsuit-against-ottawa/article23379956/.

Boynton, Sean. 2021. "Since 9/11, Islamophobia Has Been 'a Constant Feature' in Canada, Experts Say." Global News, 10 September 2021. https://globalnews.ca/news/8174029/9-11-islamophobia-canada/.

Canadian Anti-Hate Network. 2021. "The Internet's Reactions to the London Attacks." 10 June 2021. https://www.antihate.ca/the_internet_s_reactions_to_the_anti_muslim_london_attack_are_as_just_bad_as_you_d_expect_proving_that_this_is_canada_after_all.

Canadian Network for Research on Terrorism, Security and Society. n.d. "Canadian Incident Database." https://www.tsas.ca/canadian-incident-database.

Canadian Press. 2020. "Alleged Toronto Mosque Killer's Case Put Over till January." CBC News. 5 November 2020. https://www.cbc.ca/news /canada/toronto/mosque-stabbing-von-neutegam-zafis-1.5791033.

CBC News. 2021. "Man with Knife Attacks Sisters Wearing Hijabs outside Edmonton, RCMP Say." CBC News. 24 June 2021. https://www.cbc.ca /news/canada/edmonton/women-wearing-hijabs-attacked-st-albert -1.6078720.

Emon, Anver M., and Nadia Z. Hasan. 2021. *Under Layered Suspicion: A Review of CRA Audits of Muslim-Led Charities.* Toronto: Institute of Islamic Studies. www.layeredsuspicion.ca.

Epstein, Gloria. 2021. *Missing and Missed: Report of the Independent Civilian Review into Missing Persons Investigations.* 13 April 2021. https://carl-acaadr .ca/wp-content/uploads/2021/04/Missing-Persons-Report.pdf.

Fitz-Morris, James. 2015. "Peter McKay Skirts Debate on Definition of Terrorism: Look It Up." CBC News. 18 February 2015. https://www.cbc .ca/news/politics/ peter-mackay-skirts-debate-on-definition-of-terrorism-look-it-up-1.2961934.

Forcese, Craig, and Kent Roach. 2010. "Limping into the Future: The UN 1267 Listing Process at the Cross-Roads." *George Washington International Law Review* 42: 217–77.

–. 2015. *False Security: The Radicalization of Canadian Anti-Terrorism.* Toronto: Irwin Law.

–. 2018. "Yesterday's Law: Terrorist Group Listing in Canada." *Terrorism and Political Violence* 30, no. 2: 259–77.

Lachacz, Adam. 2021. "She Was Thrown to the Ground: Police Investigate Attack on Muslim Woman in Edmonton." CTV News. 14 June 2021. https://edmonton.ctvnews.ca/she-was-thrown-to-the-ground-police -investigate-attack-on-muslim-woman-in-edmonton-1.5468914.

Manitoba. 1991. *Report of the Aboriginal Justice Inquiry of Manitoba.* Winnipeg: Queens Printer.

McSorley, Tim. 2021. "The CRA's Prejudiced Audits: Counter-Terrorism and the Targeting of Muslim Charities in Canada." International Civil Liberties Monitoring Group. May 2021. https://iclmg.ca/prejudiced-audits/.

Merali, Farrah. 2018. "RCMP Spent More than $1 Million on Victoria Terror Probe." CBC News. 17 January 2018. https://www.cbc.ca/news/canada /british-columbia/rcmp-investigation-cost-more-than-one-million -1.4491219.

Missing and Murdered Indigenous Women and Girls Inquiry. 2019. *Reclaiming Power and Place.* Ottawa: Supply and Services.

Nesbitt, Michael. 2021. "Violent Crime, Hate Speech or Terrorism: How Canada Views and Prosecutes Far Right Extremism (2001–2019)." *Common Law World Review* 50, no. 1: 38–56. https://doi.org/10.1177 /1473779521991557.

Nesbitt, Michael, Kent Roach, and David C. Hoffman. 2021. "Canadian Terror: Multi-Disciplinary Perspectives on the Toronto 18 Terrorism Trials." *Manitoba Law Journal* 44, no. 1 (Special Issue).

RCMP. 2021. "London Police Service and Royal Canadian Mounted Police Provide Update on the Criminal Charges Related to the London, Ontario Vehicle Attack." 14 June 2021. https://www.rcmp-grc.gc.ca/en/news /2021/london-police-service-and-royal-canadian-mounted-police-provide -update-the-criminal.

Roach, Kent. 2003. *September 11: Consequences for Canada.* Kingston: McGill-Queen's University Press.

–. 2006. "Canadian National Security Policy and Canadian Muslim Communities." Research Paper No. 938451. *University of Toronto Legal Studies Series.* https://dx.doi.org/10.2139/ssrn.938451.

–. 2021. "Counterterrorism and the Challenges of Terrorism from the Far Right." *Common Law World Review* 50, no. 1: 3–20. https://doi.org/10.1177 /1473779520975121.

–. 2022. *Canadian Policing: How and Why It Must Change.* Toronto: Irwin Law.

Rodriguez, Sofia. 2020. "Racial Outburst in London Store Has Muslim Family Concerned and Hurt." CBC News. 1 June 2020. https://www.cbc.ca /news/canada/london/racial-outburst-in-london-store-has-muslim -family-concerned-and-hurt-1.5592502.

Scott, Marian. 2021. "Four Years after Massacre, Little Progress in Combatting Anti-Muslim Stereotypes." *Montreal Gazette*, 28 January 2021. https:// montrealgazette.com/news/local-news/four-years-after-massacre -little-progress-in-combatting-anti-muslim-stereotypes.

Singh, Inayat. 2020. "2020 Already a Particularly Deadly Year for People Killed in Police Encounters, CBC Research Shows." CBC News. 23 July 2020. https://newsinteractives.cbc.ca/fatalpoliceencounters/.

Sinnar, Shirin. 2019. "Separate and Unequal: The Law of 'Domestic' and 'International' Terrorism." *Michigan Law Review* 117, no. 7: 1333–404. https://doi.org/10.36644/mlr.117.7.separate.

Sinno, Abdulkader. 2009. *Muslims in Western Politics.* Bloomington, IN: Indiana University Press.

Standing Committee on Canadian Heritage. 2018. *Taking Action against Systemic Racism and Religious Discrimination Including Islamophobia.* 42nd Parliament, 1st Session. February 2018. https://www.ourcommons.ca /DocumentViewer/en/42-1/CHPC/report-10.

Statistics Canada. 2018. *Police-Reported Hate Crime, 2017.* https://www150 .statcan.gc.ca/n1/daily-quotidien/181129/dq181129a-eng.htm.

Woodward, Jon. 2021. "'Islamophobia Is Real': Community Leaders Express Shock after Threats, Arrest at Scarborough, Ont. Mosque." CTV News. 15 June 2021. https://toronto.ctvnews.ca/islamophobia-is-real-community-leaders -express-shock-after-threats-arrests-at-scarborough-ont-mosque-1.5471705.

14 Counter-Radicalization, Islamophobia, and the Impact on Muslim Civil Society Organizations

FAHAD AHMAD

Introduction

Since the mid-2000s, counter-radicalization policies have emerged as a novel form of security governance across Western nations to prevent the future occurrence of "domestic" terrorism – understood as attacks on domestic soil planned by Muslims who were born or raised in the same countries. With counter-radicalization, state security agencies sought to identify and prevent "radicalization," generally understood as the process through which Muslim individuals (and groups) come to harbour "extremist" beliefs that are thought to be a precursor to terrorism (Kundnani 2012, 5). This narrow understanding of "radicalization" prompted security and policing agencies to direct counter-radicalization efforts – such as community policing, targeted psycho-social interventions, and education and social programs – principally at Muslim communities. By almost exclusively targeting Muslim communities, counter-radicalization policies have affirmed the status of Muslims in the West as the "suspect community" (Breen-Smyth 2014, 223–40). Moreover, scholarship in Canada and elsewhere has shown that policing and security agencies make determinations of who is at risk of "radicalization" based on "Islamic difference," broadly interpreted as "lack of integration, a lack of secularism, the existential threat posed by Islam to the West, or external Islamic influences" (Githens-Mazer and Lambert 2010, 889). In other words, indicators of radicalization rely on Orientalist, anti-Muslim tropes (Monaghan and Molnar 2016, 394). When deployed as such, counter-radicalization policies foment Islamophobia as a "form of structural racism" that is "sustained through a symbiotic relationship with the official thinking and practices of the war on terror" (Kundnani 2012, 10). As part of counter-radicalization efforts, state security agencies have also sought the help of Muslim civil society organizations to connect with Muslim communities and implement counter-radicalization related programs. This dynamic puts these Muslim organizations in a quandary as they have to develop sophisticated strategies that strike a balance between cooperating in counter-radicalization efforts while also raising concerns with the Islamophobic nature of counter-radicalization policies.

In this chapter, I show how the ideas and practices of counter-radicalization in Canada – which were adopted in their full-fledged expression relatively recently – reproduce Islamophobia. Drawing upon my doctoral research, which examined how counter-radicalization policies shape relationships between state security agencies and Muslim civil society organizations, I highlight how counter-radicalization policies have had material impact on Muslim civil society organizations. In the next section, I provide an overview of a framework of Islamophobia in the Canadian context that informs the analysis in this chapter. I then provide a short overview of the counter-radicalization landscape in Canada, discussing the ways in which these policies have almost exclusively targeted Muslim communities. I then move to discuss the impact of counter-radicalization policies on Muslim civil society organizations. I conclude this chapter with a reflection on how the recent expansion of counter-radicalization to target wider forms of political violence risks further obscuring Islamophobia and widening securitization, thus curtailing the space in which civil society thrives.

Islamophobia: More than Just Hate

The concept of Islamophobia has received scholarly attention over the last several decades with significant interest generated in the context of the War on Terror (e.g., Beydoun 2016, 108–25; Husain 2021, 1–15; Meer and Modood 2010, 116–27; Garner and Selod 2015, 9–19; Rana 2007, 148–61). This productive scholarship has explored Islamophobia as a form of racism rooted in a historicized othering of Muslims that is engendered through the systemic actions of state institutions.

In Canada, no accepted legal definition for Islamophobia exists, and efforts by government agencies to acknowledge and define Islamophobia have proven inadequate. After the deadly Quebec City mosque shootings in 2017, a parliamentary motion to "condemn Islamophobia and all forms of systemic racism and religious discrimination" was met with resistance from prominent Conservative members of Parliament, including Andrew Scheer, Kellie Leitch, and Erin O'Toole (Maloney 2017). A parliamentary committee report released a year later, titled

Taking Action against Systemic Racism and Religious Discrimination Including Islamophobia (Standing Committee on Canadian Heritage 2018), described Islamophobia as an "irrational fear or hatred of Muslims or Islam that leads to discrimination" and acknowledged the Ontario Human Rights Commission definition of Islamophobia as "stereotypes, bias or acts of hostility" towards Muslims and Islam (22). However, these characterizations reveal a myopic, individual-centred understanding of the concept. The same report also included problematic views that expressed apprehension about defining Islamophobia based on the flimsy claim that doing so would limit "legitimate criticism of Islam" (23).

A careful consideration of Islamophobia in the Canadian context has been carried out by legal scholars Reem Bahdi and Azeezah Kanji. Using Khaled Beydoun's US-based analysis (2016) as their point of departure, Bahdi and Kanji underline that Islamophobia encompasses actions by both private individuals and state institutions which reinforce each other through a dialectical process (2018, 337). Their work affirms that Islamophobia is the belief that Muslims are "different" (alluding to racialization and othering) and "Canada needs to be protected from Muslims because they are inherently violent, patriarchal, alien, and inassimilable" (342). Arguing that state actions in Canada propagate Islamophobia in subtle ways, they propose that state-driven Islamophobia should be analysed by paying attention to the following aspects:

> i) coding or the targeting of Muslims without explicitly naming them; ii) permission or the tacit license to engage in harmful race-based practices; iii) denial or the failure to name Islamophobic tropes that underlie an impugned act or decision; iv) individualization or the presentation of Islamophobia as a manifestation of extreme and aberrant private conduct, rather than broader social practices; and, v) minimization or the diminishment of Islamophobia, partially by creating confusion or controversy about its meaning or ignoring its impacts. (323)

This provides a useful grounding for analysing how Islamophobia is encoded in national security efforts generally and counter-radicalization polices specifically. The ideas and practices that inform counter-radicalization policies ultimately foment Islamophobia in (mostly) indirect ways that are obscured by "the powerful narrative of Canada as a country that balances human rights and national security" (323). The following section provides a snapshot of the state of counter-radicalization policies in Canada.

Counter-Radicalization in Canada

Counter-radicalization emerged as a terrorism prevention policy paradigm across European nations in response to the attacks on the transit systems in London and Madrid in the mid-2000s. Despite European countries having extensive previous experience with political violence, these attacks, in the context of the War on Terror, were interpreted through the lens of the "new terrorism thesis" – a set of post-Cold War ideas which posited that political violence by Muslim perpetrators was exceptional, requiring new analyses and interventions (Kundnani 2012, 4). Consequently, counter-radicalization came to characterize a set of "soft" pre-criminal interventions – including education and social programs, messaging campaigns, requests for surveillance by non-policing agencies, and targeted psycho-social and online interventions – that seek to identify "radicalization" among Muslims and intervene early to prevent the future occurrence of political violence, an inherent unknown (Kundnani and Hayes 2018). The Prevent strategy in the UK is a paradigmatic example of counter-radicalization in Europe.

Canada has been a relative latecomer in adopting counter-radicalization policies. Nevertheless, terrorism prevention has been incorporated by the federal police, the Royal Canadian Mounted Police (RCMP), and Public Safety Canada since the mid-2000s. For example, the RCMP's National Security Outreach Program (NSCOP), launched in 2006 and still active today, seeks to build trust with and enlist Muslim and other religious and ethnic communities in counterterrorism efforts. Since 2005, Public Safety Canada has been hosting the Cross-Cultural Roundtable for Security (CCRS) with representatives from ethno-cultural and religious communities in an attempt to account for their interests in national security priorities. One of the first references to "radicalization" appears in the 2009 RCMP document titled *Radicalization: A Guide for the Perplexed*, developed after an RCMP-led delegation paid a visit to the UK to study its Prevent strategy. In 2012, the Canadian government released a counterterrorism strategy, *Building Resilience against Terrorism*, which noted "[v]iolent Islamist extremism" as the primary threat to Canada's national security. The "Prevent" component of the strategy highlighted the RCMP's NSCOP and Public Safety Canada's CCRS as examples of government actions to prevent terrorism by "building partnerships with" various communities.

While the above policy documents maintained that radicalization was not a "Muslim thing," in practice, terrorism prevention efforts were directed at Muslim communities. The RCMP and Canadian Security

Intelligence Service (CSIS) would show up unannounced at the homes and workplaces of Muslim individuals to make intimidating inquiries. This was especially alarming to Muslim communities when considered against the high profile cases of the rendition and torture of Muslim Canadians (such as Maher Arar) and the fear that CSIS had paid informants embedded in the midst of Muslim communities (El Akkad 2006). Moreover, politicians used rhetoric that affirmed the dangerousness of Muslims. In 2011, Prime Minister Harper named "Islamicism" and "home-grown Islamic radicals" as the "biggest" threat to Canada (CBC News 2011). These characteristics point to a pattern where Muslims are not explicitly named in policy documents yet the practices of national security target Muslims, bringing to light how state-driven Islamophobia, as described by Bahdi and Kanji (2008), manifests as a set of obscured practices.

Counter-radicalization policies in Canada achieved full expression in 2015 in the aftermath of attacks in Saint-Jean-sur-Richelieu and Ottawa and panic about so called "foreign fighters" – Muslim youth leaving or intending to leave Canada to participate in conflicts in Iraq, Syria, and other Muslim countries. Provinces and municipalities developed counter-radicalization responses with Quebec leading the charge. The province adopted a counter-radicalization plan and established, in partnership with the city of Montreal, the Centre for the Prevention of Radicalization Leading to Violence (CPRLV), which provides counter-radicalization trainings as well as targeted counter-radicalization interventions (CPRLV 2016). In late 2015, the Calgary Police launched the ReDirect initiative to provide mentorship and guidance to individuals deemed to be at risk of radicalization (Saba 2019). At the federal level, the newly elected Liberals under Prime Minister Justin Trudeau soon established the Canada Centre for Community Engagement and Prevention of Violence (CCCEPV). The federal Canada Centre started to coordinate counter-radicalization efforts across the country and fund existing and new counter-radicalization initiatives through the Community Resilience Fund. In 2018, the Canada Centre released a *National Strategy on Countering Radicalization to Violence* (CCCEPV 2018).

The federal counter-radicalization strategy is careful in noting that radicalization and violent extremism are not associated with a particular religious or ethnic group. At the same time, the strategy continues to identify transnational Islamist groups as the "main" terrorist threat to Canada (1). Such contradictory claims are apparent across counter-radicalization policy documents and point to a lack of acknowledgment that the entire apparatus of counter-radicalization came to existence in response to security and policing concerns about Muslims turning to political violence. As late as 2019, there were reports of RCMP and CSIS visits to Muslim student associations in universities to investigate cases of radicalization (Nasser 2019). In addition to being intimidating, such visits blur the line between outreach to Muslim communities and placing the same communities under surveillance and suspicion. An RCMP counter-terrorism training that I attended in late 2019 (as part of my dissertation research) claimed that radicalization was not endemic to Muslims while at the same time noting that RCMP national security investigations were overwhelmingly Islam-related (Ahmad and Monaghan 2022, 257). The majority of cases addressed by municipal counter-radicalization initiatives, such as Calgary ReDirect, relate to radicalization of Muslim youth and individuals (Ottis 2016). In examining radicalization indicators used by the RCMP, Monaghan and Molnar found that, despite invoking "bias-free policing" and referencing the complexity of radicalization in policy statements, the operational practice of identifying radicalization abandons nuance and continues profiling Muslims based on Orientalist caricaturizing and coding of cultural and religious expressions as dangerous (2016, 401). Together, these characteristics of counter-radicalization comport with Bahdi and Kanji's account (2018) of state-driven Islamophobia, which targets Muslims using techniques of racialization while at the same time denying the underlying role of Islamophobia. As the following section discusses, counter-radicalization policies have had a significant impact on Muslim civil society organizations.

The Complex Impact of Counter-Radicalization Policies on Muslim Civil Society Organizations

For my dissertation project, I examined how counter-radicalization policies, informed by Islamophobic ideas and practices, apply pressures upon Muslim civil society organizations, and how Muslim organizations develop responses to those policy pressures. I proposed a theoretical framework which posits that counter-radicalization policies create relations of power between state agencies responsible for national security and civil society organizations. These relations of power shape the experiences of Muslim civil society organizations and their responses. While the limited scope of this chapter does not allow a full engagement with the framework I developed, below I outline three ways in which counter-radicalization policies become salient for Muslim civil society organizations as a mode of power. The analysis that follows draws upon the perspectives of research participants from Muslim civil society organizations from across the country.[1]

The Withholding of Legitimacy

It is widely established that, for civil society organizations, legitimacy – from the constituents they serve and from state institutions – is a crucial resource (Elsbach and Sutton 1992, 700). Counter-radicalization policies have given state agencies the ability to grant or withhold legitimacy to Muslim civil society organizations based on the mere suspicion that the work of these organizations might contribute to radicalization (even though "radicalization" itself remains a contested and fuzzy concept). This withholding of legitimacy can be done through public discourse. A research participant recounted that in 2014, then Prime Minister Stephen Harper's spokesman falsely accused the National Council of Canadian Muslims, Canada's most prominent Muslim civil rights organization, of having links to terrorist entities.

Legitimacy can also be withdrawn formally, such as through revocation of charitable status. A recent report by the Institute of Islamic Studies (IIS) at the University of Toronto brought to light the case of the Ottawa Islamic Centre, an Ottawa mosque whose charitable status was revoked by the Canada Revenue Agency (CRA) because the agency assessed that speakers invited by the mosque promoted "hate and intolerance," linking the content of their past lectures to concerns about "radicalized individuals" who attended the mosque (Emon and Hasan 2021). The IIS report contends that the mosque was targeted as part of Canada's wider counter-radicalization efforts which disproportionately target Muslims who hold conservative religious beliefs. Indeed, research participants in my dissertation project reiterated the view that the CRA's targeting of Muslim charities is unjust and biased. One participant, a Muslim lawyer well-versed in the national security targeting of Muslim charities, suggested that political and media discourse about the dangerousness of Muslims directly or indirectly motivates

---

1   Though space constraints limit a full discussion of research methodology, I would like to note that between September 2018 and December 2019, I conducted anonymized semi-structured interviews with twenty individuals in decision-making positions at Muslim civil society organizations across Canada. Muslim civil society organizations refer to charities and nonprofit organizations that are either Muslim-led or Muslim serving. The findings presented in this chapter draw upon this interview data as well as an analysis of policy documents and media sources related to Canada's national security.

the CRA's targeting of Muslim charities. The actions of the CRA exemplify how seemingly neutral counter-radicalization practices end up targeting Muslim organizations (and communities).

The Almost Exclusive Focus on Muslim "Radicalization"

Research participants lamented that security and policy frameworks implicitly equate radicalization to a problem among Muslims, without offering adequate evidence to support that connection. A participant made the observation that this association is mostly ideational but so entrenched that one no longer needs to mention Islam or Muslims when talking about radicalization, for "people just know." I have argued elsewhere that radicalization is framed and constructed top-down by state institutions and imposed upon Muslim communities as an issue they must respond to (Ahmad 2020, 126). Therefore, despite assertions that state security agencies are "concerned with all forms of violent extremism, not associating this phenomenon with any particular religious, political, national, ethnic, or cultural group" (CCCEPV 2018, 2), the lived experience of Muslims and their civil society representatives makes apparent that counter-radicalization policies maintain a disproportionate focus on Muslims, thus propagating Islamophobia.

Participants highlighted that framing radicalization as a problem afflicting Muslims has ignored issues of safety facing Muslim communities, i.e., white supremacist violence. White supremacist "radicalization," as a participant described it, matters much more for Muslim communities as it produces real, deadly violence for these communities. Participants explicitly connected the neglect of white supremacist violence by state security institutions to incidents of anti-Muslim violence. Through Bahdi and Kanji's framework (2018), we understand that state and individual acts of Islamophobia exist in a mutually reinforcing relationship. Thus, when state security agencies frame Muslims as a national security threat, it fosters a climate of Islamophobia that emboldens individual Islamophobic actions. Islamophobic attacks, such as the 2017 mosque shootings in Quebec City and the 2021 truck attack that killed a Muslim family in London (Ontario), become possible in the context of racialization and othering of Muslims engendered by counter-radicalization and other state-driven national security efforts.

Islamophobia as Discourse

In the Foucauldian sense, discourse refers to a system of knowledge that structures social meaning, social practices, and social relations. To uphold counter-radicalization policies, state security institutions deploy discourse that is steeped in Orientalist ideas (of the "new terrorism thesis") wherein Muslim violence is regarded as exceptional. This has led to a narrow understanding of radicalization as a theological and psychological process of Muslims developing "extremist" religious beliefs that are assumed to be linked to political violence. Such discourse turns attention away from the structural factors of political violence (where state agencies may also be held responsible) and focuses it towards racial, religious, cultural, and political expressions of Muslims (which can readily be policed).

Research participants shared that the counter-radicalization discourse renders a "mental framework" where Muslims are the problem. The same discourse makes racialized practices of surveillance and policing of Muslims appear obvious and commonplace. Participants asserted that the security discourse is reaffirmed and proliferated through media coverage, which gives significantly greater attention to incidents of terrorism by Muslim perpetrators, framing their actions as religiously motivated attacks on the West (Kanji 2018, 7). One research participant went so far as to say that the Islamophobic discourse of Muslims being a "problem community" responsible for radicalization is so powerful that it shapes the self-perception of Muslims, even overriding their lived experience. Recognizing the harm of the state-security-driven radicalization discourse, Muslim civil society organizations are responding by educating broader publics about Islamophobia, launching anti-Islamophobia campaigns, and offering correctives to the media narratives that propagate the dangerousness of Muslims.

Conclusion

In this chapter, I have attempted to demonstrate how the ideas and practices of counter-radicalization engender the racialization and othering of Muslims, thus exemplifying state-driven Islamophobia. Using Bahdi and Kanji's framework (2018) for analysing Islamophobia, I show that counter-radicalization policies appear neutral – even denying anti-Muslim bias – but in their operationalization, rely on reductive, anti-Muslim tropes which treat Muslims as dangerous Others. I draw upon my dissertation research to show how Muslim civil society organizations are impacted by counter-radicalization policies, requiring these organizations to navigate relationships of power with state security institutions. I focus specifically on illustrating how Islamophobia is manifest in the counter-radicalization practices of state institutions that grant and withhold legitimacy to Muslim charities, the almost exclusive security attention directed at the "radicalization" of Muslims, and the use of Islamophobic discourse as part of counter-radicalization. More recently, state security agencies in Canada and elsewhere have expressed interest in deploying counter-radicalization policies to target a wide range of "ideologically motivated" extremisms, including "right wing" extremism (CSIS 2020, 13). This apparent "colourblind" turn has been used by state security agencies to defend counter-radicalization from the charge of Islamophobia. However, as Younis astutely notes, the claim of colourblindness is often performative and merely serves to push the Islamophobic underpinnings that uphold counter-radicalization policies further out of sight (2021, 5). Moreover, granting more authority and power to security agencies which have a track record of targeting racialized and Indigenous people should be cause for concern. It is contingent upon state institutions to pay attention to the concerns raised by civil society. A Canadian future safe for all is one where there is less securitization and more space for civil society to thrive unencumbered.

WORKS CITED

Ahmad, Fahad. 2020. "The Securitization of Muslim Civil Society in Canada." In *Radicalization and Counter-Radicalization*, edited by Derek M.D. Silva and Mathieu Deflem, 115–33. Bingley, UK: Emerald.
Ahmad, Fahad, and Jeffrey Monaghan. 2022. "Socializing the High Policing Métier: Exploring Counterterrorism Trainings for Frontline Workers." *Surveillance & Society* 20, no. 3: 248–63. https://doi.org/10.24908/ss.v20i3.14859.
Bahdi, Reem, and Azeezah Kanji. 2018. "What Is Islamophobia." *University of New Brunswick Law Journal* 69: 322–60. https://journals.lib.unb.ca/index.php/unblj/article/view/29035.
Beydoun, Khaled A. 2016. "Islamophobia: Toward a Legal Definition and Framework." *Columbia Law Review* 116, no. 7: 108–25. https://ssrn.com/abstract=2933156.
Breen-Smyth, Marie. 2014. "Theorising the 'Suspect Community': Counterterrorism, Security Practices and the Public Imagination." *Critical Studies on Terrorism* 7, no. 2: 223–40. https://doi.org/10.1080/17539153.2013.867714.
Canadian Security Intelligence Service (CSIS). 2020. *CSIS Public Report 2019*. Ottawa: Public Works and Government Services Canada.
Canada Centre for Community Engagement and Prevention of Violence (CCCEPV). 2018. *National Strategy on Countering Radicalization to Violence*. Ottawa: Public Safety Canada.

CBC News. 2011. "Harper Says 'Islamicism' Biggest Threat to Canada." 2011. 7 September 2011. www.cbc.ca/news/politics/harper-says-islamicism -biggest-threat-to-canada-1.1048280.

Centre for the Prevention of Radicalization Leading to Violence (CPRLV). 2016. *Annual Report: March–December 2015.* info-radical.org/wp-content /uploads/2016/11/cprlv-annual-report-2015.pdf.

El Akkad, Omar. 2006. "Muslims Say CSIS Has Spies in Many Mosques." *Globe and Mail*, 29 July 2006. https://www.theglobeandmail.com/news /national/muslims-say-csis-has-spies-in-many-mosques/article1101289/.

Elsbach, K.D., and R.I. Sutton. 1992. "Acquiring Organizational Legitimacy through Illegitimate Actions: A Marriage of Institutional and Impression Management Theories." *Academy of Management Journal* 35, no. 4: 699–738. https://doi.org/10.5465/256313.

Emon, Anver M., and Nadia Z. Hasan. 2021. *Under Layered Suspicion: A Review of CRA Audits of Muslim-Led Charities.* Toronto: Institute of Islamic Studies. www.layeredsuspicion.ca.

Garner, Steve, and Saher Selod. 2015. "The Racialization of Muslims: Empirical Studies of Islamophobia." *Critical Sociology* 41, no. 1: 9–19. https://doi.org/10.1177/0896920514531606.

Githens-Mazer, Jonathan, and Robert Lambert. 2010. "Why Conventional Wisdom on Radicalization Fails: The Persistence of a Failed Discourse." *International Affairs* 86, no. 4: 889–901. https://doi.org/10.1111 /j.1468-2346.2010.00918.x.

Husain, Atiya. 2021. "Official Antiracism and the Limits of 'Islamophobia.'" *Social Identities* 27, no. 6: 611–25. https://doi.org/10.1080/13504630.2020 .1859362.

Kanji, Azeezah. 2018. "Framing Muslims in the 'War on Terror': Representations of Ideological Violence by Muslim Versus Non-Muslim Perpetrators in Canadian National News Media." *Religions* 9, no. 9: 274. https://doi.org/10.3390/rel9090274.

Kundnani, Arun. 2012. "Radicalisation: The Journey of a Concept." *Race & Class* 54, no. 2: 3–25. https://doi.org/10.1177/0306396812454984.

Kundnani, Arun, and Ben Hayes. 2018. "The Globalisation of Countering Violent Extremism Policies: Undermining Human Rights, Instrumentalising Civil Society." Transnational Institute (TNI). 6 March 2018. www.tni.org /files/publication-downloads/cve_web.pdf.

Maloney, Ryan. 2017. "Anti-Islamophobia Motion Easily Passes House of Commons." Huffington Post Canada. 24 March 2017. www.huffpost.com /archive/ca/entry/m-103-anti-islamophobia-motion-house-passes _n_15567120.

Meer, Nasar, and Tariq Modood. 2010. "Analysing the Growing Scepticism towards the Idea of Islamophobia." *Arches Quarterly* 4, no. 7: 116–27.

thecordobafoundation.com/wp-content/uploads/2011/01/arches_vol_4
_edition_7.pdf.

Monaghan, Jeffrey, and Adam Molnar. 2016. "Radicalisation Theories, Policing Practices, and 'the Future of Terrorism?'" *Critical Studies on Terrorism* 9, no. 3: 393–413. https://doi.org/10.1080/17539153.2016.1178485.

Nasser, Shanifa. 2019. "When CSIS Comes Knocking: Amid Reports of Muslim Students Contacted by Spy Agency, Hotline Aims to Help." CBC News. 7 August 2019. www.cbc.ca/news/canada/toronto/csis-students-university -muslim-campus-1.5229670.

Ottis, Peter. 2016. *The Promises and Limitations of Using Municipal Community Policing Programs to Counter Violent Extremism: Calgary's Re-direct as a Case Study.* Master's thesis, Norwegian University of Life Sciences. nmbu.brage. unit.no/nmbu-xmlui/handle/11250/2443196.

Rana, Junaid. 2007. "The Story of Islamophobia." *Souls* 9, no. 2: 148–61. https://doi.org/10.1080/10999940701382607.

Saba, Rosa. 2019. "No Pressure, No Watchlists: How a Calgary Team Helps Steer Youth Away from Radicalization." *Toronto Star*, 24 June 2019. www .thestar.com/calgary/2019/06/24/calgarys-radical-solution-to-youth -radicalization-friendship-support-and-understanding.html.

Standing Committee on Canadian Heritage. 2018. *Taking Action against Systemic Racism and Religious Discrimination Including Islamophobia.* 42nd Parliament, 1st Session. February 2018. https://www.ourcommons.ca /DocumentViewer/en/42-1/CHPC/report-10.

Younis, Tarek. 2021. "The Psychologisation of Counter-Extremism: Unpacking PREVENT." *Race & Class* 62, no. 3: 37–60. https://doi.org/10.1177 /0306396820951055.

15 Immigration and Systemic Islamophobia

NASEEM MITHOOWANI

The importance of immigration to the Canadian way of life and the future of our country cannot be overstated. Immigration accounted for 80 per cent of our country's population growth between 2017–18 (IRCC 2020, 5). By the early 2030s, it is expected that Canada's population growth will rely exclusively on immigration as domestic population growth stagnates (Thevenot 2020).

Given its importance to the growth of our society and shaping the make-up of our country, it is imperative that immigration policies are scrutinized to ensure that they model Canada's commitment to inclusiveness and equality, racial and otherwise. Not only is this the right thing to do, it is in our country's best interest. Having a fair immigration system – and importantly, one that is perceived internationally as such – is vitally important to our ability to attract sought-after immigrants in a fierce international competition driven by the fact that many other Western countries are also experiencing stagnant population growth. It is therefore vital to our economic well-being and future prosperity.

At times, Canadian immigration policies have appeared both free of the bias that plagued other nations, and openly defiant to any such bias. Examples which showcased the Canadian immigration system at its most open include the historic speed at which our country admitted thousands of Syrian refugees in 2015 (Houle 2019), or the creation of a special public policy to assist the entry to Canada of those who were affected by the infamous US "Muslim ban" under the Trump administration.

However, it would be a mistake to assume that racial bias – and particularly Islamophobia – does not exist within Canadian immigration law. Rather, I would argue that it is entrenched within it. On this point, I write this essay not as an academic but rather as an immigration lawyer in Canada, drawing on my experience litigating issues of immigration law, working within the legal system of Canada's immigration law landscape, and interacting with clients having to find their way through what can be a complicated system. That complication is only compounded by the operation of bias in what are otherwise discretionary decisions by duly authorized administrators. Over the past decade, there have been numerous examples of immigration and refugee law policy that have been overtly Islamophobic and have been criticized as such.

Public policies forcing women to remove the religious facial covering (*niqab*) during citizenship ceremonies were ultimately dismantled by the judiciary and rightly called out as xenophobic by politicians, media, and the Canadian public (*Canada v. Ishaq*, 2015 FCA 194; Gelowitz 2015; CBC News 2015).

Similarly, the RCMP was forced to cease using an interview guide to assess the potential security risk that refugee claimants posed upon entry to Canada when it became apparent that the directions were tainted with blatant Islamophobia. Examples of questions included asking refugee claimants about their views on women who do not wear hijab or how often they prayed (Peritz and Leblanc 2017).

Despite the eventual reversal of these highly problematic governmental policies, overt forms of Islamophobia still persist within immigration policy. For example, the 2021 Canadian citizenship test study guide still contains superfluous reminders to potential citizens that "Canadian openness" doesn't extend to "barbaric cultural practices" such as honour killings or female genital mutilation (IRCC 2021, 9). The phrase "barbaric cultural practices" recalls the 2015 federal election campaign in which this phrase was central to the Conservative Party, and from which members of the party have since recanted (Bronskill 2021).

Likewise, the revival of draconian security certificates after 9/11 has been used to detain almost exclusively Muslim men, with little regard to their due process rights (Roach 2006). Despite the critique of security certificates as an Islamophobic response in the so-called "War on Terror," the practice continues today (Ahmad 2019). At the time of writing, the sole individuals that continue to live under security certificates are Muslim men.

These are but a few examples of *overt* Islamophobia in Canadian immigration law. However, this chapter will concentrate on more *subtle* ways in which Muslims feel targeted within the Canadian immigration system. These more subtle forms of Islamophobia have not attracted the same level of attention and are arguably more indicative of entrenched institutional bias.

For example, recent immigration initiatives to allow unlimited numbers of Ukrainian refugees into Canada using expedited measures (some of which include the removal of security clearance requirements for Ukrainians that are deemed low risk) have been watched closely by refugee advocates in Canada. While these initiatives are laudable, it is difficult not to contrast this spirit of innovation and problem-solving against the inaction or limited response in the resettlement or rescue of refugees in the Muslim world. The Canadian government has acknowledged genocide against Rohingya and Uighur Muslims. Despite this extraordinary pronouncement, these groups have not benefited from any targeted program to allow them to leave their countries to seek safe haven in Canada.[1] Similarly, Afghan and Syrian refugee numbers have been closely capped and, particularly in the case of Afghans, refugee lawyers have witnessed extremely detailed security screenings which have resulted in significant delays. This is the case even for Afghans that the Canadian Armed Forces had previously screened and deemed safe to work with, in the context of seeking military and interpretation aid.

While the potential unconscious bias against Muslim refugees demands further study, the scope of this chapter is limited to two concerns of Islamophobia within the immigration system – first, the bias inherent in the adjudication of temporary resident visas in Muslim-majority countries and second, the manner in which inadmissibility findings are made against Muslims on the basis of their membership to a "terrorist organization."

Temporary Residency

Allowing individuals to come to Canada on a temporary basis – to visit, work, or study – is a key component of Canadian immigration law.

Currently, the citizens of all Muslim-majority countries (with the exception of the United Arab Emirates) are required to obtain temporary status from Immigration, Refugees, and Citizenship Canada (IRCC) (Pollara 2021) prior to entering Canada, through the form of a temporary resident visa (colloquially known as a "visitor visa"), student permit, or work permit. For individuals overseas, these applications are assessed in Canadian visa offices or embassies abroad. The ultimate decision to approve or deny a temporary resident application rests with an individual visa officer who enjoys broad discretion in the carrying out of their task.

Securing temporary residence approvals has become increasingly important to foreign nationals. Visitors to Canada from abroad are

---

1 In June 2022, private member motion M-62 was introduced, calling for expedited entry of ten thousand Uighur refugees. The motion was debated in October 2022. At the time of writing, M-62 is not law.

often coming to reunite with friends or family members, in an effort to maintain social and familial bonds. For prospective Canadian immigrants, a history of work or study in Canada has become a focal point in our economic immigration programs, necessitating obtaining work or study permits.

Student permits create a particularly attractive pathway to securing Canadian permanent residency as international students are able to work in Canada following graduation and apply to specialized immigration avenues accordingly.

Statistics obtained from 2016 to November 2020 show an average acceptance rate of 64 per cent for all study permits, filed across all countries (Basiri 2021, para. 4). When we look closer, however, the grant rate for study permit applications emanating from Muslim-majority countries falls far short of this mark. The highest approval rate for Pakistan for this time period, for example, was no more than 32 per cent.

It is particularly difficult to understand the rationale behind the low rate of acceptances of student permit applications from Pakistan in 2019 and 2020, given that the government appeared to be courting Pakistani international students during the same time period. For example, in July 2019, Pakistan joined the list of only four other countries that could benefit from a Student Direct Stream application process which boasted promises of faster processing times and more efficient processing (IRCC 2019).

The implicit message in elevating Pakistan to the short list of countries benefiting from a dedicated student permit application stream would be that these applicants are high quality candidates that Canada ought to court. Indeed, in press releases announcing the inclusion of Pakistan in the Student Direct Stream, the government noted that such a move supported "the Government's goal of attracting students from a more diverse range of countries" (IRCC 2019). This measure suggests that acceptance rates for student permit applications from Pakistan should be high.

The fact that the approval rates are so low, despite the government support of Pakistani student permit applications, raises important questions about the possibility of bias on the part of the individual officers in the application process. This aligns with the anecdotal experience of Muslims feeling disadvantaged in the study permit approval process but being unable to articulate exactly why.

Given that officers are required to provide very little in the way of reasons to justify a refusal, and that their decisions will be upheld by a reviewing court so long as they meet the marker of being "justified, transparent and intelligible," it is near impossible for an individual applicant to identify or expose any underlying bias. It may, therefore, run unchecked within our immigration systems.

It may be tempting to disregard this concern as mere speculation or fantasy. But it isn't. A June 2021 report on workplace racism in IRCC exposed a culture of systemic racism within the department, including micro-aggressions, bias in hiring and promotion, and bias in the delivery of immigration programs (Pollara 2021). Racialized employees expressed concern over an "us versus them" attitude when it came to the clients the department serviced, leading to the use of racist terms that would not ordinarily be tolerated in the broader Canadian society, discriminatory processing policies that affect individuals applying from certain countries, and a lack of anti-racism training for employees.

In addition to individual officer bias, other structural barriers exist for Muslim applicants. For example, citizens in a number of Muslim-majority countries (such as, at the time of writing, Pakistan[2]) have their temporary resident applications assessed in countries other than the countries of their citizenship, due to closures of embassies or visa offices there. Pakistani and Afghan applications for temporary residency to Canada are assessed, for example, in Abu Dhabi. Algerian applications are assessed in Paris. Bangladeshi applications are assessed in Singapore. In these cases, visa application officers lack any connection or awareness of the applicant's country conditions. Nonetheless, when appealing visa application decisions, courts presume as a matter of law that visa officers have specialized knowledge of local conditions earning them judicial deference in their fact-specific determinations. Removal of the decision-making process from the countries where individual applicants live may result in unconscious bias with respect to the perception of local country conditions by individuals who do not live there.

Another pressing issue for those concerned with anti-Muslim bias in temporary resident applications is the increased use of automation by IRCC. In March 2018, IRCC implemented the Chinook computer software that automates processing temporary resident permits.

Alarmingly, Chinook was developed without any recognition of how it may create or further racial equity in immigration systems, despite a general awareness in Canadian society that machine learning and artificial intelligence systems are rarely "neutral" and can be riddled with

---

2 After much lobbying, in November 2022, Canada announced an Indo-Pacific Strategy which promises to enhance visa processing capacities in Islambad, Pakistan, thereby signaling a move of visa processing from Abu Dhabi. This change has not yet been implemented.

assumptions and unconscious bias. Indeed, the increased use of automation was cited in the aforementioned May 2021 study on workplace racism in IRCC as a concern of racialized staff for its potential to "embed racially discriminatory practices in a way that will be harder to see over time" (Pollara 2021; Dawson 2022).

Despite these warnings, Chinook was developed ad hoc by individual visa officers as a tool to increase efficiency. Its creation did not involve legal or technical experts in data collection (Ziaie 2021; Tao 2021).

Its implementation was similarly casually undertaken, without critical assessment or qualitative study. This is highly relevant when considering that Chinook is not uniformly used among visa offices. Rather, its adoption has been left as a matter of choice by individual visa offices and was initially taken up largely to process applications from the Global South. Where it has been implemented, a sharp increase in refusal rates has resulted. For example, study permit approval ratings for Iran (where Chinook is used) decreased from a rate of 69 per cent in 2016 to 44 per cent in 2019 and 42 per cent in 2020.[3]

Part of the way in which Chinook is being used by visa offices is to search for and flag particular words or risk indicators in applications, bringing those applications to an officer's attention. There is a fair amount of secrecy involved in this process, as the words and flags that are used are selected individually by the local visa office and are not publicly available or even identified in a particular file when that file is refused. There is no evidence of oversight as to how words are chosen or why.

Another important feature of Chinook is that visa officers who refuse applications can select their justification from a drop-down menu of automated, standardized justifications. If a visa officer chooses from the list of prepopulated reasons to justify their refusal, their reasons for refusal will read as a generic assessment, and their personalized working notes on the file will not appear in the file. This further obfuscates the actual decision-making process, producing a fertile environment for bias to flourish.

In non-Muslim-majority countries where anti-Muslim sentiment is on the rise, a different concern arises: the use of locally engaged staff in the automation process. As part of the way in which Chinook streamlines the application process, locally engaged staff are tasked with the vital role of previewing files and creating a prescreen. They select the information they deem most important for inclusion in the prescreen that a visa officer would ultimately review when approving or rejecting

---

3   Data analysis on file with the author.

the application. The visa officer may choose to review the application in its entirety but could also rely solely on the prescreened information that appears on Chinook to render his or her decision. By allowing locally engaged staff the unfettered discretion to pick and choose which information is highlighted for review on a file, we have outsourced enormous influence over the perception of a particular application to a temporary, non-Canadian employee who may never have benefited from anti-racist training.

The use of locally engaged staff creates significant unease among Muslim applicants in countries dealing with increasing Islamophobia, such as India. And in fact, since the use of Chinook, study permit approval ratings from Indian nationals have dipped from 68 per cent in 2016 to 43 per cent in 2020 – much lower than the global average (Stacey 2022). Since IRCC does not track refusals by religion, it is impossible to know whether religion had any bearing on refusals. However, that is not enough to assuage the concern that it may have.

Despite these warning signs, it does not appear that any study was undertaken by IRCC on how Chinook may further discrimination within IRCC processing. This is important to study further, as IRCC has signalled an intention to rely more heavily on automation and artificial intelligence to assist with its workload.

Inadmissibility

Another way in which Muslims appear to be disproportionately impacted in immigration policy is in the uneven use of the so-called "security grounds" to find someone inadmissible to Canada.

A finding of inadmissibility under security grounds carries severe consequences, including the inability to access discretionary relief of the finding through humanitarian and compassionate grounds, the lack of appeal mechanisms for permanent residents who lose their status in Canada, and the ineligibility to have a claim for protection heard through a hearing at the Refugee Protection Division.

Section 34(1)(f) of the Immigration and Refugee Protection Act (SC 2001, c. 27) provides that a permanent resident or a foreign national is inadmissible on security grounds for "being a member of an organization that there are reasonable grounds to believe engages, has engaged or will engage in acts of terrorism."

Canada Border Services Agency (CBSA) officers – acting as delegated decision makers by the minister of public safety – have been tasked with determining whether to pursue an allegation that an individual is inadmissible pursuant to section 34(1)(f).

There are very few publicly available guidelines to CBSA officers to assist in determining which groups may be properly labelled as organizations that have engaged in acts of terror or how CBSA ought to make that assessment. The term "terrorism" is not even defined in the immigration legislation, and a universal definition for the purposes of section 34(1)(f) has not emerged in the case law. What we do know from case law on the Bangladesh National Party (BNP) is that CBSA officers are not bound to restrict their assessment to organizations that have been identified as terrorist organizations in lists that the government uses for other purposes, or those organizations whose characterization as a terrorist group is subject to agreement in the international community.

As a result, the CBSA has expanded the definition of terrorist groups beyond rogue actors to entrenched political parties in Muslim majority countries (Waldman 2021). The BNP is one of two main political parties in Bangladesh and has formed government in the past. When in power, the Canadian government recognizes the BNP as a legitimate government, and when the group remains in opposition, it continues to engage with its key members. Despite the BNP's legitimacy in Bangladeshi politics, the CBSA has made a policy decision to deem the BNP a terrorist organization (Ahmed 2021; Meurrens 2021) for the purposes of section 34(1)(f).

The allegation that the BNP engages in terrorism revolves around the political party's employment of "hartals" as a way of expressing displeasure over perceived corruption in election results. Hartals aim to shut down the country in protest by blocking roads, closing businesses and schools, and encouraging broad civil disobedience. The violence that has sometimes erupted as a result of these hartals, and the BNP's goal of disrupting the country's economy, informed the CBSA's claim that the political party engages in terrorism (Meurrens 2021).

This analysis is a huge shift from the definition of terrorism as it has been defined in our criminal system and appears to penalize legitimate political involvement or protest. Regardless, the CBSA's view that the call for hartals can be classified as an act of terrorism has been accepted by the immigration division. This, combined with the broad definition of "membership" means that any individual who holds any role in the BNP – no matter how removed their actions are from the hartals or how limited their involvement in the party may be – can be found inadmissible to Canada.

Judicial oversight of such determinations is minimal. Given that these are administrative proceedings, the findings of the immigration division are subject only to judicial review on reasonableness grounds by the federal court, a deferential standard that acknowledges that there might be a number of possible outcomes. The findings of inadmissibility on the basis of membership in the BNP have been upheld as reasonable in a number of federal court applications for judicial review (*Ahmed v. Canada (Citizenship and Immigration)*, 2020 FC 791).

This lack of effective judicial or legislative guidance translates to an enormous amount of discretion on the part of individual CBSA officers to reach their own conclusions as to which groups have engaged, or will engage, in terror. This is concerning given that allegations of racism have long plagued the CBSA, which is not subject to any form of civilian oversight. In fact, it appears that the CBSA has used its discretion over-broadly when it comes to Muslim organizations. The CBSA has a history of defining established political parties of Muslim-majority countries (Ahmed 2021) as falling within the definition of terrorist organizations in ways that can only be described as puzzling.

The Muttahida Quami Movement is a political party in Pakistan that has come under scrutiny by the CBSA for alleged acts of terror. Similarly, the CBSA has recently sounded the alarm bells (for the first time) over membership in the Muslim Brotherhood. In the very recent case of *Elmady v. Canada*, the Applicant unsuccessfully sought to challenge the use of Islamophobic tropes and biased evidence by the CBSA in its assessment that the Muslim Brotherhood is a terrorist organization (Sawyer 2021).

So far, only with respect to Muslim-majority countries has the CBSA targeted individuals as belonging to terrorist organizations for their membership in otherwise mainstream political parties. On this basis, it seems that Canadian immigration law and policies consider politically active Muslims as inherently suspect on terrorism grounds.

Conclusion

Immigration policy and laws – like all government policy and law – are scrutinized through a gender-based analysis known as Gender-based Analysis Plus (GBA+). GBA+ is an intersectional analytical process that involves examining disaggregated data and conducting targeted research to better understand the impacts that any individual law or policy has in either furthering or hindering the government's goal of ensuring gender equity. Putting gender equity at the forefront of policy creation has resulted in specific programming changes, new initiatives to better address gender *in*equity, and increased training for IRCC staff. These are laudable changes and deserving of praise.

When it comes to ensuring racial equity in immigration laws and policy – and particularly in disassembling structural Islamophobia within IRCC – the lack of any equivalent analysis has been devastating. Entrenched Islamophobia has been identified in many government departments, including within Canadian security structures and the Canada Revenue Agency. Its existence in immigration law and policy has attracted less attention and study.

Such study has the potential to bring welcome change to immigration processes and policies that appear to operate in defiance of racial equity. At the very least, increased study would instil public confidence that immigration systems – the very tools used by largely racialized individuals to gain status in Canada – operate in transparency and have been assessed for racial bias.

WORKS CITED

Ahmad, Fahad. 2019. *Securitization and the Muslim Community in Canada.* Broadbent Institute. 17 July 2019. https://www.broadbentinstitute.ca/atlast_atweet/securitization_and_the_muslim_community_in_canada.

Ahmed, Washim. 2021. "Canada's Immigration System Is Tainted by Prejudice." iAffairs. 21 August 2021. https://iaffairscanada.com/2021/canadas-immigration-system-is-tainted-by-prejudice/.

Basiri, Meti. 2021. "ApplyInsights: Study Permit Approval Rates for Canadian Universities and Colleges Returning to Pre-Pandemic Levels." ApplyBoard. 13 December 2021. https://www.applyboard.com/blog/applyinsights-study-permit-approval-rates-for-canadian-universities-and-colleges-returning-to-pre-pandemic-levels#:~:text=The%2068%25%20approval%20rate%20for,rebound%20alongside%20the%20market%20growth.

Bronskill, Jim. 2021. "Conservative MP Tim Uppal Sorry for Role in 'Divisiveness' of Harper-Era Politics." CBC News. 14 June 2021. https://www.cbc.ca/news/politics/uppal-harper-conservative-muslim-niqab-1.6065058.

CBC News. 2015. "Zunera Ishaq, Who Challenged Ban on Niqab, Takes Citizenship Oath Wearing It." CBC News. 5 October 2015. https://www.cbc.ca/news/politics/zunera-ishaq-niqab-ban-citizenship-oath-1.3257762.

Dawson, Fabian. 2022. "Immigration Canada Acts to End Racism, Cultural Bias among Employees." CTV News. 5 April 2022. https://www.ctvnews.ca/politics/immigration-canada-acts-to-end-racism-cultural-bias-among-employees-1.5848940.

Gelowitz, Mark. 2015. "*Canada v. Ishaq*: Guidance from the Federal Court of Appeal on Motions for Intervener Status." Osler. 19 October 2015. https://www.osler.com/en/blogs/appeal/october-2015/canada-v-ishaq-guidance-from-the-federal-court-o.

Houle, René. 2019. "Results from the 2016 Census: Syrian Refugees Who Resettled in Canada in 2015 and 2016." Statistics Canada. 12 February 2019. https://www150.statcan.gc.ca/n1/pub/75-006-x/2019001/article/00001-eng.htm.

Immigration, Refugees and Citizenship Canada (IRCC). 2019. "Student Direct Stream Expanded to Pakistan." Newsroom. 26 July 2019. https://www.canada.ca/en/immigration-refugees-citizenship/news/2019/07/student-direct-stream-expanded-to-pakistan.html.

–. 2020. *2020 Annual Report to Parliament on Immigration.* https://www.canada.ca/content/dam/ircc/migration/ircc/english/pdf/pub/annual-report-2020-en.pdf.

–. 2021. *Discover Canada: The Rights and Responsibilities of Citizenship.* https://www.canada.ca/content/dam/ircc/migration/ircc/english/pdf/pub/discover.pdf.

Meurrens, Steven. 2021. "The Bangladesh Nationalist Party." Steven Meurrens: Canadian Immigration Lawyer (blog). 13 April 2021. https://meurrensonimmigration.com/the-bangladesh-nationalist-party/#:~:text=While%20not%20designated%20by%20Public,acts%20or%20instigate%20the%20subversion.

Peritz, Ingrid, and Daniel Leblanc. 2017. "RCMP Accused of Racial Profiling over 'Interview Guide' Targeting Muslim Border Crossers." *Globe and Mail*, 12 October 2017. https://www.theglobeandmail.com/news/national/rcmp-halts-use-of-screening-questionnaire-aimed-at-muslim-asylum-seekers/article36560918/.

Pollara Strategic Insights. 2021. "IRCC Anti-Racism Employee Focus Groups: Final Report." Immigration, Refugees and Citizenship Canada. Government of Canada. https://epe.lac-bac.gc.ca/100/200/301/pwgsc-tpsgc/por-ef/immigration_refugees/2021/122-20-e/POR_122-20-Final_Report_EN.pdf.

Roach, Kent. 2006. "National Security, Multiculturalism, and Muslim Minorities." *Singapore Journal of Legal Studies* (December): 405–38. https://www.jstor.org/stable/24869087.

Sawyer, Ethan. 2021. "Activist's Deportation Case Adds to Increased Calls for Oversight of Border Services." CBC News. 8 April 2021. https://www.cbc.ca/news/canada/british-columbia/deportation-vancouver-1.5978332.

Stacey, Viggo. 2022. "Africa's Visa Refusal Rate an 'Urgent Challenge' for Canadian Higher Education." Pie News. 8 February 2022. https://thepienews.com/news/africas-visa-refusal-rate-an-urgent-challenge-canadian-higher-education/.

Tao, Will. 2021. "A Closer Look into Chinook, Module 4: The Refusal Notes Generator and How It Works." Heron Law Offices. 29 August 2021. https://heronlaw.ca/a-closer-look-into-chinook-module-4-the-refusal-notes-generator-and-how-it-works/.

Thevenot, Shelby. 2020. "Immigration to Drive Canada's Population Growth as Global Birth Rates Fall." CIC News. 18 July 2020. https://www.cicnews.com/2020/07/immigration-to-drive-canadas-population-growth-as-global-birthrates-fall-0715086.html#gs.x2rtyv.

Waldman, Lorne. 2021. "Ten Unsolved Mysteries of Immigration Law: Celebration of the 50th Anniversary of the Federal Court." Unpublished manuscript, last modified 2021. Microsoft Word file.

Ziaie, Zeynab. 2021. "Chinook and Canadian Immigration: An Efficiency-Enhancing Tool or Cause for Concern?" CILA. 6 December 2021. https://cila.co/chinook-and-canadian-immigration-an-efficiency-enhancing-tool-or-cause-for-concern/.

16 The Motive Requirement in Canada's Definition of Terrorist Activity: Heuristics and Movements as Surrogates for Definitional Certainty

MICHAEL NESBITT

Introduction

Canada differentiates "ordinary" crime from terrorism primarily through the prism of whether a "terrorist activity" was planned or has taken place. Canadian criminal law defines terrorist activity in three parts, but the most controversial and least understood element is whether the act was motivated by religion, politics, or ideology. This motive requirement has never been defined by Parliament or the courts. Perhaps as a result, it seems that this motive requirement is the key sticking point for officials and, more generally, the public in making sense of whether ordinary crime should instead be charged as terrorism.

The result of this definitional uncertainty, I argue, is a focus on movements as surrogates for motives; in particular, social understandings (and heuristics) develop around in-group and out-group movements. These social understandings can then implicitly place out-group movements inside the crosshairs of terrorism, while in-groups remain outside its crosshairs. This has had two perverse effects. First, it has led to a disproportionate focus on certain "known" (socially accepted or understood) out-groups like al Qaeda. But in so doing it has also necessarily resulted in a real and/or perceived over-surveillance of Canada's Muslim population. By placing Canada's Muslim population in the crosshairs of terrorism investigations in a way that other racial and/ or religious groups are not, the use of surrogates has in turn contributed to the perception (and/or reality) that Islamophobia rather than objective national security imperatives are driving Canada's approach to investigating and prosecuting terrorism. This brings us to the second point, which is that such an approach will have adverse national security outcomes; simply put, a disproportionately large focus on any one community – in this case the Muslim population – means, taking into account budget and resource constraints, an underappreciation for other dangerous movements, most recently the far right. Until the motive requirement is properly dealt with – whether that be by clearly defining and explaining it or a complete reworking of Canada's terrorism framework – this dynamic seems bound to repeat itself: those associated in peripheral ways with "out-group" movements will come under threat of over-surveillance while emerging threats will be slow to attract the attention that they deserve.

A Critique of Canada's Collective Approach to Terrorism's Motive Requirement: Setting the Stage

When Canada passed the Anti-Terrorism Act (ATA, SC 2001, c 41) in 2001, it brought into effect Canada's anti-terrorism criminal offences regime. The offences were introduced in a new Part II.1 of the Criminal Code (R.S.C. 1985, c. C-46), entitled "Terrorism"; however, the "Terrorism" section of the Code notoriously does not define "terrorism" (Criminal Code, s. 83.01). Instead, Canada created a complex web of definitions and discrete terrorism offences, each of which is predicated on first proving either an association with a "terrorist entity" or with a "terrorist activity." Combined, the definition of these two predicates function as the practical alternative to defining terrorism.

A terrorist entity or group is then defined, in part, as "an entity that has as one of its purposes or activities facilitating or carrying out any terrorist activity" (Criminal Code, s. 83.05).[1] As such, to determine if a group is terrorist, we must first determine if they have facilitated a "terrorist activity." The definition of "terrorist activity" is thus the central ingredient in proving a terrorism offence in Canada; as such, it is the organizing principle that generally allows us to differentiate between an "ordinary" crime and terrorism (Roach 2003, 31).[2]

Terrorist activity is, in turn, defined most relevantly by three further elements. First, the serious consequence clause, which sets as a minimum threshold that the terrorist act results in death, serious bodily harm, or economic damage likely to lead to bodily harm. In other

---

1   A terrorist group may also be listed under the Criminal Code, s. 83.05. However, at trial the group *should* by law nevertheless be proven to be terrorist, meaning once again we return to the definition of terrorist activity.
2   As Kent Roach said shortly after the passage of the ATA, "The requirement for proof of such motive was defended on the basis that it helps ensure that 'ordinary crimes' are not prosecuted as terrorist crimes."

words, only the most serious of consequences – mostly associated with human death – will "count" as terrorism. Second, the purpose/intent clause, being, roughly, that for something to be "terrorist activity," the accused's *purpose* must be clearly shown to be changing the behaviour of a group, for example, coercing a government into changing its foreign and defence policy. Third is the motive clause (religious, political, and/or ideological) (Criminal Code, s. 83.01 (1)(b)), which is unclear and complicated to say the least. Of these three elements of terrorist activity, the consequence clause is generally *very* straightforward – for example, one merely has to ask, was a person or persons killed, or was that the intention? The purpose clause is *fairly* straightforward: generally speaking, was the attack focused on the victim (revenge), or about the perpetrator (money), or was it perpetrated to send a message to a third group (e.g., the government, a religious group) in order to coerce them to change their policies or practices? But the *motive* requirement has always been more complicated than the other two, in large part because it has remained undefined since it was first conceived. Moreover, the inclusion of a motive clause in the first place is exceedingly rare in Canadian criminal law. To prove murder, for example, one must prove a purpose/intent (to kill), and a consequence (death). While the motive (*why* the murder was committed) might explain the crime or might help tie an accused to the murder victim, or it may be relevant for moral culpability on sentencing, proving such motive is not required in murder and most other crimes the way it is with terrorism.

As a result, Canada's approach to defining terrorist activity rather than terrorism, and then including the motive requirement as an element, was extremely controversial from the very beginning. During legislative debates, then-Conservative MP Vic Toews offered a representative refrain in criticizing the motive requirement: "I'm very concerned about our government, and our agencies, and our courts, looking at the personal views of individuals, religious views, because I don't want our courts to go on religious witch hunts or ideological witch hunts" (Standing Committee on Justice and Human Rights 2001a). Likewise, Mr. John Russell, then-vice president of the British Columbia Civil Liberties Association (BCCLA), raised concern about the breadth of the terrorism motive requirement: "The idea that 'terrorist activity' will be committed for political, religious, or ideological purposes is enormously vague and broad, and it could capture a lot. It would be possible under this legislation to place under preventive detention our version of a Mahatma Gandhi or a Martin Luther King" (Standing Committee on Justice and Human Rights 2001b). But perhaps Kent Roach put it most precisely – and most presciently – shortly after Canada's anti-terrorism criminal offences came into effect in late 2001: "Terrorism trials in Canada will be political and religious trials" (Roach 2003, 27).

Such concerns about religious trials and the undefined motive clause were justifiable, both at the time and especially with the benefit of hindsight. But in 2001 (as now) it was Muslim Canadians in particular who were in the crosshairs both because of their status as a minority-religious group in Canada (if religion would be targeted, minority groups would surely be most at risk), and because Muslims in general were all-too-often wrongly and disturbingly associated with the 11 September 2001 terrorist attacks. Indeed, 9/11 was not just front of mind, it was the very impetus for Canada's ATA, with al Qaeda forming the prototype for what a terrorist group would look like: somewhat hierarchical and organized; group- (or "entity") based as opposed to "lone wolves"; and, perhaps most saliently, religiously motivated.

It was thus of little surprise that Canada's very first terrorism trial tested the above concerns, those being that such trials would be religious inquiries or even inquisitions, and more pointedly that the disproportionate focus would be on the Muslim faith in particular. In *R. v. Khawaja*, the court was called to answer whether the definition of terrorist activity's "motive requirement" was constitutionally void for both over-breadth and vagueness as Mr. Russell of the BCCLA had feared during legislative debates (*R. v. Khawaja*, 2006 CanLII 63685 (ON SC)).

At first instance, the Ontario Superior Court disagreed that the definition of terrorist activity was overly broad or vague, though significantly, as the parliamentarians before it, the court failed to explain how the motive should be properly defined and circumscribed. However, the court was also presented with another constitutional challenge, that being that the focus on religion and ideology in the motive requirement offended section 2 of the Charter, which protects freedom of speech and religion. Here, the court did strike down (and out) the motive requirement from the definition of terrorist activity (*Khawaja*, para. 80, 87), though it did so *not* on the basis that the definition of "terrorist activity" offended section 2 expression, conscience, thought, and religious rights, but because those that shared or could be seen as sharing some religious, political, or ideological beliefs associated with those that commit terrorist activity would experience a chilling effect in their speech and associations. As the court put it:

> Canadians who might share the political, religious or ideological stripe of the foreign groups under scrutiny could not help but fall under some sort of shadow. It is exactly that sort of phenomenon that has given rise to

concerns for racial or ethnic profiling and prejudice in the aftermath of the notorious terrorist actions in a number of countries around the world in recent years. (*Khawaja*, para. 52)

The case then went to the Ontario Court of Appeal, which again held that the definition of terrorist activity was not overly broad or vague, though it yet again failed to define or circumscribe the motive requirement or any of the three elements. It also reversed the Superior Court's decision on freedom of religion (Charter, s. 2), finding that there was no constitutional infringement because the so-called "chilling effect" on broader communities was neither self-evident (and thus the court could not take "judicial notice" of the fact) nor was it proven with evidence at trial (*R. v. Khawaja*, 2010 ONCA 862 (CanLII), paras. 118–35).

And so it was that *Khawaja*'s constitutional challenge was appealed to the Supreme Court – the first and, to date, only time that court has dealt with the motive requirement. The result was less than satisfying, at least for one looking to understand the motive requirement. On these issues, the Supreme Court agreed with the Court of Appeal and found that the motive was neither too vague nor too broad, nor did it offend freedom of expression, conscience, religion, and thought. In concluding, the court neither defined the motive requirement nor any of its constituent elements, but it did assert that

> Criminal liability should not be based on a person's political, religious, or ideological views. Police should not target people as potential suspects solely because they hold or express particular views. Nor should the justice system employ improper stereotyping as a tool in legislation, investigation, or prosecution. In the present case, the impugned provision is clearly drafted in a manner respectful of diversity, as it allows for the non-violent expression of political, religious or ideological views. It raises no concerns with respect to improper stereotyping. (*R. v. Khawaja*, 2012 SCC 69, para. 83)

In theory, one supposes that the Supreme Court in *Khawaja* was not necessarily or at least inevitably wrong in the result. Perhaps the motive requirement could serve to further limit the application of Canada's terrorism laws while, at the same time, providing a principled basis on which to differentiate ordinary crime from terrorism that does not tend to discriminate or create a chilling effect on broader communities. But in failing to define precisely what was meant by the motive requirement – what the terms "political," "religious," or "ideological" might mean, and how they might be proven *in a court of law* – it left open the soon-to-be realized possibility that, in the absence of a principled distinction between violence and ideologically/politically/religiously motivated violence, prosecutions would tend to focus on what the system knew: terrorism cases would be those that looked to be motivated by religious extremism where individuals were *also* purportedly affiliated directly or inspired by a movement ("entity") like al Qaeda (or later ISIS), which in turn associated itself with the Muslim religion.

The subsequent section will evaluate the fallout of Canada's approach thus far to the motive requirement. In particular, it will consider how a motive requirement left undefined – both by Parliament and then by the Supreme Court in *Khawaja* – has contributed to what I argue is a focus on movements as surrogates for motives. Such a focus on extremist movements without a concomitant understanding of how precisely to define the motive clause has put Canada's Muslim community in the line of fire and, at the same time, has meant that Canada has been slow to adapt to new and emerging extremist threats – that is, slow to react to new movements and lone wolves. The result is a picture of a system and particularly a motive requirement in need of legislative and/or judicial review.

How Movements Are Motives and What This Means for In-Groups and Out-Groups

In the time since Canada's first terrorism prosecution in *Khawaja* there have been over thirty prosecutions (as of writing). Not a single case has defined the motive requirement in terrorist activity, nor has a government department (police, prosecution, CSIS) offered a workable definition of ideologically, politically, or religiously motivated terrorist acts (Nesbitt, Amarasingam, and West 2023).[3] Perhaps this should not come as a surprise: neither Parliament nor the Supreme Court, as we have seen, felt the need to define and circumscribe the motive requirement, so why should future trial court judges?

The result, however, is a necessarily precarious situation: if one does not know, specifically, how to recognize religiously or ideologically motivated terrorism when one sees it, how does one determine when to investigate ideologically motivated cells as potential cases of terrorism, whether to charge a person holding any strong religious or ideological

---

3   For a more thorough examination of how the motive requirement has been dealt with in Canadian criminal law and, importantly, how future courts might seek to define its terms, see Nesbitt, Amarasingam, and West (2023).

belief with terrorism, and when to prosecute as such? More pointedly: how does one do these things – investigate, charge, and prosecute – without relying on stereotypes and heuristics (implicit rules of thumb) around what religions and ideologies count as terrorism without clarity as to how we are counting?

The answer, it would seem, is not at all surprising: what Canada saw in the courtroom was fully consistent with what Canada implicitly "knew" post-9/11: fifty-nine of the first sixty individuals charged with terrorism in Canada were al Qaeda- or ISIS-inspired, which is to say, religiously motivated.[4] Similarly, only two of the first sixty listed terrorist groups under the Criminal Code were associated with any far-right movement, and these two groups (Blood and Honour, Combat 18) were not listed until 2019 – meaning the first eighteen years of listing was of primarily religiously and politically inspired groups – and both groups were already largely inactive in Canada at the time of listing. In fact, both far-right groups were only added to the terrorism list as a result of pressure from abroad, particularly the Christchurch Call for Action in response to the terrorist attack on mosques in Christchurch, New Zealand. In its listings and its prosecutions, Canada was reproducing what it "knew" while seemingly failing to target that which it did not know, that being emerging threats. In other words, Canada seemed to be relying on some implicit understandings about what terrorism looked like rather than purely legal and/or definitional understandings of what it was.

It must be said that such a single-minded focus might be defensible if the Canadian terrorism threat over that period was, indeed, exclusive, that is, related only to al Qaeda-inspired extremism. But we know that is not the case: government, news media, and any awareness of what was happening in the country in the 2010s suggests that ideologically motivated far-right extremism was a similar, equal, or at times even greater threat in Canada since at least around 2015 (Nesbitt 2019).[5] So why no terrorism convictions of far-right actors over the first twenty years since the terrorism laws hit the books?

A review of how Canada has handled its emergent far-right problem is illuminating. In 2015, then-Justice Minister Peter MacKay asserted that Lindsay Souvannarath, a self-described Nazi sympathizer who plotted to shoot up a Halifax mall on Valentine's Day of that year, was

---

4 For an overview of all the individuals charges – and all the charges – between 2001 and the date of writing, see Nesbitt and Nijjar (2021).
5 For a more detailed discussion of this point see Michael Nesbitt (2019, 129–31).

not charged with terrorism because her actions were not "culturally motivated." In subsequent explanations it became clear then-Minister MacKay was confusing the motive predicate in the definition of terrorist activity, and particularly imputing to it a non-existent cultural component (Paperny 2015). Mackay's confusion was unfortunate for a minister of justice, but it was perhaps no surprise. It followed official explanations that Justin Bourque – who in 2014 killed three RCMP officers after expressing anti-establishment and anti-state sentiments – could not be charged with terrorism because his actions were not religiously motivated (as though ideological motivation would not have sufficed) (Paperny 2015). Shortly thereafter, and as late as 2017, Canada's RCMP was still expressing doubt as to whether far-right extremism could amount to terrorism (Bell 2018). In particular, the RCMP again pointed to the "ideological basis and motivation for the act" as the source of their confusion. Even if investigators could find evidence of far-right motive, were far-right ideologies "coherent" enough to merit terrorism charges (Bell 2018; Bronskill 2020)?

Three things became clear in the wake of each of these pronouncements: first, there is no denying that there was confusion at the highest levels (police chiefs, ministers of justice) about what the motive requirement meant and how it applied; second, existing terrorist movements like al Qaeda or those linked ideologically were *implicitly* captured by the motive requirement, a conclusion that follows straightforwardly from the fact that we have dozens of terrorism convictions where motive was proven without ever directly defining what the motive meant or how it was to be proven; and third, emergent threats were not immediately understood as terrorism even where all indicators suggested they might be.

When looking at the empirical prosecution record over a twenty-year period, it is difficult to escape the conclusion that the Ontario Superior Court in *Khawaja* (2006) was on to something when it feared that "Canadians who might share the political, religious or ideological stripe of the foreign groups under scrutiny could not help but fall under some sort of shadow," which in turn gives "rise to concerns [of] racial or ethnic profiling and prejudice." Even if the Ontario Court of Appeal was right that the motive requirement was "clearly drafted," and that police should not "employ improper stereotyping," by failing to engage and articulate the clarity in the motive requirement that they saw, and by failing to explain how to avoid stereotyping (the use of implicit understandings) without knowing precisely what one is looking for, the courts have contributed to a result they saw as not necessarily flowing from the legislative text.

Moreover, the flip side to this threat of over-surveillance is a failure to adequately protect against emerging movements around which there are few(er) broad social understandings as concerns terrorism. Simply put, on this theory, investigative agencies will be slow to respond to new and/or emerging threats because the proxies (and heuristics) that help in understanding those emerging threats as terrorism have not been socially constructed. Further, if investigators are focusing largely on long-recognized threats, then they are, by dint of resource allocation if nothing else, more likely to be slow to react to emerging threats. And if the focus is on ill-defined movements, meaning those that share a "political, religious or ideological stripe" come into focus, then much time will be spent on non-threats, time which could be better allocated elsewhere. Of course, if the focus has always been on movements and groups – which is why a predicate to terrorism offences is proving "terrorist group," as discussed above, and why listed terrorist entities tend to be groups, even if in theory they might be individuals – then so-called lone wolves also become troublesome for the law to prosecute.

Consider the following: On 23 April 2018, Alek Minassian used a van to run down his victims in Toronto, resulting in ten dead on the scene and another person dead years later in hospital, as well as eighteen others injured. Minassian was a self-described "Incel" or "Involuntary Celibate" and became known for his post-attack interview where he asserted that his misogynistic beliefs drove his actions. He was not charged with terrorism (Bell and Russell 2019). Subsequently, there was widespread engagement by criminal law commentators and in the media about whether the then-relatively new and little-known Incel ideology could or should justify terrorism charges. Slowly, it appears a societal consensus emerged that an Incel ideology could meet the motive requirement for terrorist activity. The very next Incel attack in Canada was perpetrated by a young man (Toronto Youth, unnamed because he was seventeen-years-old at the time of the attack) who attacked three people, killing one at a Toronto spa. He was charged with murder-terrorist activity (and two counts of attempted murder). In explaining the charges, authorities explicitly noted the Incel ideology as the basis for the distinction between an "ordinary" murder charge and a murder-terrorist activity charge (Bell, Russell, and McDonald 2020).

Perhaps even more notoriously, on 29 January 2017, Alexandre Bissonnette entered a Quebec Mosque and opened fire, killing six people and injuring nineteen others. At trial (*R. c. Bissonnette*, 2019 QCCS 354), the court found that Bissonnette had researched

the Ku Klux Klan (para. 78), notorious far-right mass killers including Dylann Roof and Elliot Rodger (para. 11), as well as Marc
Lepine, who killed fourteen women in 1989 at the Ecole Polytech-
nique de Montréal (para. 78). Bissonnette clearly held anti-Muslim,
anti-immigrant, and misogynist beliefs. Despite widespread media
inquiries into whether his actions amounted to terrorism, he was
never charged as such. The case was debated in government, legal
circles, and media outlets for the next several years. Then, as with
the approach to Incel violence, a societal understanding seemed to
emerge around xenophobic and racist views sufficing to form the
ideological (motive) basis for terrorism charges: on 6 June 2021,
Nathaniel Veltman drove a truck into a Muslim family in London,
Ontario, killing four and leaving a young boy as the sole survivor;
Veltman was charged with murder-terrorist activity (Coletta 2021).
As with the Minassian-Toronto Youth timeline, Veltman seemed to be
the *very next* clear far-right murder after the Bissonnette attack; once
again, officials identified Veltman's ideological motive as that which
allowed the "ordinary" murder charge to become one of terrorism as
well (Bell and McDonald 2021).

   In both the Toronto Youth and Veltman cases, it appears social understandings eventually coalesced around whether an ideological commitment to the Incel movement or the rather amorphous racist and
xenophobic world view (nominally far right) movement, respectively,
could turn "ordinary" criminal (murder) charges into terrorism charges.
But in this process, we see the weaknesses of a "social understandings
of movements" model of terrorism rather than one built on clear legal definitions and understandings. First, it took time for these social
understandings to emerge around these movements, meaning that the
law was seen to apply disproportionately – and thus unfairly – for a
period of years while actions that *looked* like terrorism were not charged
as such. Perhaps more to the point, because the social understandings
are implicit and based on heuristics rather than clear definitional lines,
they necessarily rely on a variety of biases held by all officials, meaning that the law very well could have applied unfairly because biases
(including Islamophobia, race bias, or Orientalism, or biases like tunnel
vision) were getting in the way of treating ISIS terrorism and far-right
terrorism in a similar fashion.

   Moreover, while the majority of al Qaeda-associated terrorism
charges have actually been laid against individuals at the planning
stages – that is, while individuals are preparing to act but not having
acted – there are still no preventive charges against Incel or far-right
actors for terrorism. This is notable because, at the end of the day, the

greatest perceived benefit of Canada's anti-terrorism criminal regime was to allow for pre-emptive (inchoate) charges to ensure that plans were foiled before the damage was done. Clearly, there are attendant security risks to this devaluation of threats as we wait for social understandings to develop.

One final caveat is in order. That is, while we might laud the move to finally recognize far-right and Incel violence as terrorism in the Veltman and Toronto Youth cases, it is far from ideal to do so without first defining how such a move to charging terrorism came about in a principled rather than a reactive manner. One unfairness is not resolved with another.

The above cases have left us with little understanding of how to draw the line between ordinary crime and terrorism in a principled fashion. This has created security concerns whereby it appears officials may take too long to recognize new or non-movement (lone actor) threats as rising to the level of terrorism; it raises fairness concerns, whereby it looks like certain out-groups – and significantly those associated in tangential ways with terrorist movements, such as a shared belief in a religion – are treated differently than those of other races, religions, and so on. Finally, waiting for implicit understandings to develop about terrorist threats makes it extremely difficult to project what will happen with future out-groups, which again might cause us to move too cautiously on a violent actor associated with a group like QAnon or too hastily and unfairly on a political protest ("out") movement. As usual, the broader the social understanding of terrorism, the more out-groups (including minority and disadvantaged groups) should be concerned – as should be those of us who care about protecting the rights and equality of all.

Conclusion

Neither the terms "ideology," "political," nor "religious," like the term "terrorism" before them, are defined directly in Canadian law, meaning that the motive requirement – thought central to the coherence of the term "terrorist activity" – has been left to be identified as something approximating "we know it when we see it." Whether we like to admit it or not, Canadian law has thus relied on implicit social understandings rather than explicit definitions to differentiate between terrorism and ordinary crime.

In practical terms, these "implicit understandings" are buoyed in the courtroom – and, presumably, during investigations – by heuristics or rules of thumb to try and fill the definitional void. Actions that meet the consequence and purpose clauses of the definition of terrorist activity whereby the actors have written a manifesto, raised a flag, or had access to propaganda that might associate them with a pre-existing religious group or recognized ("out") movements are treated as also meeting the motive element, and thus the definition of terrorist activity. New groups and lone actors become problematic because there are no social understandings around how they should implicitly be treated and no definitions explicitly making clear how they should be treated; as such, their terrorism *bona fides* are treated with suspicion – despite a long history of lone actor and far-right terrorism in North America. This theory reveals itself in the empirical reality we see today in Canada: those tangentially associated by religion or beliefs with "out" movements are in danger of being swept into the pool of suspect actors and feel over-policed and/or over-surveilled. Meanwhile, emergent ideological and lone wolf actors are not pre-empted and rarely (or only too late) charged, leaving society at risk.

There will be those who favour a response to this problem centred on definitional reform, whether that be via legislative reform or judicial challenge. Such individuals will have to offer workable definitions that, taking legal practice seriously, do not fall back on heuristics and movements as surrogates (proxies) for terrorism, and then watch carefully to see, first, if anyone listens, and second, if Canada's approach rights itself with any new definitional certainty. These definitions will have to straddle the line between opening the barn doors to terrorism charges, on the one hand, and so limiting the scope that terrorism is only associated with one group, religion, or belief. Others will prefer breaking down the foundations of terrorism law and starting from scratch. Such individuals will have to provide a viable alternative to deal with terrorism, which sadly seems here to stay. These start-anew advocates will have to address the concern, thought central to justifying the criminal terrorism regime by the drafters, that Canada needed – and still needs – criminal authority of the very type contained in the terrorism provisions of the Criminal Code in order to pre-empt another 9/11 at the planning stage.

Both approaches have benefits and drawbacks. Surely other options exist too. What is clear is that Canada's current approach falls short. How Canada defines terrorism is central to how it polices and charges terrorism. If the definition of terrorist activity is unclear – even if only one element is unclear – then that lack of clarity will flow into the policing and charging of terrorism. What is needed then is serious study of how we define and thus police terrorist activity, what it means to implicate religion, politics, and ideology in criminal offences, and what it means for investigations and trials when religion, politics, or ideology are at the very centre of legal contestation.

WORKS CITED

Bell, Stewart. 2018. "What Does It Take to Lay Terrorism Charges? An Internal Government Document Explains the RCMP View." Global News. 27 April 2018. https://globalnews.ca/news/4173552/canada-terrorism-charges -rcmp-document/.
Bell, Stewart, and Andrew Russell. 2019. "Day of Retribution: Toronto Van Attack Suspect Describes Hatred towards Women as Motive." Global News. 29 September 2019. https://globalnews.ca/news/5954272/toronto-van -attack-suspect-motive-interrogation-video/.
Bell, Stewart, and Catherine McDonald. 2021. "London Attack Suspect Charged with Terrorism." Global News. 14 June 2021. https://globalnews .ca/news/7942926/london-attack-suspect-terrorism/.
Bell, Stewart, Andrew Russell, and Catherine McDonald. 2020. "Deadly Attack at Toronto Erotic Spa Was Incel Terrorism, Police Allege." Global News. 19 May 2020. https://globalnews.ca/news/6910670/toronto-spa-terrorism -incel/.
Bronskill, Jim. 2020. "Scope of Right-Wing Extremism Vexed Security Officials, Documents Show." CBC News. 27 January 2020. https://www.cbc.ca /news/canada/edmonton/right-wing-extremism-1.5441464?__vfz =medium%3Dsharebar.
Coletta, Amanda. 2021. "Four Muslim Family Members in Canada Killed in 'Targeted' Attack, Police Say." Washington Post, 8 June 2021. https://www .washingtonpost.com/world/2021/06/07/canada-london-vehicle-attack -hate-veltman/.
Nesbitt, Michael. 2019. "An Empirical Study of Terrorism Charges and Terrorism Trials in Canada between September 2001 and September 2018." Criminal Law Quarterly 67, no. 1: 96. https://ssrn.com/abstract=3325956.
Nesbitt, Michael, and Harman Nijjar. 2021. "Counting Terrorism Charges and Prosecutions in Canada Part 2: Trends in Terrorism Charges." Intrepid (blog). 6 June 2021. https://www.intrepidpodcast.com/blog/2021/6/24 /counting-terrorism-charges-and-prosecutions-in-canada-part-2.
Nesbitt, Michael, Amarnath Amarasingam, and Leah West. 2023. "The Illusive Motive Requirement in Canada's Terrorism Offences: Defining and Distinguishing Ideology, Politics and Religion." Osgoode Hall Law Journal 60, no 3. https://doi.org/10.2139/ssrn.4177368.

Paperny, Anna Mehler. 2015. "Halifax Plot: So What Is 'Terrorism,' Anyway?" Global News. 14 February 2015. https://globalnews.ca/news/1830795/halifax-plot-so-what-is-terrorism-anyway/.

Roach, Kent. 2003. *September 11: Consequences for Canada*. Kingston: McGill-Queen's University Press.

Standing Committee on Justice and Human Rights. 2001a. *Evidence*. 37-1 No 29 at 1650 (Hon. Vic Toews). 18 October 2001. https://www.ourcommons.ca/DocumentViewer/en/37-1/JUST/meeting-29/evidence.

Standing Committee on Justice and Human Rights. 2001b. *Evidence*. 37-1 No 36 at 0950. 30 October 2021. https://www.ourcommons.ca/DocumentViewer/en/37-1/JUST/meeting-36/evidence.

17 Guilt by Association: The Shaky Foundations of Canada-US Intelligence Sharing and Its Consequences for Muslim Canadians' Mobility

YOUCEF L. SOUFI

Over the last two decades, we have become accustomed to hearing news of Muslim Canadians having trouble crossing the American border. It is typically reported in the media to call attention to the discrimination that Muslims experience in the post-9/11 era. For instance, in 2015, the CBC reported that Abdelkrim Boulhout, a Winnipeg resident, father, and Canadian citizen since 1992, was detained for seven hours at the Pembina border crossing between Manitoba and North Dakota with his wife and young children before being ordered to turn back to Winnipeg (CBC 2015). Perhaps the most striking example of cross-border discrimination in the media is the case of Syed Adem Suleiman, who at the age of six missed his flight to Boston with his father because Air Canada had him flagged as DHI (Designated High Profile) (Murphy 2016, paras. 1–3). But what is the rhyme or reason behind Muslim Canadians' refusal for entry into the US? What role does the Canadian state play in this refusal? Is it justified to guarantee the safety of Canadian and American citizens? And what impact does it have on Muslim Canadian lives?

In this chapter, I shed light on how Canadian security agencies' sharing of information with the US Department of Homeland Security (DHS) has impacted the lives of Muslim Canadians. My study shows that Canadian intelligence sharing relies on a model of "guilt by association." The individuals in my study were neither charged with crimes nor has their mobility been restricted by the Canadian government's own No-Fly List. In other words, the Canadian government does not itself see these individuals as national security threats. In fact, many of my participants have been told by CSIS agents and/or RCMP officers that they are no longer individuals of interest to their agencies. But despite serving little to no benefit to national security, the information shared with the US continues to have severe consequences on my participants' livelihoods and has brought about serious emotional harm that extends beyond them into their familial and social orbits.

My conclusions are based on three case studies of CSIS and RCMP terrorist investigations. I came across my participants' stories in the course of another study that focuses on Winnipeg Muslims' experience of the War on Terror. My participants from these three case studies were not the primary focus of investigations but knew the person who was. While each participant's degree of closeness to the terrorist suspect varied (from roommate to family member to friend), their stories all share one common feature: they claim that it is their acquaintance with a terrorist suspect rather than any illegal action they might have committed that led to their loss of mobility. In other words, I am interested in cases where CSIS or the RCMP relies on the model of guilt by association to undercut citizens' freedoms. In each of these investigations, particular patterns emerge: my participants were questioned by CSIS and the RCMP, then later attempted to travel internationally but found themselves unable to do so because of information shared between the RCMP and/or CSIS and the US. Often the discovery involved being held for several hours and questioned by American customs authorities. My participants then found themselves in the precarious situation of finding a mechanism for redress.

Below, I proceed by presenting the existing literature on Muslim Canadians' travel restrictions in the context of the War on Terror. I then present my participants' experiences in the three case studies. Based as they are on a small sample, my conclusions are preliminary. I recommend that future researchers gather more data on this topic to identify the various ways this model of guilt by association has impacted Muslim Canadians.

The Academic Literature on Muslim Canadians Travel Restrictions

Studies on travel restrictions placed on Canadian Muslims can be divided into two broad categories. First, some studies focus on Canada's No-Fly List. For instance, Nagra and Maurutto examine Muslim Canadians' perceptions of the Canadian No-Fly List (Nagra and Maurutto 2020; Nagra 2017). They show that many Muslims view the No-Fly List as arbitrary, that it impacts their life pursuits, and that it erodes basic rights like the presumption of innocence. Uzma Jamil also examines the Canadian No-Fly List, providing a genesis of its politico-legal evolution and contending that it is ineffective in keeping Canadians safe (Jamil 2017). And Colin Bennett compares the US No-Fly List and Canadian No-Fly Lists, placing them in the context of a broader pre-9/11 trend towards increased state surveillance at airports (Bennett 2008; Lyon 2006).

Second, several scholars have focused on the racialization of the US-Canadian border. In their article "Crossing Borders and Managing Racialized Identities," Nagra and Maurutto survey fifty Muslims in Vancouver and Toronto to bring to light how racialization at the border impacts Muslim Canadians (Nagra and Maurutto 2016, 165–94). They shed light on their Muslim participants' experiences of being demeaned and discriminated against, leading to a sense of "diminished citizenship." Sherene Razack presents the Canadian border as a "zone of exception," where the law renders Muslims objects of abandonment by their government (2010, 87–107). Similarly, Nandita Sharma pays attention to the ways that the Canadian border functions to construct a Canadian nation by policing racialized subjects (2008, 121–43), and Davina Bhandar historicizes the racial experience of Asians at the Canadian-US border in the early twentieth century to critique the characterization of the pre-9/11 Canada-US border as a "friendly border" – at least for people of colour (2008, 281–302). Jane Helleiner surveys white residents of a Canadian border town to highlight attitudes that legitimate racial profiling (2012, 109–35), and Anna Pratt critiques the criteria of "reasonable suspicion" in the assessments of risk among border officers (Pratt 2010, 461–80; Pratt and Thompson 2008). These studies shed light on the regime of racialization and suspicion that serves to identify and detain Muslims at borders. They also show the consequence of this suspicion on Muslims' sense of belonging in Canada.

But studies on the Canadian No-Fly List and the racialization of the Canada-US border also leave questions unanswered. What of Canadians who are not on Canada's No-Fly List but still find their travel mobility constrained because of information shared between Canadian and US intelligence? What is their experience and what redress do they have when the government that denies them mobility is not their own? As for studies on the racialization of the Canada-US border, they leave unanswered *which* Muslim citizens are turned away from crossing the US border. Whereas the racialized nature of the border makes all Muslims potential objects of suspicion, detention, and humiliation, the refusal to travel across borders is typically predicated on bureaucratic justifications, even if often shoddy ones. Moving forward, I would encourage scholars to shed further light on the bureaucratic mechanisms used to reject particular Muslims attempting travel to the US. Equally important, scholars should ask what role the Canadian state plays in creating these travel restrictions and what impact these restrictions have on Muslim citizens' lives. Only after doing so can scholars, citizens, and government officials make specific recommendations to change Canadian bureaucratic norms.[1] In the next section, I begin to answer these questions by tackling three case studies. For each case study, I present CSIS and the RCMP's investigation, then describe what happened to one or more Muslim acquaintances of the national security suspect. I conclude each section by noting the patterns in my participants' loss of mobility.

Case Study 1: Ferid Imam, Miawand Yar, and Muhanad El Farekh

In 2007, Ferid Imam, Miawand Yar, and Muhanad El Farekh left Winnipeg, Manitoba without informing family or friends (McArthur et al. 2010). All three were undergraduate students at the University of Manitoba, and their disappearance naturally worried their families, who contacted law enforcement authorities to tell them of their mysterious disappearance.[2] Shortly thereafter, the RCMP discovered that three men had left for Pakistan. Both the RCMP and CSIS launched an investigation to determine the men's intent. Eventually, Imam, Yar, and El Farekh would be charged with supporting terrorism. There is evidence that drone strikes killed Imam and Yar in the years after their disappearance. El Farekh was captured and convicted of terrorism-related charges in the US in 2017.

At the time of the disappearance in March 2007, CSIS and the RCMP began investigating whether the three men had accomplices in Winnipeg. Both security agencies took an interest in young Muslim students who were members of the University of Manitoba's Muslim Student Association. According to Mahdi, who was a science student with aspirations to become a medical doctor, CSIS and the RCMP interviewed Muslim students widely. CSIS took a particular interest in the men's previous Muslim roommates and Muslim travel companions. Mahdi had been a roommate of El Farekh and had travelled with him to China in the summer of 2006. He became the object of frequent CSIS interviews throughout the spring and summer of 2007. Mahdi answered the CSIS agents' questions as best he could. Then, in the summer of 2008,

---

1   For an example of a group that has documented and petitioned the government to change its bureaucratic norms, see the group No-Fly List Kids (NFLK). In 2017, NFLK successfully lobbied the government to include in Bill C-59 a mechanism of redress for those impacted by false positives on Canada's No-Fly List. https://noflylistkids.ca/en/home/.

2   *USA v. Muhanad Al Farekh*, Eastern District of New York, 2017, Case No. 1:15-cr-00268(BMC).

Mahdi planned to travel by car to the US for a vacation when he was stopped at the border. He explains his traumatic experience: "As soon as I gave them my passport, they surrounded my car, guns pointed at me. They then strip-searched me and detained me overnight." His treatment at the border has left him with deep psychological scars: "I was a kid, a nineteen-year-old. I want you to imagine what that does to a person." Mahdi speaks of the years of depression and therapy that have followed in the wake of CSIS's investigation. From that point onwards, Mahdi was unable to travel to the US. And yet, Mahdi has neither been charged with a terrorism crime nor has he been, to the best of his knowledge, the object of CSIS's investigation since the summer of 2007. In fact, in a 2010 interview with the *Globe and Mail*, the RCMP shared its conclusions that Imam, Yar, and El Farekh had acted alone (McArthur et al. 2010).

Malik, who was twenty-two when Imam, Yar, and El Farekh left for Pakistan, corroborates Mahdi's account of the CSIS investigation in his interview with me. He too became an object of RCMP and CSIS suspicion after going on a pilgrimage with the three men in 2006, the year before their departure. Despite his frequent questioning by CSIS, Malik did not initially feel threatened or even bothered by CSIS's investigation. At the time, Malik had little reason to travel to the US, and he did not suspect that information about him had been transmitted to the DHS. However, in 2016 this began to change. Malik had recently left his employment as an engineer for a large Alberta oil company and tried his hand as a small entrepreneur. For years, Malik had trained in martial arts and now decided to translate his passion into a livelihood by establishing a martial arts school. Malik had planned to train and be tested in the US by a foremost authority in martial arts, someone who could confer upon him the highest-ranked belt. With two of his most eager students, Malik attempted to board a plane from Calgary to New York. When he arrived at the airline counter, he was told he could not collect his ticket. Malik immediately felt the intense humiliation of needing to explain to his two non-Muslim students why he could not travel. On his drive home, he also worried about how this news might impact his business. His other students would ask why the group did not travel to New York. His reputation was now at risk, and Malik would see the impact on his business in the subsequent months and years. The inability to train with and compete against American martial artists limited his credentials and his ability to attract students. The threat to Malik's livelihood intensified in 2020 when a US martial arts master that had been a guest at Malik's academy was pulled aside by US Customs officials during a return flight to the US. "They not only questioned him about me, but they also told him I was a bad person and not to associate with me." Malik now worries about his reputation in his wider martial arts community. He sometimes wonders when students abruptly abandon a class if they had perhaps heard something that associated him with terrorism. Like Mahdi, Malik has never been charged with a crime and has not been interviewed by CSIS or the RCMP since 2008.

Five relevant points emerge from this case study. First, CSIS and/or the RCMP either sometimes or often (depending on the collection of further data) share information about Canadian Muslim citizens with the US DHS because of association rather than acts committed by these Muslims (Abu-Laban and Nath 2007).[3] Association plus being Muslim is suspicious enough. Second, this information bars these Muslim Canadians from crossing the Canada-US border, even after Canadian law enforcement loses interest in them (Whitaker, Kealy, and Parnaby 2012).[4] Third, no Canadian official notifies Canadian citizens of their inability to cross the border; instead, they learn of their travel restrictions during their travels, which makes them vulnerable to intimidation by customs officers and public embarrassment. Fourth, restrictions on cross-border travel to the US impact the livelihoods of Muslim citizens, whether through lost training and business opportunities, or because of tarnished reputations and associations with terrorism. Fifth, Canadian security agencies are unwilling to help these Canadians find redress for their situation. In the next two case studies, I show how these patterns repeat.

Case Study 2: Hiva Alizadeh

Hiva Alizadeh was an Ottawa resident arrested in August 2010 (White, Friesen, and McArthur 2010). Alizadeh was suspected of fundraising for terrorist groups in Iraq and Iran and, more seriously, of planning to detonate explosives on Canadian soil. In November, Alizadeh pled guilty to possessing explosives intending to cause harm as part of a terrorist conspiracy.

Eight months before his arrest, Alizadeh spent a weekend with a friend named Adam in Toronto. Adam had met Alizadeh in Winnipeg before Adam relocated to Toronto with his family. Adam had not

---

3 This pattern of targeting Muslims based on association was the basis upon which Maher Arar found himself the object of extraordinary rendition in 2002.
4 The difficulty in finding redress after being wrongfully associated with terrorism has been a pervasive pattern in the War on Terror.

spoken to Alizadeh much in the preceding four years, though both men's wives continued a close friendship until Alizadeh's arrest. When Adam hosted Alizadeh at his home, Alizadeh was already under surveillance by the RCMP. The RCMP therefore obtained a warrant to tap Adam's phone calls. After Alizadeh's arrest, Adam and his wife, Samantha, were questioned by both the RCMP and CSIS in the company of their lawyer. The lead RCMP officer on the case informed Adam that the investigation had made plain that Adam did not collaborate with Alizadeh in his plot and did not share Alizadeh's violent political commitments. The officer went so far as to describe Adam as an "upstanding citizen." And yet, the travails of Adam and Samantha were just beginning. During their investigation of Alizadeh, the RCMP and/ or CSIS passed information to the US about Adam and Samantha that would bar them from travelling to the US. Neither Adam nor Samantha knew of this border restriction and neither had reason to travel to the US soon after Alizadeh's arrest. But they discovered that Canadian security agencies' sharing of information could have serious consequences beyond the inability to travel to the US.

Adam's extended family lived in Turkey, and he frequently travelled from Istanbul to Toronto. Adam soon realized he could not travel from Istanbul to Toronto because the DHS barred him from taking any flights to and from Canada that used US territory as an emergency landing (Jamil 2017). At one point, Adam found himself stranded in London, unable to join his family in Toronto. With the help of his lawyer, Adam managed to obtain a modest form of redress to his predicament. He applied to the US Travel Redress Inquiry Program (TRIP), which gave him a redress number after some months (Homeland Security, n.d.). After receiving this letter, Adam could use this number when booking international flights, though he remained barred from travel to the US.

The inability to travel to the US has often had unpredictable and negative impacts on Adam and Samantha's lives. For instance, in 2012, the family attempted to board a flight from Istanbul to Vancouver to visit Samantha's parents and brother who live in British Columbia. However, Samantha did not know at the time that she had been barred from travelling to the US as well. She was therefore denied boarding. While her lawyer recommended that she file a TRIP application, the hefty cost of the family's tickets to Vancouver was lost. In addition, Samantha speaks of the emotional toll the experience took on her: "I was scared I'd never be let back into Canada. My kids saw their Mom as an utter mess. Finally, we booked a flight from Istanbul to Edmonton because it bypassed all American airspace. We then drove from Edmonton to BC." Samantha speaks of the difficulty the episode caused for her relationship with her family. "Relations with my family were already strained after my conversion (to Islam), and now I had to worry about them thinking we were terrorists. It doesn't help that my grandmother still gets detained every time she crosses the US border because I had travelled with her to the US before [Alizadeh]'s arrest."

Likewise, Adam has had to pass up several career opportunities over the years. At one point, the Turkish government considered him for a position as a diplomat working in the US. Knowing that he could not travel to the US, Adam had to pass up on the opportunity. Moreover, Adam notes how information the Canadian government shared with the US has ended up in the hands of other foreign governments. He explains that the government of Taiwan has denied him entry after inviting him to a conference on municipal governance (Adam has held the prestigious position of Deputy Mayor in a municipality in the suburbs of Istanbul), and the Serbian and Israeli governments have also detained and questioned him at their borders.

Adam and Samantha's story mirror accounts from Mahdi and Malik. They too were under suspicion because of the actions of an acquaintance. They too cannot travel to the US despite the lack of charges or ongoing investigations by Canadian security agencies. And they too have suffered both financial and emotional costs. Adam and Samantha's story also highlights the limited possibility of redress for Muslim Canadians whose information has been shared with US authorities. The Terrorism Redress Inquiry Program provides Canadian acquaintances of terrorist suspects sufficient redress to be able to use US airspace and emergency landings in their international travels, but not enough to allow them to travel to the US (Freeze 2011).

Case Study 3: Fouad[5]

My final case study supports two conclusions I have made throughout this chapter. First, Canadian agencies share information with the DHS about Muslim Canadians who are soon cleared domestically of being national security threats. The sharing of information about Muslim Canadians who are acquaintances of national security suspects does not therefore appear to provide genuine safety against the threat of terrorism. Second, this sharing of information has had harmful effects on Muslim Canadians, both emotionally and financially. But more than the

---

5   For the sake of the anonymity of my research participant, Fouad is a pseudonym.

other two, this third case study suggests that black Muslim Canadians with lower socio-economic means are particularly vulnerable to CSIS and the RCMP's assumptions of guilt by association.

Fouad was a Winnipeg man from an East African country who arrived in Canada at the age of eight. In his twenties, he worked odd hours at a call centre in Winnipeg but supplemented his yearly income by frequently visiting his East African birth country, where he sold cell phones from Canada. Fouad married a woman from this East African country and began to spend more time there. His travels caught the attention of CSIS, who worried about his travel intentions and, according to Fouad, contacted the security agency of this East African country. At the time, this East African country had a long suspicion of Fouad's ethnic community because of its strong secessionist movement in its ranks. It therefore needed little more to arrest Fouad than a sign of suspicion from Canadian security agencies.[6] Fouad was imprisoned for the next four years, allegedly on charges of espionage. His family in Canada found themselves largely ignored by the government of former Prime Minister Stephen Harper, with officials even telling the family that publicizing the case in the media would make it more difficult for the Canadian government to negotiate Fouad's release.

Immediately prior to Fouad's imprisonment, CSIS contacted Fouad's eldest brother Dawud to ask him about his brother. Dawud had moved and settled in Toronto four years earlier and had minimal contact with his brother. Dawud answered the CSIS agents' questions as best he could. To his knowledge, he himself was never the object of the agents' investigation or suspicion. At the time that Fouad was imprisoned, Dawud was recently enrolled at Harvard University in a graduate program in architectural sustainability. Until then, Dawud had worked for various architectural firms in Toronto where he assessed the environmental sustainability of proposed building projects. Dawud's graduate degree was meant to further his skills, ensuring greater job stability and higher pay. Dawud's program enabled him to take courses remotely, but Harvard also required students to spend a term on campus. As Dawud prepared to leave for Harvard in 2014 to complete his degree requirements, he discovered that he could no longer travel to the US. Dawud could not complete his degree or advance his career, despite submitting a TRIP request.

---

6   Human Rights Watch has highlighted the political repression and suspicion of Fouad's ethnic community.

Dawud came from humble socio-economic means. He nonetheless had worked hard to climb the social ladder. He had put himself through an undergraduate degree on his own; he had networked with architectural firms through the Greater Toronto Area; and he was on his way to finishing a graduate degree at one of the most prestigious universities in the world. But Dawud was not yet established and CSIS was well aware of the family's lacking economic means, which made it impossible to provide Fouad with the recourse to lawyers or political pressure that might have led to his release. Would Dawud have been a target of Canadian agencies' sharing of information with the US if he had greater socio-economic means? Did his belonging to a new and vulnerable East African immigrant community embolden agents to disregard the consequences of sharing information with their US counterparts? What is clear is that once again Canadian intelligence agencies deployed a model of guilt by association to lump Dawud in with his brother – despite clear reasons to doubt the validity of the charges against his brother.

Rethinking the Smart Border Declaration

CSIS and the RCMP share information with the US under the Smart Border Declaration (Klassen 2014; Koslowski 2005; Pratt 2005; Shultz 2009). This Declaration was a product of the post-9/11 era when fears swirled about the porousness and therefore the vulnerability of the Canadian-American border to terrorist infiltration. The year before 9/11, Ahmed Ressam had been arrested at the border between British Columbia and Washington, his car carrying explosives destined for Los Angeles International Airport (Livermore 2018). After 9/11, some erroneous reports claimed that the plotters had crossed over the border from Canada. The Smart Border Declaration was a means to ensure that the US government knew of any possible threats that might slip through the Canadian border unidentified. This policy has its merits: Imam, Yar, El Farekh, and Alizadeh were all proven in courts of law to be legitimate objects of suspicion. These individuals might reasonably have harboured the desire to harm the US. But this chapter has shown that Canadian security agencies have taken a wide latitude in interpreting what constitutes a terrorist threat. In particular, part of their standard practice relies on identifying Muslim acquaintances of suspects and sharing information about them with the US DHS.

We might ask: do CSIS and the RCMP know that their information sharing with the US leads to innocent Muslim Canadians being barred from travel to the US? In other words, is it possible that they share information about Canadian Muslim citizens during their investigations and expect that the US will clear these citizens of suspicions once Canadian agencies conclude that they are not credible security threats? The preliminary evidence suggests that Canadian agencies fully know they are hanging citizens out to dry. For instance, when Adam and Samantha found themselves unable to travel to Vancouver from Istanbul, they reached out to the RCMP officer who had called Adam "an upstanding citizen." The RCMP officer expressed sympathy for their grievance and helped them find a route that would enable them to fly to Canada. But when Adam expressed that sharing information with the US had unfairly placed him and his family in a precarious situation, the RCMP officer turned defensive. According to Adam, the officer told him, "if we don't do this work, then the US will come up here themselves to do it."[7] Regardless of the veracity of the RCMP officer's claim, the answer shows both an institutional awareness and acceptance that "upstanding" Canadians can suffer consequences to their mobility, livelihood, sense of security, and belonging.

Mahdi shares a similar story. During the early 2010s, Mahdi attempted to board a domestic Air Canada flight. At the time, Air Canada used the US DHS's database to produce its own list of admissible and inadmissible passengers. Mahdi was therefore denied boarding. He called the RCMP officer who had interviewed him years earlier for help. The RCMP officer told Mahdi that he could not help remove him from the US's database or from Air Canada's own list, but that he knew how he could circumvent the system to fly domestically, telling Mahdi to go over to the rival WestJet counter to purchase a ticket to his destination. Again, the RCMP officer in this case was fully aware of the unfair consequences that Muslim Canadians face after the RCMP and CSIS share information with the US, but he was unwilling to help change that system.

Some may argue that CSIS and the RCMP's sharing of information is a necessary evil for the greater safety of Canadians and Americans. However, "associations" are too tenuous to prove common purpose or activities between individuals. The recourse to association is therefore dangerous to the individual rights cherished by liberal democratic societies. Historically, common law has relied upon mechanisms such as conspiracy, incitement, or aiding and abetting to punish group

---

7   The comment reflects the suggestion after 9/11 of integrating security between Canada and the US.

criminality (Freedman 2006). Even Canadian legislation against terrorism is careful not to criminalize mere association with terrorist organizations. Rather, some form of ideological or material support to a terrorist organization is necessary to charge one with a crime (Forcese and Roach 2015). It seems the sinister cunning of the Smart Border Agreement is that CSIS and the RCMP do not even have to disclose their infringement of Muslim citizens' rights because the US is a foreign and sovereign government and, as such, it does not owe mobility rights to citizens of other states.

Conclusion

In this chapter, I have sought to shed light on the sharing of information between Canadian security agencies and the US DHS regarding Muslim Canadian security threats. I have contended that this system of information sharing is at least sometimes based on a model of guilt by association rather than the commission of criminal actions. The model of guilt by association creates psychologically, emotionally, and financially perilous effects on those trapped within it. But this pain seems little warranted to ensure the security of Canadian or American societies. In fact, Canadian agencies know that despite being cleared of suspicions domestically, its Muslim citizens will continue to suffer from the information that they passed to the US DHS. In other words, the model of guilt by association does not actually protect Canada or the US, despite punishing citizens, who by all measures would otherwise be considered paradigmatic contributing members of society – engineers, entrepreneurs, doctors, civil servants, and architects.

I encourage scholars to develop the conclusions of this short study in two future directions. First, there is a need for more data to assess the pervasiveness with which Muslim Canadians have had their mobility constrained because of mere association. Based on my preliminary research, national security investigations over the last two decades have likely led to other Muslim Canadians being denied entry to the US based on association. But how many? This data remains unknown. We need to determine the extent of the problem before making the case to the Canadian government that the way Canadian agencies share information with the US needs to be rethought to protect Canadians from humiliation and adverse impacts on their livelihoods. Increased data will allow us to confirm whether instances in which Canadian security agencies' share information based on mere association are rare mistakes in the pursuit of national security, or, as I have suggested, are foundational to how Canadian security agencies operate.

Second, I encourage researchers to pay greater attention to whether CSIS and/or the RCMP feel emboldened to share information with the US depending on the racial and socio-economic background of Muslim Canadians. It is telling that the RCMP spoke cordially with Adam and Samantha. The couple was not only represented by a lawyer, but one of Samantha's parents is also an RCMP officer. In contrast, Dawud and his family found themselves with little government support after Dawud's brother was arrested. Ultimately, Adam and Samantha still found themselves in a similar predicament as Dawud. Thus, the question of race and socio-economic background in the liberties that Canadian agencies take in sharing information with the US remains an open question. In the end, this chapter is meant to prod researchers to shed greater light on the mechanisms through which Muslim Canadians are targeted as objects of suspicion and denied mobility for associations that would not hold up in court. By gaining greater insight into these mechanisms, we can better understand how the War on Terror has burdened, discriminated against, and attacked Muslim Canadians. And perhaps we can begin to properly redress the uneven ways that our national security apparatus is wielded against some Canadians over others.

WORKS CITED

Abu-Laban, Yasmeen, and Nisha Nath. 2007. "From Deportation to Apology: The Case of Maher Arar and the Canadian State." *Canadian Ethnic Studies* 39, no. 3: 71–98. https://doi.org/10.1353/ces.0.0049.

Bennett, Colin J. 2008. "Unsafe at Any Altitude: The Comparative Politics of No-Fly Lists in the United States and Canada." In *Politics at the Airport*, edited by Mark B. Salter, 51–76. Minneapolis: University of Minnesota Press.

Bhandar, Davina. 2008. "Resistance, Detainment, Asylum: The Onto-Political Limits of Border Crossings in North America." In *War, Citizenship, Territory*, edited by Deborah Cowen and Emily Gilbert, 281–302. New York: Routledge.

CBC News. 2015. "RAW: Abdelkrim Boulhout on Being Detained for 7 Hours at the U.S. Border." 13 October 2015. https://www.cbc.ca/player/play/2677073906.

Forcese, Craig, and Kent Roach. 2015. "Criminalizing Terrorist Babble: Canada's Dubious New Terrorist Speech Crime." *Alberta Law Review* 53, no. 1: 35–84. https://doi.org/10.29173/alr280.

Freedman, David. 2006. "The New Law of Criminal Organizations in Canada." *Canadian Bar Review* 85, no. 2: 171–219. https://cbr.cba.org/index.php/cbr/article/view/4049/4042.

Freeze, Colin. 2011. "Easy to Get onto No-Fly List, Harder to Get Off." *Globe and Mail*, 2 June 2011, A10.

Helleiner, Jane. 2012. "Whiteness and Narratives of a Racialized Canada-US Border at Niagara." *Canadian Journal of Sociology* 37, no. 2: 109–35. https://doi.org/10.29173/cjs10016.

Homeland Security. n.d. "DHS Traveler Redress Inquiry Program (DHS TRIP)." United States of America. Accessed 7 October 2021. https://www.dhs.gov/dhs-trip.

Jamil, Uzma. 2017. "Can Muslims Fly? The No Fly List as a Tool of the 'War on Terror.'" *Islamophobia Studies Journal* 4, no. 1: 72–86. https://doi.org/10.13169/islastudj.4.1.0072.

Klassen, Jerome. 2014. *Joining Empire: The Political Economy of the New Canadian Foreign Policy*. Toronto: University of Toronto Press.

Koslowski, Rey. 2005. "Smart Borders, Virtual Borders or No Borders: Homeland Security Choices for the United States and Canada." *Law and Business Review of the Americas* 11, no. 3/4: 527. https://scholar.smu.edu/lbra/vol11/iss3/9.

Livermore, Daniel. 2018. *Detained: Islamic Fundamentalist Extremism and the War on Terror in Canada*. Kingston: McGill-Queen's University Press.

Lyon, David. 2006. "Airport Screening, Surveillance, and Social Sorting: Canadian Responses to 9/11 in Context." *Canadian Journal of Criminology and Criminal Justice* 48, no. 3: 397–411. https://doi.org/10.3138/cjccj.48.3.397.

McArthur, Greg, Patrick White, Joe Friesen, Christie Blatchford, Marten Youssef, and Colin Freeze. 2010. "The Lost Boys of Winnipeg." *Globe and Mail*, 1 October 2010, A14.

Murphy, Jessica. 2016. "Father of Canadian Six-Year-Old on No Fly List: Our Family Is Not Alone." *Guardian*, 4 January 2016. https://www.theguardian.com/world/2016/jan/04/canada-six-year-old-no-fly-list-syed-adam-ahmed.

Nagra, Baljit. 2017. *Securitized Citizens: Muslim Canadians' Experience of Race Relations and Identity Formation Post-9/11*. Toronto: University of Toronto Press.

Nagra, Baljit, and Paula Maurutto. 2016. "Crossing Borders and Managing Racialized Identities: Experiences of Security and Surveillance among Young Canadian Muslims." *Canadian Journal of Sociology* 41, no. 2: 165–94. https://doi.org/10.29173/cjs23031.

Nagra, Baljit, and Paula Maurutto. 2020. "No-Fly Lists, National Security and Race: The Experiences of Muslim Canadians." *British Journal of Criminology* 60, no. 3: 600–19. https://doi.org/10.1093/bjc/azz066.

Pratt, Anna. 2005. *Securing Borders*. Vancouver: University of British Columbia Press.

Pratt, Anna, and Sara K. Thompson. 2008. "Chivalry, 'Race' and Discretion at the Canadian Border." *British Journal of Criminology* 48, no. 5: 620–40. https://doi.org/10.1093/bjc/azn048.

–. 2010. "Between a Hunch and a Hard Place: Making Suspicion Reasonable at the Canadian Border." *Social & Legal Studies* 19, no. 4: 461–80. https://doi.org/10.1177/0964663910378434.

Razack, Sherene. 2010. "Abandonment and the Dance of Race and Bureaucracy in Spaces of Exception." *States of Race: Critical Race Feminism for the 21st Century*, edited by Sherene Razack, Sunera Thobani, and Malinda S. Smith. Toronto: Between the Lines.

Sharma, Nandita. 2008. "White Nationalism, Illegality and Imperialism: Border Controls as Ideology." In *(En)gendering the War on Terror: War Stories and Camouflaged Politics*, edited by Krista Hunt and Kim Rygiel, 121–44. Farnham: Ashgate.

Shultz, Jessica. 2009. "The Role of Integrated Border Enforcement Teams in Maintaining a Safe and Open Canada-United States Border." Master's thesis, University of Windsor.

Whitaker, Reginald, Gregory Kealy, and Andrew Parnaby. 2012. *Secret Service: Political Policing in Canada: From the Fenians to Fortress America.* Toronto: University of Toronto Press.

White, Patrick, Joe Friesen, and Greg McArthur. 2010. "Hard Worker Felt He Couldn't Get Ahead." *Globe and Mail*, 27 August 2010, A9.

Contributors

Melanie Adrian is an associate professor in the Department of Law and Legal Studies, where she holds the inaugural Chair of Teaching Innovation at Carleton University. She is author of *Religious Freedom at Risk: The EU, French Schools, and Why the Veil Was Banned* (2016) and co-editor of *Producing Islams in Canada: On Knowledge, Positionality, and Politics* (2021). Adrian serves as senior editor of the *Oxford Encyclopedia of Islam in North America*. Her op-eds have been published in the *Globe and Mail* and the *Ottawa Citizen*. Dr. Adrian was invested in the Order of Ontario in 2019.

Fahad Ahmad is a postdoctoral fellow at the Centre for Criminology & Sociolegal Studies in the University of Toronto and an incoming assistant professor of Criminology at Toronto Metropolitan University. As an interdisciplinary scholar, his research intersects critical terrorism/radicalization studies; racialized practices of national security policing and surveillance; civil society and resistance; and justice philanthropy. He obtained his PhD from the School of Public Policy and Administration at Carleton University where his doctoral research – supported by the Social Sciences and Humanities Research Council (SSHRC) and the Pierre Elliott Trudeau Foundation – comparatively examines the securitization of Muslim civil society organizations under national security regimes in Canada and the UK. His scholarship is informed by fifteen years of work experience in community and non-profit organizations in Canada and the US.

Rabiat Akande is an assistant professor at Osgoode Hall Law School. Rabiat Akande is a legal historian and works in the fields of law and religion, Islamic law, constitutional law, and comparative law. Prior to her time at Osgoode, Rabiat Akande was a postdoctoral fellow at Harvard

University Academy for International and Area Studies, where she remains an academy scholar. She is a graduate of the University of Ibadan and Harvard Law School.

Natasha Bakht is a full professor of law at the University of Ottawa and the Shirley Greenberg Chair for Women and the Legal Profession. She was called to the Bar of Ontario in 2003 and served as a law clerk to Justice Louise Arbour at the Supreme Court of Canada. Her scholarship explores the intersection between religious freedom and women's equality. She served as the English language editor-in-chief of the *Canadian Journal of Women and the Law* (2014–20). Natasha is a member of the Law Program Committee of the Women's Legal Education and Action Fund (LEAF). She was named one of the top fifty people in city by Ottawa Life Magazine (2009), received a Femmy Award by International Women's Day Ottawa for being a thought leader in the region (2017) and received the South Asian Bar Association's Legal Excellence Award (2019). Her book *In Your Face: Law, Justice and Niqab-Wearing Women in Canada* (2020) was featured on *The Hill Times'* 100 Best Books in 2020 and received the 2020–1 Huguenot Society of Canada Award. She is also an award-winning dancer and choreographer.

Faisal A. Bhabha is an associate professor at Osgoode Hall Law School, York University, in Toronto, Canada, where he also serves as the faculty director of the Canadian Common Law LLM degree program. He researches and publishes in the areas of constitutional law, multiculturalism, human rights, and legal ethics. In conjunction with his academic research and teaching, Faisal maintains a small law practice, advising and representing a variety of individuals and public interest organizations in matters pertaining to constitutional law and human rights. He appears before administrative boards and tribunals and at all levels of court, including the Supreme Court of Canada. In particular, he has frequently acted as counsel to the National Council of Canadian Muslims (NCCM) in constitutional cases. Faisal previously served as vice-chair of the Human Rights Tribunal of Ontario (2008–11). He has appeared as an expert witness before Canadian parliamentary and senate committees and served as a member of the Equity Advisory Group (EAG) of the Law Society of Ontario (2005–8). He has lived and worked in the Middle East and South Africa, and he has lectured and taught in many countries.

Anver M. Emon is a professor of law and history in the Faculty of Law and Department of History, University of Toronto. He holds the

Canada Research Chair on Islamic Law and History and directs the Institute of Islamic Studies. He principally researches Islamic legal history and has published books such as *Islamic Natural Law Theories* (2010) and *Religious Pluralism and Islamic Law* (2012). He works comparatively across legal traditions to interrogate the epistemologies of distinct legalities, as in his edited collections *Islamic and Jewish Legal Reasoning* (2014) and *Islamic Law and International Human Rights Law* (2012). His recent work examines the ways in which Islamic history and Islamic law operate under the surface of contemporary legal problems. His co-authored *Jurisdictional Exceptionalisms* (Cambridge University Press, 2021) with Urfan Khaliq examines the intersection of Islamic law and international law in the contemporary legal dynamics of parental child abduction, while his report with Dr. Nadia Z. Hasan, *Under Layered Suspicion* (www.layeredsuspicion.ca), examined implicit biases in Canada Revenue Agency audits of Muslim-led charities in Canada.

Zeinab Farokhi holds a PhD in women and gender studies and diaspora and transnational studies at the University of Toronto. Farokhi is currently an SSHRC postdoctoral fellow at Concordia University (2022–4) and an assistant professor at the University of Toronto Mississauga. Her dissertation, "Digital Islamophobia: A Comparison of Right-Wing Extremist Groups in Canada, the United States, and India," via qualitative discourse analysis investigated and tracked the gendered, affective, and transnational digital strategies, rhetorics, and affinities of anti-Muslim extremist actors on Twitter. Farokhi's postdoctoral research will conduct a mix-methods comparison of Hindu nationalist and white supremacist accounts on YouTube to assess the affective and affinitive alignments among extremist groups and their exploitation of audio-visual affordances. Dr. Farokhi's work emphasizes feminist approaches to extremism, digital media, and transnational and diaspora studies and highlights the urgent need to better understand how national and transnational extremist rhetoric manifests, spreads, and persuades across digital ecologies.

Wafaa Hasan is an assistant professor at the Women and Gender Studies Institute, University of Toronto, St. George campus. Hasan is a community activist, author, and public speaker. Her academic research is primarily based in decolonial, transnational feminist studies with a particular focus on anti-racist solidarity and dialogue practices.

Syed Adnan Hussain is an associate professor of religious studies at Saint Mary's University. Hussain's research interests centre on modern

Islam in South Asia and North America. He has extensive experience working with not-for-profit groups, including the Kenya Human Rights Commission and the LAWS program at the University of Toronto Law School. His other areas of interest include Islam in North American since 9/11, human rights law, film, post-colonial theory, modern Islamic law, Islam in South-East and East Asia, gender and queer theory, juvenile delinquency, and the laws of apostasy and blasphemy. Dr. Hussain holds degrees from McGill University, the Candler School of Theology and Emory University School of Law in Atlanta, GA, and a PhD in Religious Studies from the University of Toronto.

Sheliza Ibrahim is an assistant professor at the University of Toronto at Mississauga (UTM). She holds a PhD in science education from York University, a MSc in science communication from Queen's University Belfast, and a Hons. BSc in biology from the University of Toronto. She has taught and conducted research in the field of Mathematics Education and Science Education, examining pedagogical approaches that support traditional ecological knowledge, reinhabiting place, and critical awareness of the nature of science and mathematics. Currently her research focuses on higher education and the design of socially just practices in the field of numeracy and other STEM fields, and she conducts various international research projects across the Caribbean in higher education. She also works in partnership with the Faculty of Medicine at UTM to support student achievement. Ibrahim's teaching practice and research is informed by place-based learning, culturally responsive pedagogy, knowledge mobilization, environmental studies, social justice education, enactivism, conscientization, computational thinking, numeracy, and cognition.

Yasmin Jiwani is a full professor in the Department of Communication Studies, and a Concordia University Research Chair on Intersectionality, Violence, and Resistance. Her research interests focus on the discursive ways in which racist-sexism is conceptualized and ideologically utilized in popular discourse. The particular sites which she has examined include media reportage of violence against Indigenous or racialized immigrant women, representations of Indigenous and Muslim youth in the popular press, as well as discourses of resistance articulated by marginalized groups in film and other popular media. Her most recent project is centred on cyber-memorials and virtual graveyards as reflections of the vernacular. Here, her analysis attends to race, gender, and belonging as expressed in the narratives posted on these sites. She is the author of *Discourses of Denial: Race, Gender and Violence,* and co-editor of *Girlhood, Redefining the Limits,* as well as *Faces of Violence in the Lives of Girls.*

Maryam Khan is an assistant professor at the Faculty of Social Work at Wilfrid Laurier University. Khan has more than ten years of clinical, community-based, and activist experience working with diverse individuals, families, and communities in mental health, addictions, VAW, and LGBTQ+ social and health care settings. In 2021, Khan won the nationally competitive inaugural "CBRCanada Emerging Community-Based Researcher Award" from Community Based Research Canada. At the present time, Khan is leading two SSHRC funded community-based projects: one on queer Muslims and their families, the other on the experiences of queer Muslims in social services. Khan works with racialized LGBTQ+ individuals and communities, religious and spiritual sexual minorities, and Islam and Muslim women. She is passionate about producing critical knowledges in LGBTQ+ policy and education, gender variance and (dis)ability, social construction and representation of race and otherness, sex workers, HIV/AIDS, and intersectional identities. Theoretically, Maryam draws on critical pedagogies such as Intersectionality and Standpoint feminisms, Indigenous-centred and decolonization perspectives, Transnational and critical race feminisms, Liberatory Islamic perspectives, and anticolonial and postcolonial approaches to Social Work practice, education, and research.

Zarah Khan is a PhD student at the Women and Gender Studies Institute at the University of Toronto. Khan holds a master of arts in gender studies and feminist research from McMaster University, and bachelor's degrees in Cultural Studies, English Literature, and Art History from McMaster University.

Naseem Mithoowani is a graduate of Osgoode Hall Law School. She was called to the Bar of Ontario in 2008. Since 2010, she has practised exclusively in the areas of immigration and refugee law, currently with Mithoowani Waldman Immigration Law Group. Naseem has appeared before all levels of the Immigration Division and Refugee Protection Division and regularly argues judicial review applications before the Federal Court. Outside of her legal practice, Naseem is an adjunct professor at Osgoode Hall Law School, where she teaches immigration and refugee law. In 2021, Naseem was appointed by the federal government to the Canadian Human Rights Tribunal, where she serves as a part-time adjudicator for a five-year term. Named a top lawyer under forty by Lexpert magazine and a social change maker (2021) by the *Peak* magazine, Naseem also serves on the board of directors for Islamic Relief Canada and the Crescent Town Community Club. She also provides assistance as an advisory committee member for a national security hotline at the University of Toronto and the Jewish Immigrant Aid Society.

Michael Nesbitt, LLB, LLM, SJD, is an associate professor of law at the University of Calgary, Faculty of Law. Nesbitt teaches and researches in the areas of criminal law, national security law, and international organizations and human rights. Before joining the Faculty of Law in July 2015 he practised law and worked on Middle East policy, human rights, international sanctions, and terrorism for Canada's Department of Foreign Affairs. Previously, he completed his articles and worked for Canada's Department of Justice, where his focus was criminal law. Michael has also worked internationally for the United Nations' International Criminal Tribunal for the Former Yugoslavia in the Appeals Chamber. While completing his doctorate Michael was an SSHRC Joseph-Armand Bombardier CGS Scholar, executive editorial assistant to the *University of Toronto Law Journal*, and taught in the legal research and writing program.

Kent Roach, CM, FRSC, is a professor of law at the University of Toronto. He formerly served as a law clerk to the late Justice Bertha Wilson. He has been editor-in-chief of the *Criminal Law Quarterly* since 1998. In 2002, he was elected a Fellow of the Royal Society of Canada by his fellow academics. in 2015, he was appointed a member of the Order of Canada. In 2017 the Canada Council awarded him the Molson Prize for his career contributions to social sciences and the humanities. Acting pro bono, he has represented civil liberties and Indigenous groups in several landmark Charter cases including *Ward, Latimer, Sauve,* and *Khawaja.* He was also co-editor of an interdisciplinary collection of essays on the Toronto 18 trials published in volume 44, no. 1 of the *Manitoba Law Journal.* His most recent books are *Remedies for Violations of Human Rights: A Two Track Approach to Supra-national and National Law* (2021) and *Canadian Policing: Why and How It Must Change* (2022).

Moska Rokay is a PhD student at the University of Toronto's Faculty of Information and is a recipient of an SSHRC CGS-D Scholarship (2022–5). Rokay's research interests lie in the interdisciplinary crossroads of archives, critical race and ethnicity studies, media studies, and identity formation in diaspora communities of war and trauma. She is an advocate for community-centred, activist archives and archives of diaspora/

migrant communities. She was the inaugural archivist of the Muslims in Canada Archives (MiCA) at the Institute of Islamic Studies, University of Toronto from 2019–22. As a refugee and settler on Turtle Island, she is actively involved in the Afghan Canadian diaspora community. In 2020, she was the recipient of the Association of Canadian Archivists' New Professional Award as well as the *Archivaria* Gordon Dodds Student Paper Prize. She completed her master of information at the University of Toronto in 2019.

Sarah Shah (they/them) received a doctoral degree from the University of Toronto in Sociology. They are a Research Fellow at the Institute of Islamic Studies, the University of Toronto, an Assistant Professor at the Department of Sociology, the University of Toronto, Mississauga, and a Research Consultant for Canadian Muslim organizations. They are a lead researcher at the Muslims in Canada Data Initiative (MiCDI). In addition to diasporic Muslim demographics, Shah's research unpacks how religion dialectically structures and is structured by gender and family relations, immigration and racialization processes, and mental health. In their current project on Pakistani Canadian Muslim families, Shah looks at Muslim religious reflexivities or the critical ways in which diasporic Muslims navigate and negotiate their religious identities and practices.

John Smith is the pseudonym of an academic who has published widely on issues related to Indian history and politics in accordance with high standards of research excellence. The author's most recent work on Hindutva politics has led some Hindutva activists to issue threats against the author's person and well-being, including death threats. As such, the author uses this pseudonym here to ensure the primacy of academic freedom, support an informed citizenry, and protect against the unfortunate reality of surveilling trolls.

Youcef L. Soufi is a research associate at the Institute of Islamic Studies at the University of Toronto. His forthcoming book traces the rise of classical debate gatherings in Iraq and Persia between the tenth and thirteen centuries. Previous publications have appeared in *The Oxford Handbook of Islamic Law*, *the Journal of Islamic Studies* (32, no. 2), *Journal of the American Oriental Society* (141, no. 4), and *Islamic Law and Society* (28, no. 1–2), among others. His new project is on Islamophobia and state surveillance since 9/11.

Ingram Content Group UK Ltd.
Milton Keynes UK
UKHW040744290523
422376UK00019B/24